S0-BXL-556

Leisure Service Delivery System: A Modern Perspective

ORGANIZATIONS

SOCIAL ENVIRONMENT

PHYSICAL ENVIRONMENT

PARTICIPANTS

JAMES F. MURPHY

JOHN G. WILLIAMS

E. WILLIAM NIEPOTH

PAUL D. BROWN

Leisure Service Delivery System:

A Modern Perspective

Health Education,
Physical Education, and
Recreation Series

Ruth Abernathy, Ph.D., Editorial Adviser,
Professor, Physical and Health Education,
University of Washington, Seattle, Washington 98105

Leisure Service Delivery System: A Modern Perspective

JAMES F. MURPHY, Ph.D.

Assistant Professor, Department of Recreation and Leisure Studies California State University, San Jose, California

JOHN G. WILLIAMS, M.S.

Director, Department of Parks and Recreation Sunnyvale, California

E. WILLIAM NIEPOTH, Ed.D.

Professor, Department of Recreation California State University, Hayward, California

PAUL D. BROWN, Ed.D.

Professor and Chairman, Department of Recreation and Leisure Studies, California State University, San Jose, California

LEA & FEBIGER · *Philadelphia, 1973*

Library of Congress Cataloging in Publication Data

Main entry under title:

Leisure service delivery system.

(Health education, physical education, and recreation series)
1. Recreation leadership. 2. Recreation—Administration.
J. Murphy, James Fredrick, 1943-
GV14.5.L4 1973 658′.91′79 73-7851
ISBN 0-8121-0434-X

Library of Congress Catalog Card Number 73-7851

Published in Great Britain by Henry Kimpton Publishers, London

Printed in the United States of America

PREFACE

The provision of recreation opportunity satisfies a basic human need and is an essential community function in today's complex post-industrial society. To understand human behavior as it is manifested in recreation activity, attention must be directed toward the cultural similarities and differences of individuals and social groups in a leisure environment. Each individual and social aggregate approach leisure differently, depending upon various cultural, organizational, environmental and sociopsychological influences. Additionally, society, participants, and the functioning of institutions are all subject to constant change.

Almost every text written for recreation and park curricula conceives of the various important aspects of leisure service as separate, distinguishable parts. A customary practice is the publication of texts on programming, leadership and administration to provide students and practitioners with an understanding of the particular phases of the overall delivery of leisure services. However, this disjointed approach does not provide any meaningful guidance to the reader since each of the various aspects of the delivery system are not seen as complementary and mutually supportive. They are typically viewed as requiring separate attention in different courses at various levels within the major curriculum. Therefore, the purpose of this text is to provide the prospective leisure manager a relevant system for understanding and implementing the philosophy, management principles and standards and guidelines of recreation opportunity.

By utilizing an ecological perspective of the leisure service delivery system the authors' intent in this book is to provide the reader with an understanding of its internal structure, the functions performed by the various management aspects (planning, organizing, staffing, directing and controlling), and the changes and variations in participant response or environmental (social and physical) conditions within a community. The primary elements of the delivery system–participants, the social environment, the physical environment, leisure service organizations—are all interrelated and fundamental to a successful and meaningful leisure experience.

Ecology in the context of this book is concerned with the interrelationships among people in their physical and social setting, and the way these relationships influence, or are influenced by, particular social processes. The ecological configuration used in the book is intended to lead to an understanding of the internal structure of the leisure service delivery system; the functions performed by the various management aspects of leisure service organizations (planning, organizing, staffing, directing and controlling); and the changes and variations in participant response or environmental conditions (social and/or physical) within a community.

The term leisure services is used to represent all of the various youth-serving, voluntary, private and public recreation and park agencies. It is seen by the authors to be more fully representative of the nature of recreation opportunity. Leisure service is viewed in this text in a holistic sense. It represents all of the potential free-time opportunities that confront people and behavior which is potentially convertible to wholesome and pleasureable recreation experience. This means that leisure service has as much responsibility to provide a well-baby clinic in Watts or Detroit as it has to run a tennis class in suburban Westchester County, New York or Palm Beach, Florida. The delivery of leisure services is aided when it is viewed from a systems perspective and is best understood by recognizing the interrelationship between the participant, the agency or organization, and the social and physical environment.

Although the authors have maintained a continued interchange of ideas and criticisms concerning each of the chapters of the book, Dr. Murphy was primarily responsible for the chapters entitled Recreation and Leisure in Post-Industrial Society, Recreation and Leisure Service: Meeting Basic Human Needs, Recreation and Leisure Service: A Social Concern, and Basis for the Leisure Service Delivery System; Dr. Niepoth assumed responsibility for the treatment of the chapters primarily concerned with socio-psychological considerations, The Recipient of Leisure Service: The Participant and A Conceptualization of Leisure Services; Dr. Brown was responsible for the chapter entitled Standards and Guidelines for the Effective Delivery of Leisure Service; and Mr. Williams assumed the major responsibility for the discussion on the management concerns of the delivery system, which included the chapters on planning, organizing, staffing, directing and controlling.

San Jose, California	James F. Murphy
Sunnyvale, California	John G. Williams
Hayward, California	E. William Niepoth
San Jose, California	Paul D. Brown

CONTENTS

INTRODUCTION

The Ecology of Leisure Service

The ecology of the leisure service delivery system is concerned with the interrelationships among people in their physical and social environment, and the way these relationships influence, or are influenced by, particular social processes. It is therefore understood that the relationships of each component of the delivery system within any community are viewed as an ecological unit. It is holistic in the sense that any change in the population being served will affect the nature of programming and vice versa. Each component is an integral part of the overall delivery system and each influences another segment of the unit. All the elements mutually modify one another. Gist and Fava state that human ecology:

> is also concerned with interactive relationships between individuals and groups and the way these relationships influence, or are influenced by, particular spatial patterns and processes. It is concerned with cultural, racial, economic, and other differences insofar as preferences and prejudices associated with these differences serve to bring people socially or spatially together or keep them apart. It is concerned with social organization insofar as the organization of human activities influences, or is influenced by, the spatial distribution of people or of institutions. Above all, it is concerned with the dynamics of the social order insofar as change in the structure and functions of institutions, or changes in patterns of human relationships, bring about ecological changes, and vice versa.[1]

Any discussion of participants, social issues and concerns, the physical environment or the structure of leisure service organizations requires a corollary understanding of the relationships of each aspect of the delivery system.

Elements of the Delivery System

The Participant

It is recognized that the participant is the essential factor in the provision of recreation and leisure service. Participants have individual traits and characteristics which affect their involvement in a program and their adjustment to community life. Recreation behavior is influenced

---

[1] Gist, Noel P., and Fava, Sylvia F. *Urban Society*. 5th ed., New York, Thomas Y. Crowell Company, 1964, p. 96.

by a number of conditioning factors (which will be discussed in Chapter 6) including individual differences such as age, sex, self-concept, etc., and by an external *opportunity system* such as laws, mores and folkways, norms, geography, income level, etc. These factors operate in an interrelated fashion.

Movement, with respect to mobile or permanent residency within cities or between cities and rural areas, is another important characteristic of participants. It has been noted by many urbanologists that the ebb-and-flow movement in the city resulting from the separation of work place and place of residence is a significant aspect of urbanization. The tendency of central city residents to be highly mobile within the ghetto but fairly stationary with respect to the social and physical environment outside the ghetto lessens the extent and degree of potential recreation experience and resources.[2] Since it is recognized that residents of deprived urban neighborhoods are almost entirely dependent upon public recreation facilities, it is necessary for the leisure service manager to be conscious of deficiencies in transportation, income, knowledge, etc., of such a population. Residents of more affluent neighborhoods are more highly mobile both within and outside the context of their social and physical milieu; thus, a wider range of recreation alternatives is more likely to be at their disposal.

It is necessary to view the entire context of population groups, and as noted by Moore, for example, the study of a particular sociocultural clientele will provide the manager with important information upon which to effect the delivery of leisure service:

> Study of disadvantaged environments reveals that a matrix of interwoven configurations tends to influence development and support of recreation efforts, and to evoke participation patterns of the particular milieu. Although each geographic area and residential grouping may vary with local circumstances, the environment of disadvantagement frequently includes such social problems as community isolation, high concentration of one minority group, poverty and/or low-income levels, contrasts of social apathy and social activism, diverse cultural modes in conflict with the dominant society, residenital mobility, broken and incomplete families, unemployment and low-status employment, poor health conditions, population density, frequency of school and social dropout, inadequate and below-standard housing, inefficient and ineffective municipal services, high crime and delinquency rates and insufficient leisure opportunities.[3]

The movement and involvement of population groups in city, village, or country life are also conditioned by various needs, motives, drives and goals. The relationship of leisure pursuits to overall civic participation

---

[2] Moore, Velva. "Recreation Leadership with Socioculturally Handicapped Clientele," *Recreation and Leisure Service for the Disadvantaged: Guidelines to Program Development and Related Readings.* Edited by John A. Nesbitt, Paul D. Brown and James F. Murphy, Philadelphia, Lea & Febiger, 1970, p. 167.

[3] Ibid., p. 166.

must therefore be viewed within a holistic configuration. While the basic goals of the experience of recreation are enjoyment and satisfaction, the means, attitude and perception of the participant are unique for each population grouping.

The Physical Environment

Population groupings exist in a given natural environment which includes location, climate, natural resources, topography, flora and fauna, etc. It is recognized that geographical considerations must be considered in the planning of programs. Individuals must cope with the environment to exist. "Environment sets limits on the size and density of the population, but the process of adjustment is continuous and reciprocal because man in turn modifies the environment via his technology and culture."[4]

While man has increased his ability to cope with the natural environment through modification of the climate, topography and flora and fauna, the quality of the cities and the countryside is being reduced because of overpopulation, smog, congested transportation systems, polluted streams and waterways and a variety of human and industrial waste. Kraus has stated that the concern for a quality environment supersedes urban renewal:

> Instead, they [the cities] . . . must be rebuilt [by environmental planners and designers, including leisure service managers] so that they provide environments where people can live on a human scale, with opportunities for meaningful human contact and a sense of neighborhood . . . Green areas bordering parkways, small parks in the midst of business districts, municipal and commercial structures that are set into large open plazas, transforming lots into vest-pocket parks—all these help to make communities more livable.[5]

Recreation and leisure service plays a chief role in the physical environment by contributing to the aesthetics of the visual environment and by providing a useful and pleasing milieu for leisure opportunity.

Land is the foundation of the environment which shapes our lives. There is a relationship of people and pollution to the quality of land use. Too many people cause air and water pollution, make excessive noise, emit harmful chemicals, crowd open space, cause traffic congestion and otherwise reduce the quality of the natural environment.

We have increasingly recognized the great need for parks, wilderness areas, beaches, open space and other recreation areas. The combination of population increase, higher incomes, shorter working hours and ever greater concentration in ever larger metropolitan centers has re-

---

[4] Gist and Fava, Op. cit., p. 98.

[5] Kraus, Richard. *Recreation and Leisure in Modern Society.* New York, Appleton-Century-Crofts, 1971, p. 361.

sulted in a demand for more natural landscape—for beauty, a glimpse of wildlife, or a picnic table in the woods. In the words of Aldo Leopold:

> All conservation of wilderness is self-defeating, for to cherish we must see and fondle, and when enough have seen and fondled, there is no wilderness . . .

The Social Environment

It is generally conceived that an essential purpose of leisure service is to improve the quality of neighborhood and community life. Recreation and leisure service offerings are generally regarded as being more than an amenity of life. According to Kraus[6] public recreation has significant social value and for blacks it is seen as a method for improving the quality of urban life, reducing social pathology, building constructive values and generally making communities a better place to live. Recreation serves as a *threshold* or entry to other forms of social service and action in the community setting. If it is effective, it can provide an opportunity for neighborhood organization and group action for poor urban blacks, physically disabled groups or senior citizens unable to get meaningfully involved otherwise.

Harrington[7] has noted that the poor are caught in a vicious cycle of poverty. Poverty breeds despair, social ignorance, health problems and a low educational profile. These conditions prevent the poor from competing for jobs, finding decent housing and attaining educational success. Combined, these factors reduce income-earning potential and consequently result in a low socioeconomic status. The despair of the poor is often compounded in a leisure setting, particularly when cultural differences may prohibit certain ethnic groups from participating in the programs in which subordinate leisure habits and attitudes are found to be inappropriate or contradictory to values and norms of the dominant group.[8]

Common preferences, values, attitudes and beliefs are all considered preparatory for certain groups of people to engage in similar activities or to have a predisposition to act. Certain cultural, economic and/or religious affiliation may enhance or deter participation in certain leisure offerings because of social pressures, attitudes, motives, public opinion or discrimination by other groups in the community. The pattern of black residential segregation in American communities is illustrative of this element in human ecology. Spatial segregation of blacks in central city slums is related to their limited economic means, but as noted by

---

[6] Kraus, Richard. *Public Recreation and the Negro: A Study of Participation and Administrative Practices.* New York, Center for Urban Education, 1968.

[7] Harrington, Michael. *The Other America: Poverty in the United States.* Baltimore, Penguin Books Inc., 1963, pp. 21-22.

[8] Moore, Op. cit., p. 167.

Harrington, their low economic position is in turn related to many social environmental factors, including restricted recreation opportunities.

Moore states:

> Restricted childhood play experiences . . . implies an undeveloped recreation repertoire. The disadvantaged population seldom has the opportunity to gain leisure "know-how" in the realms of the dominant society's positively sanctioned leisure and play activities.[9]

Leisure Service Organizations

Leisure service agencies structure opportunities for participants within an ecological framework. The leisure service delivery system revolves around the organization of the physical and social environment. Human beings engage in social relations because they cannot exist on a sustaining basis apart from other human beings.

Societal relations revolve around the organization of the regular activities of people. Social organization denotes the totality of normatively regulated and patterned interrelationships among population groupings. The process by which the assemblage of differentiated and independent aspects of the delivery system attempts to integrate the physical environment (including natural areas, facilities, equipment, etc.), the social environment (health, education, housing, etc.), and the human concerns (motivation, communication, individual variation, instruction, etc.) is through effective organizational management. Without some form of organization, the social order would break down, and the leisure service delivery system would be disrupted.

The concern of this text is focused upon those aspects of social organization which affect the delivery system at the community level. Since the leisure service delivery system is based on a commitment to provide opportunities which encourage and facilitate a wide range of recreation interests (behaviors and desires), it is necessary for agencies to be cognizant of the whole network of human activity that exists in communities. Social organization involves economic, political, physical and technological factors. Each aspect of the overall organization of human activity mutually modifies the other, an interaction which expresses the dynamic process which serves to bind a community together.

The implication of social organization in an ecological framework indicates that leisure service is not a static entity. It creates a sense of community as a result of people's engagement in activities that demand interrelationships of efforts. "What usually binds a community together is a state of mind on the part of its members, a sense of interdependence and loyalty; a result of a dynamic on-going process."[10]

---

[9] Ibid., p. 167.

[10] Murphy, James F. "Community Recreation: A Dynamic Process," *California Parks and Recreation* 28:14, April/May, 1972.

CHAPTER 1

Recreation and Leisure in Post-Industrial Society

The Leisure Nexus

As America enters the last third of the twentieth century, it is faced with unequaled opportunities for achieving what no other culture has ever before realized—a society dominated by free time. The necessary goals required for life maintenance will be satisfied for the great majority of Americans. Subsistence will not be a persistent drive.

It is extremely difficult for most Americans to comprehend a society oriented almost exclusively to non-work concerns. The stock market states that leisure is a $150 billion business[1] and Kraus[2] suggests that even a conservative estimate places it at $223 billion but most Americans have been unable to shed the Puritan work ethic which has glorified labor and demeaned idleness. If one is to engage in recreation, it has to somehow be constructive, tangible activity. The segmentation and compartmentalization of American culture into different organizational forms —work, leisure, education, religion, etc., have resulted in the separation of values once attributed to life maintenance and sustenance.

The individual unprepared for leisure may well serve as an ominous guidepost for the future. Urbanization and industrialization have created an era of abundance in American society, both of wealth and leisure. However, as noted by Gist and Fava, "the commitment of the masses to a philosophy of work has left many unprepared for the judicious use of either the New Wealth or the New Leisure."[3]

They suggest that individual unpreparedness for abundant leisure in modern urban society may stem from two sources:

1. the inability of many people to disassociate and detach themselves from the work ethic to enjoy leisure without feelings of sin or guilt. Such persons have not developed a style of life and set of values that include leisure as a major element, and

---

[1] *Leisure: Investment Opportunities in a $150-Billion Market.* New York, Merrill Lynch, Pierce, Fenner and Smith, Inc., 1968.

[2] Kraus, Richard. "The Economics of Leisure Today," *Parks and Recreation* 6:62-66, 83-86, August, 1971.

[3] Gist, Noel P., and Fava, Sylvia F. *Urban Society.* 5th ed., New York, Thomas Y. Crowell Company, 1964, p. 414.

2. the confusion stemming from a seemingly unlimited number of possible choices to be made during free time. In this respect most most modern urban areas provide a cafeteria-like [refer to Chapter 5] approach to leisure opportunities for citizens, but usually without sufficient qualitative information concerning the value or worth of each "dish" or its personal or social implications. "Commonly he has neither the knowledge nor intellectual sophistication to make a crucial evaluation of these leisure offerings, but relies, perhaps unconsciously, on the 'taste makers' and the 'motivators.' That he often becomes an avid but undiscriminatory consumer is not surprising."[4]

With an unprecedented amount of free time available to the masses, particularly many middle-class and working-class employees, there has developed a changing view of the philosophy of work and leisure as they relate to people's central life interests. According to Roberts:

> People no longer have to seek an ulterior motive in order to justify having fun. The new emerging cultural attitudes towards leisure were given intellectual justification by Huizinga, who argued in his book, *Homo Ludens*, that play was a type of activity that met basic human needs and was therefore an indispensable element in all human civilizations.[5]

As we move into a post-industrial society in which the economy has moved away from production-oriented to consumer-oriented characteristics, leisure has become a distinct part of the social structure. A society is said to become *leisure-based* when the self-consciousness of man depends primarily upon the interests and activities associated with leisure. It is in their leisure lives that individuals express their real personalities. In large measure, the individual's self-concept is based upon, and reinforced by, the activities he pursues during his leisure. Dumazedier[6] has argued that it is man's leisure that is the major determinant of his self-consciousness, and that it is the style of life the individual develops during his leisure that forms the basis for adoption of values and attitudes that influence his behavior in all other aspects of life.

While work is still an essential component of man's social orientation, it has increasingly demanded less reverence. For example, when an individual is at work, he now feels relatively detached from the role that he is playing and does not identify his own personality with the qualities which his job demands that he display. Therefore, we may expect that as other institutions accommodate their own values and structures to conform to the emerging leisure-based orientations, leisure will become the

---

[4] Ibid., p. 414.

[5] Roberts, Kenneth. *Leisure.* London, Longman Group Limited, 1970, p. 90.

[6] Dumazedier, Joffre. *Towards a Society of Leisure.* New York, Collier-Macmillan, 1967, pp. 17-32.

source of man's sense of self-identity, and the basis of all social life. It has been noted in a number of studies of the youth subculture that the behavior and attitudes of the young emphasized the leisure-centeredness of their lives.[7] David Riesman argued in *The Lonely Crowd* that the "other-directed" man, a product of the industrial state, has incorporated leisure and consumption as central life interests.[8] The national character in America exemplifies, according to Riesman, middle-American, middle-class consumption patterns. While leisure-oriented behavior is expressed differently by various age, sex, income and other forms of conditioning factors, the important issue for study by sociologists has been that increasingly these leisure activities relate to people's central life interests.[9] Leisure has become the part of life to which people attach the greatest interest and importance.

Views of Leisure

Leisure is viewed differently by various individuals, depending primarily upon their value orientation and preference. Leisure evolved during the period of ancient Greece when the Hellenic concept of the "cultivation of the self" was made by Aristotle. The *traditional* or *classical* view of leisure places heavy emphasis upon contemplation, engagement in debate and politics in a search for knowledge and cultural enlightenment. Leisure in this sense is seen as freedom from the necessity of being occupied. De Grazia[10] and Pieper[11] are advocates of this model which identifies leisure as a condition or state of being or a condition of the soul which is divorced from time. According to Gray, the traditional or classical model of leisure "is an act of aesthetic, psychological, religious and philosophical contemplation."[12]

The most popular model of leisure, the *discretionary time* concept or quantitative perspective, holds that leisure is the portion of time which

---

[7] Refer to Ambrosino, Lillian. *Runaways.* Boston, Beacon Press, 1971; Houriet, Robert. *Getting Back Together.* New York, Coward, McCann and Geoghegan, Inc., 1971; Murphy, James F. "The Counter Culture of Leisure," *Parks and Recreation* 7:34, 41-42, February, 1972; Stickney, John. *Streets, Actions, Alternatives, Raps.* New York, G. P. Putnam's Sons, 1971; and *Voices From the Love Generation.* Edited by Leonard Wolf, Boston, Little, Brown and Company, 1968, for discussions of the youth culture in America.

[8] Riesman, David, Glazer, Nathan, and Denney, Reuel. *The Lonely Crowd: A Study of the Changing American Character.* Garden City, New York, Doubleday and Company, Inc., 1953, pp. 327-338.

[9] Feldman, Saul D., and Thielbar, Gerald W. *Life Styles: Diversity in American Society.* Boston, Little, Brown and Company, 1972.

[10] De Grazia, Sebastian. *Of Time, Work and Leisure.* Garden City, New York, Doubleday and Company, Inc., 1964.

[11] Pieper, Josef. *Leisure: The Basis of Culture.* New York, The New American Library, 1963.

[12] Gray, David E. "This Alien Thing Called Leisure." Speech delivered at Oregon State University, July 8, 1971.

remains after work and the basic requirements for existence have been satisfied. Fabun[13] suggests that at present we have only a single view of how time should be spent, exemplified by the industrial workers with hours to get through in order to receive sustenance.

We have constructed a society in which participation in work has traditionally been the goal of life itself. According to Fabun, the challenge of our economic system is to recognize and then implement the consequences of the changed energy flow of production and with it the demand for new ways of looking at work and leisure and the role each plays in society.

Staffan Linder uses economic analysis to examine the changing uses of time. He finds that contrary to expectations, economic growth has not resulted in an abundance of time and a leisurely life. It has, in fact, produced a scarcity of time (a result of persistent consumption needs requiring man to work more and therefore cancelling out excess leisure) and a more hectic life tempo. The scarcity of time, he suggests, corrupts the pleasure of cultivating our minds.[14]

Linder points out the ramifications of the relationship between increasing goods and decreasing time in our economy. As time becomes necessarily scarce, there is a need to continually reallocate it among competing goods and needs. Inevitably, values begin to change in the reallocation process and the whole quality of our life is altered and we are trapped in the consumption-oriented complexities of modern living which limit the potential enrichment of man. The problem of leisure, then, is that people engage in consumption in order that they can fill their free time with utility to show something for their toil.

Two models of leisure developed by Kaplan[15] actually appear to represent leisure as a *social instrument.* Leisure in this view is seen as a means of meeting needs of the poor through VISTA and Community Action Programs and as a *threshold* for the disadvantaged to help them actualize social needs and develop self-help skills. Additionally leisure is seen as an epistemological device, related to the activities and meanings of an assumptive, analytic and aesthetic nature. This view would entail examining the world from a political standpoint; painting a picture or even engaging in a protest march.

A model suggested by Gray is the *anti-utilitarian* view, which was articulated by Walter Kerr in *The Decline of Pleasure.*[16] This view sug-

[13] Fabun, Don. *The Dynamics of Change.* Englewood Cliffs, New Jersey, Prentice-Hall, Inc., 1966.

[14] Linder, Staffan B. *The Harried Leisure Class.* New York, Columbia University Press, 1970.

[15] Kaplan, Max. "Aging and Leisure." Speech delivered at a meeting of the American Psychological Association, Washington, D. C., September 4, 1971.

[16] Kerr, Walter. *The Decline of Pleasure.* New York, Simon and Schuster, Inc., 1962.

gests that leisure is a state of mind that is a worthy end in itself. This concept rejects the "position that every investment of human energy must produce a useful result. It rejects the work ethic as the only source of value and permits the investment of self in pursuits that promise no more than the expression of self."[17] "Doing your own thing" has merit according to this view of leisure, with the industrial and technological revolutions having been an antagonistic influence.

Finally, there is a fifth view of leisure, a *holistic* model, which sees leisure as a construct "with such elements as an antithesis to the work of the participant, a perception of the activity as voluntary or free, a pleasant expectation or recollection, a full range of possibilities from withdrawal in sleep or drink to highly creative tasks."[18]

According to this conceptualization, elements of leisure are to be found in work, family, education, religion, etc. Conversely, elements from these constructs are often to be found in leisure.

This latter view of leisure seems most appropriate for identification by leisure managers, since it eliminates the unnecessary dichotomy drawn between work and leisure which has been a formidable barrier in the path to enjoyment of leisure. Work and leisure are inextricably related to each other. We can no longer conceive of leisure, according to this model, as solely discretionary time and work as action. Leisure must be viewed as action too. There is need for a value reorientation which will confer honor on leisure as it did on work during the nineteenth century.

Our social system has created longer adolescence, more years of retirement and monotonous assembly-line jobs—but our value system has not allowed the moral or ethical response which will confer honor on increased free time.[19] Leisure service managers will have the dubious task of making interpretations about people's non-work behavior with emphasis upon the facilitation of opportunities for recreation that cover the full range of commitment and intensity.

Recreation in an Electric Age

The changing focus of society noted by McLuhan[20] has pushed advanced industrial societies into an electric age in which a synthesis of thought and the five senses has integrated information into a single form. At the same time, social change has made newcomers of us all.

The traditional approach of equating recreation solely with activity

---

[17] Gray, Op. cit.

[18] Kaplan, Op. cit.

[19] Berger, Bennett. "The Sociology of Leisure: Some Suggestions," *Work and Leisure: A Contemporary Social Problem*. Edited by Erwin O. Smigel, New Haven, Connecticut, College and University Press, 1963, pp. 21-40.

[20] McLuhan, Marshall and Fiore, Quentin. *The Medium is the Massage*. New York, Bantam Books, Inc., 1967.

has little meaning in an era in which words, equipment, life styles, work and leisure have become interchangeable. A totally new form of recreation is emerging which is predicated upon human interaction.

Dr. David Gray has suggested that the traditional conception of recreation (usually as a leisure activity voluntarily engaged in which provides immediate satisfaction) is inappropriate.[21] He investigated the semantics of the recreation concept among leisure service practitioners and educators and arrived at a definition of recreation which is in agreement with the philosophy of the leisure service system described in this text. According to Gray:

> Recreation is an emotional condition within an individual human being that flows from a feeling of well being and satisfaction. It is characterized by feelings of mastery, achievement, exhilaration, acceptance, success, personal worth and pleasure. It reinforces a positive self image. Recreation is a response to esthetic experience, achievement of personal goals or positive feedback from others. It is independent of activity, leisure or social acceptance.[22]

According to Gray, there are several implications with this proposed definition which will conceivably require most leisure service agencies to alter their present orientation and focus. The authors of this text agree that such a conceptualization of recreation experience is necessary for leisure service managers to consider, particularly since recreation is constantly paired inappropriately with activity. Current definitions and application of recreation by leisure service agencies ignore or give little attention to the psychological aspects of Gray's contemporary approach to conceptualizing recreation experience. The following are some of the implications of Gray's definition of recreation:

1. If recreation is an emotional response to a stimulus, it is what happens to people during the activity rather than the activity that counts.
2. Activities should be organized to provide maximum opportunity for esthetic experience, achievement of personal goals and positive feedback from others.
3. The *primary* purpose of a recreation agency is human development; the product is self-satisfaction.
4. Recreation may occur at any time, at any place and in any activity.
5. Recreation agencies must learn to recognize and hopefully measure at least indirectly their contribution to development and self-satisfaction.[23]

The previous equation of recreation with activity within a "leisure

---

[21] Gray, David E. "Recreation: An Interpretation." Summary of Research Findings, December 12, 1971, California State University, Long Beach, California.

[22] Ibid.

[23] Ibid.

time" reference stressed quantitative outcomes. How many people were engaged in activities? How many teams were organized for the softball league? How many children were present at the arts and crafts class? A definition of recreation which recognizes individual potential and responds to the developmental traits of each participant seeking optimal satisfaction is qualitative and underscores the view articulated by Gray, which seeks to promote the realization of self-worth by each individual participant.

Leisure Service as an Institution

The emergence of recreation and leisure service as a separate, distinguishable institution in America to provide opportunities for leisure expression for the public is a major social development in the twentieth century. That the people are willing to support a group of professional organizers and community catalysts for the sole function of encouraging the fostering of leisure interests has aided the process whereby leisure service agencies have evolved into an identifiable institution.

At the outset of the twentieth century, in response to an urbanizing industrial economy, leisure service agencies emerged to meet the various social, recreation and community needs of a diverse population.

Since its emergence, recreation has become an important social institution involved in the control of people's leisure lives. As we move toward the year 2000 it can be claimed that leisure is becoming a central aspect of social control. Since leisure service has thrust itself more securely within the framework of local, state and national governmental organization, it has the potential of exerting significant influence upon the lives of citizens.

We have witnessed the application of Jim Crow laws to blacks in the South which prohibited them from enjoying city parks, playgrounds, theaters, amusement centers, etc.[24] Leisure service had a direct impact upon the regulation of amusement, entertainment and the pursuit of leisure expression for large numbers of people who were excluded from an aspect of social life in various communities. While there were no legal sanctions against blacks per se in the North, *de facto* segregation kept them restricted to certain areas of town which had only limited play spaces and recreation offerings.[25] While there was no official national professional sanction (by the National Recreation Association, the American Recreation Society, etc.) for prohibiting blacks from engaging in leisure experiences, the movement tacitly supported local and regional

---

[24] Woodward, C. Vann. *The Strange Career of Jim Crow.* 2nd Ed., New York, Oxford University Press, 1966.

[25] Murphy, James F. "Egalitarianism and Separatism: A History of Approaches in the Provision of Public Recreation and Leisure Service for Blacks, 1906-1972." Unpublished Doctoral Thesis, Corvallis, Oregon, Oregon State University, 1972.

statutes which discriminated against blacks in the use of recreation areas and facilities and inhibited them from advancing within the profession by excluding them from attending key leadership and administrative institutes and conferences.[26]

Recently, local sanctions have been instituted by various city, county and state governmental units which have prohibited rock concerts from being held. Some of the ordinances adopted were a generalized response to disorder and general chaos that existed in prior large gatherings of young people (Altamont, Vortex, Woodstock, etc.). However, others have been initiated in response to stereotypes of youth in general as bearded, hippie-like, drug-oriented, boisterous, unruly, insensitive delinquents whose activities must be carefully observed and controlled. While both reactions may in fact be appropriate responses, what has occurred has been a substantial lack of understanding from leaders within the leisure service field, and a failure to point out, one way or another, the characteristic symptoms and causes of the behavior of the young.

Roberts has suggested two ways in which leisure service can be meaningfully related to a society's processes of social control:

> Firstly, leisure can perform a latency function within society, enabling people to express feelings and relieve tensions that are aroused by other social institutions. By allowing people to "let off steam" leisure can help to preserve the stability of the individual's own personality and the structure of the society to which the individual belongs . . . Secondly . . . leisure can operate as an agency of social control by exposing people to values upon which their whole life style and patterns of social interaction become based.[27]

Roberts' suggestions for leisure as a means of social control imply that leisure service agencies should realize that recreation opportunity should not be too rigidly structured. The wider the opportunities are for different personalities to work off frustrations and tensions that confront them, the more effective is the latency function.

Secondly, since the maintenance of the modern social system depends upon its members possessing certain types of values, beliefs, knowledge and attitudes, the control of leisure is an important element in the preservation of social stability. By preserving certain desired patterns of norms and roles in the social order, it requires that leisure service agencies stimulate and encourage appropriate uses of leisure. While it is important for government and its representatives to exercise control over people's leisure lives if they are disruptive, it is also necessary to recognize that leisure is becoming a central element in our lives and should not be overly routinized.

A newly acquired sophistication of citizens has resulted in their ques-

[26] Ibid., pp. 53-113.
[27] Roberts, Op. cit., p. 83.

tioning of the value and relevance of goods and services provided through the current leisure service delivery system. They have become aware of the disparity between what is promised in the way of involvement and opportunity and what is actually provided. Leisure service organizations can make a major contribution to the public through which democracy is enlarged, individual dignity enhanced and personal expression and fulfillment are manifested through meaningful recreation opportunity.

A national forum entitled "Educating Tomorrow's Leaders in Parks, Recreation and Conservation" convened by the National Recreation and Park Association, the major voice and stimulus for leisure service in America, stated that the role of parks and recreation in American life indicates that perhaps a change in the concept of the leisure manager is required. Not only should he possess imagination, adaptability and durability in crisis situations. Today's social trends demand another dimension for prospective leisure service managers:

> It simulates empathy, awareness, and sensitivity. It demands an awareness of what is going on beyond the day-to-day mechanics of the field operation. It necessitates involvement with people, a sensitivity to their needs and interests which are often not expressed, and a dedication to humanity that is "above and beyond" the job description.[28]

Kraus suggests that the leisure service field must consciously shift its priorities in the direction of making significant social contributions to urban life. Since the complexity of life in contemporary American society requires a response which extends beyond the traditional view of recreation as activity pursued for its own sake, Kraus indicates that there are three plausible approaches[29]:

1. Park and recreation departments must develop new sets of objectives which encompass programs aimed at reducing social pathology and promoting social welfare. In many cases, this will mean deliberately developing services which incorporate educational and vocational elements, or which service those in the community who have special problems or handicaps.
2. In the past, minority group and other disadvantaged neighborhoods have had the least adequate facilities and most limited recreation programs in many large cities. Today, it is essential that this imbalance be redressed by giving increased emphasis to developing enriched programs and services in such neighborhoods.

---

[28] *Educating Tomorrow's Leaders in Parks, Recreation and Conservation.* Edited by Peter J. Verhoven, Washington, D.C., National Recreation and Park Association, 1968.

[29] Kraus, Richard. *Urban Parks and Recreation: Challenge of the 1970's.* New York, Community Council of Greater New York, 1972, p. 22.

3. Park and recreation departments should undertake special programs aimed at working with delinquent or pre-delinquent youth, the physically and mentally handicapped, the aging, and similar populations. If they do not undertake these responsibilities themselves, they should work closely with those agencies that do, in order to insure a total range of leisure-oriented social services in community life. All major institutions in the modern city—including government, religious agencies, business and industry, schools and colleges, and other civic groups—should be mobilized to cooperate in this effort.

Presently there are 170,000 identified full- and part-time leisure service personnel, with 81,289 full-time year-round practitioners engaged in service to provide leisure opportunities to the public. There are over 16,000 active members in the National Recreation and Park Association, the nation's largest nonprofit organization in the leisure service field.[30] Kraus[31] notes that an additional 150,000 to 200,000 individuals are employed today in full-time, year-round nonprofit public and private agencies which have a primary concern for the provision of recreation facilities and services.

Recreation and leisure service has changed markedly since its official beginning in 1906, with the founding of the Playground Association of America. It progressed through the World War I, the Depression, World War II, the civil rights movement and the general turmoil in the nation's cities. While the concept of leisure opportunity has remained unchanged over the years, the nature of the social and physical environment has been greatly altered. The whole complexity of life challenges the professional leisure service manager to meet these issues with a response that invites involvement, action and self-satisfaction.

[30] "Leisure—A New Dawn in America." *Parks and Recreation* 6: Whole Issue, August, 1971.

[31] Kraus, Richard. *Recreation and Leisure in Modern Society.* New York, Appleton-Century-Crofts, 1971.

CHAPTER 2

Recreation and Leisure Service: Meeting Basic Human Needs

Human Service Organization

Organizations are socially devised. This distinguishes them from machines and the human organism. According to Nigro,[1] organizations are "open systems." The traditional theory of organizations places considerable emphasis upon individual adjustment to the organization; the design of the structure of the organization came first and was the primary consideration. The principles of the traditional approaches (or machine model) of organizational theory developed by Frederick W. Taylor at the turn of the century emerged during an era in which the worker was seen as an instrument of production, a means rather than an end. These are in basic conflict with *industrial humanism,* which was evolved in the 1920's as a result of the Hawthorne studies. Since then, efforts have been made in an increasing number of industries and organizations to redesign jobs and the work environment to meet the needs of the human personality. It is suggested by Nigro that "minute task specialization makes the work repetitive and deadening, narrow span of control and centralized decision making practically eliminate the opportunities for worker self-determination."[2]

The work flow in contemporary organizations is approached from a holistic perspective—each worker engages in a fairly complete work cycle in which whole stages of the job are created for the employee. Leisure service delivery systems which incorporate such a process conceivably increase the possibility of enhancing community spirit and enabling the community to participate at a meaningful level.

This process encourages managers to develop their own solutions to problems at each level in the hierarchy of the organization. Supervisors, center directors and program leaders are encouraged and freed to develop day-to-day work procedure. The process also discourages managers from passing the buck upwards and encourages them to give more discretion to their own subordinates and community participants. This sharing of power and decision making fosters a moral sensitivity and

[1]Nigro, Felix A. *Modern Public Administration.* 2nd ed., New York, Harper and Row, Publishers, 1970, p. 100.

[2] Ibid., p. 96.

increases the possibility of an adequate output and citizen and employee satisfaction with program services.

Eliminating Social Distance

Since the initiation of the War on Poverty in the early 1960's when "maximum feasible participation" became a guiding principle of many urban leisure service organizations, organizations have attempted to bring service closer to the people. This has encouraged the decentralization or "flattening" of the agency to bring about a less rigid and more sensitive response to people who have felt isolated and cut off from the mainstream of public and private services. These outreach efforts have consisted of field offices, mobile fun wagons, traveling play leaders, detached and roving leaders, portable pools and a whole host of program services designed to close the gap between the agents of human services and the recipients of these service offerings.

The intent of leisure service provisions, in large part, has been directed toward the development of programs that meet the needs of the various neighborhoods. It has been increasingly recognized that most human service operations have really functioned only on "lip service," without really effecting a viable relationship with potential participants, particularly the socially and economically deprived central city dweller.

Nigro has referred to the Chicago Park District as an example of a

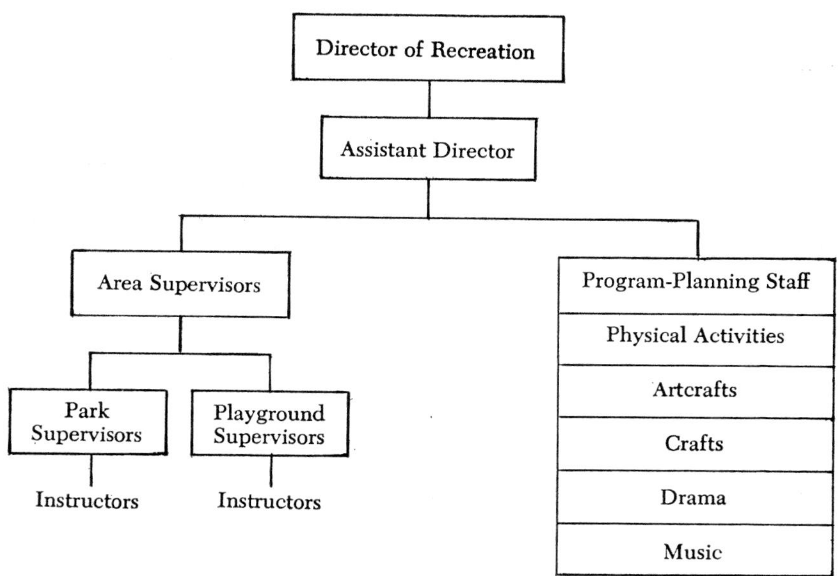

Figure 2-1. Headquarters—Field Organization, Chicago Park District (From Nigro, F. *Modern Public Administration*. 2nd Ed., Copyright 1965, 1970 by Felix A. Nigro. By permission of Harper & Row, Publishers, Inc., p. 128).

decentralized leisure service organization which has attempted to bring service closer to the people and to make provision of special facilities that may be required in any one area.[3] Figure 2-1 shows the headquarter—field office organization of a recreation department. At the head of the department the director and assistant director are shown to have responsibility for providing overall direction from the headquarters office for the city-wide program and services. Thus, the headquarter's staff formulates the broad policies governing the kinds of programs to be offered throughout the city.

The program-planning staff are experts in the different leisure specialties. They make their skills and knowledge available to the instructors in the field locations. The area supervisors serve primarily as administrative coordinators of the various parks and playgrounds in their neighborhoods and as liaison between the neighborhood and headquarters. They do not have direct supervisory control over each community center in the area. The park and playground supervisors serve this function and are responsible for overseeing the various activities and programs offered at each park and playground.

This format is being adopted by more and more municipal leisure service agencies. People of the local community look to the park supervisor for the development of recreation programs that meet their needs. It is his job to develop a balanced program of leisure opportunities in the park or playground that he supervises. The facility supervisor makes the final decisions concerning the work schedule and programming for the park or playground. As viewed by the headquarter's staff, the facility supervisor is the community representative. They rely upon him for the implementation of the rules and policies instituted at the central office.

The decentralization of leisure service operations is viewed as a necessary management technique by some progressive operations in order to facilitate the satisfaction of basic human needs. "It has been increasingly recognized that too much rigidity in formal communication systems is undesirable. So long as normal situations flow through the area supervisor, flexibility of operations is encouraged."[4]

The need for a more informal, people-oriented operational structure has been effectively articulated by Dr. David Gray. He has stated that we presently operate leisure service programs on a "chain-link fence" philosophy which is facility-oriented. Such a concept views leisure service personnel to be primarily concerned with surveillance of the grounds of the recreation center or playground; developing a master program schedule for the facility; assuring superiors and the com-

---

[3] Ibid., p. 128.
[4] Ibid., pp. 130-131.

munity that compliance with rules, safety and proper use of facilities is being met; and coordination of maintenance activities of the facilities.[5]

In contrast to this view, there is a more recent and pertinent concept of the role of leisure service personnel as community figures. This concept identifies leisure service staff as *encouragers of community development* concerned about people, human interaction and preservation of the quality of neighborhood life. This view perceives the dispenser of leisure services as an *encourager* or *enabler* (refer to Chapter 5 for a discussion of the differences between direct service and enabler approaches in recreation and leisure service) who initiates a process that enables the community to satisfy basic human needs, grow in dignity and self-fulfillment.[6]

The changing urban environment requires a new response on the part of leisure service agencies to meet the needs of people. The administrator of a large western city concluded that a "standardized, city-wide program was not adequate to the times." The city was divided into three major areas and a continuing attempt was, and is, being made to tailor recreation programs and activities to the needs of the areas, and in some cases, to the neighborhoods within the areas.[7]

The decentralization of the city's leisure services enabled each of the three service areas to establish its own local programs, although there were still some city-wide programs and events common to all three areas. In the evaluation of this process, recreation leadership positions were re-structured to become *front line contacts* in all neighborhoods of the city, with the additional assignment of becoming information and resource people for the population of the neighborhoods which they served. The development of a community encourager profile by the city's leisure service personnel reflects a trend by some public recreation agencies and many youth-serving organizations which desire to make their services more meaningful. It has been an attempt to *reverse* the process which ordinarily developed unnaturally in communities when recreation programs evolved from the biases, comforts or conveniences of city management and leisure service administration.

More than most other public, voluntary or private agencies, the leisure service function can help reduce alienation of many confused and frustrated people. It can help citizens to develop identity and a sense of community. It allows for the identification of basic human needs which

---

[5] Gray, David E. "The Tyranny of the Chain-Link Fence," *California Parks and Recreation* 10:10, August, 1968.

[6] Refer to Biddle, William W., and Biddle, Loureide J. *Encouraging Community Development.* New York, Holt, Rinehart and Winston, Inc., 1968, for a discussion of the role of community encouragers.

[7] Holman, Howard. "Urban Recreation Today," *California Parks and Recreation* 12:7-8, April, 1970.

are largely unmet. The efforts of leisure service community encouragers working out of centers or in the streets must be directed to help people with their social and psychological problems.

As Cunningham states:

> There is general belief that government is overly centralized, and there is uneasiness over such great concentration of public power. In the face of this distance, people have a feeling of impotence and insignificance. Distance is particularly great between ghetto dwellers and their city government, a fact brought ever more clearly into focus during the [last] . . . decade.[8]

Cunningham also states that citizen involvement is part of a deliberate national trend to transfer certain functions of government to local community control. While no clear overall advantage has emerged as a result of studies that have been conducted of various local operations, it is generally recognized that the great expansion of urban centers has made it necessary to consider new forms of governmental organization. This trend has implications for the leisure service field. "Greater citizen involvement in the meaningful recreation programs which our departments conduct will help to bridge the social distance between the governed and the governing."[9]

Centralized versus Decentralized Operation

It is recognized that centralization frequently reflects too much bureaucratization and a desire to preserve the status quo. The centralized system typically has proved itself incapable of responding effectively to the diverse needs of the population. It has taken a series of violent citizen outbursts to bring home the severity of the day-to-day problems faced by deprived and alienated groups. Reluctantly public and voluntary agencies have realized that the differences in the backgrounds of middle-class and deprived people call for a greater variety of methods than any centralized bureaucracy can authorize, let alone devise and encourage.

It has been further realized that the forces of the establishment leisure service agencies—the boards and commissions, the professional hierarchy, the civil service process, certification and placement, etc.—have for the most part fostered standardization instead of diversity. The net effect has been to create a centralized system which with its commitment to the status quo functions in isolation from the community.

The goal of decentralization efforts by contemporary leisure service agencies is to close the social distance between them and their constituents and to make their services more accessible to the public. The intent is to

---

[8] Cunningham, Ross. "Bases for Urban Recreation Services," *California Parks and Recreation* 12:5-6, April, 1970.

[9] Holman, Op. cit., p. 6.

bring agents of leisure service closer to the community and to improve the quality of community life in order to regain citizen confidence.

Self-Actualization Through Leisure

Maslow developed a theory of human motivation in which he stated that human needs arrange themselves in hierarchies of prepotency.[10] Man is a wanting animal. Every drive is related to the state of satisfaction or dissatisfaction of other drives. He arranged his need-hierarchy in the following ascending order: physiological needs (food, rest, exercise, shelter, protection from the elements); safety needs (protection against danger, threat, deprivation); social needs (need for belonging, for association, for acceptance by his fellows, for giving and receiving love and friendship); ego needs (self-esteem needs, self-confidence, independence, achievement, competence, status, recognition); and self-fulfillment and self-actualization (needs for realizing one's own potentialities, for continued self-development, for being creative).

Self-actualizing people are gratified in all their basic needs (of belonging, affection, respect and self-esteem). They do not feel anxiety-ridden, insecure, unsafe, rejected or unwanted, nor do they have debilitating feelings of inferiority or worthlessness. Maslow also found that self-actualizing people did not feel the frustration that has been exhibited by alienated youth and adults.[11] He suggests that a self-actualizing person transcends the dichotomizing of work and play. Maslow also suggests that a real problem with cultural determinism and the essentially materialistic values which pervade our culture is that many people, particularly the young, are deprived of intrinsic values and frustrated by a society they see mistakenly motivated by only material needs. Leisure service agencies that conceivably focus entirely upon lower-level or "materialistic" needs serve to deprive higher-motivated individuals who seek to satisfy deeper, more intrinsic needs. The full definition of human nature, and therefore, of human needs must include a consideration of intrinsic values.

It is fairly clear that the conditions of modern life give only limited opportunity for people to obtain expression of self-actualization. The deprivation most people experience (both in work with organizations and as private citizens) with respect to the other lower-level needs diverts their energies into the struggle to satisfy those needs, and the higher-order needs of self-esteem and self-fulfillment remain unactivated. Maslow suggested that the average person is 85 percent satisfied in his

---

[10] Maslow, Abraham H. "A Theory of Human Motivation," *Psychological Review* 50:370-396, July, 1943.

[11] ———. "A Theory of Metamotivation: The Biological Rooting of the Value-Life," *The Age of Protest*. Edited by Walt Anderson, Pacific Palisades, California, Goodyear Publishing Company, Inc., 1969, pp. 246-254.

physiological needs, 70 percent satisfied in his safety needs, 50 percent satisfied in his belonging needs, 40 percent in his egoistic needs and only 10 percent in his self-fulfillment needs.

Insofar as only few people achieve the highest need plateau, we know very little about its behavior manifestations. It is suggested by Maslow that the self-actualizing person has a sharpened perception of reality. He is free from the fears and inhibitions which cause others to cover up and mask reality. He accepts himself, others and nature. There is a pervasiveness of spontaneity and creativity among self-actualizing persons.

It has been suggested by Farina that self-actualization is the goal of leisure.[12] He sees leisure as the state or condition of being free from the urgent demands of the lower-level needs. To Farina, leisure is personal, and consists of activities not directly related to utilitarian goals except insofar as they promote self-realization. He sees the essence of his concept of leisure as being free to express oneself through activity—be it intellectual, spiritual, or physical—in order to strive toward one's full potential as a human being.

This view of leisure fits consistently with Maslow's theory of human motivation which recognizes that while behavior is almost always motivated, it is also almost always biologically, culturally and situationally determined. Farina's conceptualization of leisure also is corroborated by Ellis's arousal-seeking theory of play.[13] According to Ellis, play is seen as a class of behaviors that are concerned with increasing the level of arousal of the human organism. Man has a need to maintain arousal and also an incessant need for interaction with the environment in a way that produces arousing stimuli. Ellis puts it thus:

> This idea draws attention to the fact that when the more potent needs of survival have been satisfied the organism is then driven into interactions of increasing complexity with the environment. This is an optimistic statement for recreation professionals. The natural state of man requires arousing interactions with the environment, and to the extent that these are not met by work, they will have to be met through play.[14]

It is therefore understood that the leisure service manager is involved in facilitating the delivery of opportunities for man to *optimize* his arousal level. This theory of play reinforces Maslow's theory of human motivation in that it recognizes the idea that the organism has a need for optimal arousal and arousal-elevating behaviors which are necessary, not surplus or trivial.

---

[12] Farina, John. "Toward a Philosophy of Leisure," *Convergence* 2:14-18, April, 1969.

[13] Ellis, M. J. "Play and Its Theories Re-Examined," *Parks and Recreation* 6:51-55, 89-91, August, 1971.

[14] Ibid., p. 55.

It is suggested by Theobald that as people move toward self-actualization they become more fully human:

> The first step on this route is a search for a degree of security in their life styles. They demand . . . the right to develop their lives for themselves in terms of what is meaningful for them.[15]

As our society becomes more and more affluent, all of the previous dominant drives of the human being—drives for food, clothing and shelter—are in the process of being replaced by a much higher drive, a drive toward the right to be "human." At the same time there are millions of Americans who do not possess the adequate food, clothing and shelter they need for minimal existence. They must constantly divert their energies toward attaining the material necessities of life. This is particularly manifest in central city communities and in outlying rural areas.

If the basic needs can be fulfilled, man is then driven by his own internal necessities to try to discover what will allow him to develop his own capabilities. Conceivably, leisure service agencies can provide *all* of the conditions which will create an environment which is conducive to self-development. If younger people, senior adults, handicapped individuals and socially and economically deprived people are frustrated in their attempts to maximize their potential, there is an increasing likelihood that they will vent their anxiety in negative ways and seek to draw attention to their needs through withdrawal or protest.

The extremely rigid rules and regulations often applied to participants in leisure service programs serve as an example of bureaucratic mania with respect to the suppression of large numbers of individuals from contributing as they could to the development of themselves and of society.

The loss of a sense of community and of any personal contact with one's living environment has depreciated the quality of the neighborhood living space. Man functions best when he understands his actions and when he is able to determine and participate in the entire process. Community life in urban America has had a disintegrating effect for more and more people. The relationship between work, school, family and recreation has become fractionalized. One's perception of his neighbors is often limited, simply because he lacks first-hand knowledge and experience with them in primary group relationships.[16]

The emergence of the need by a growing number of people for self-actualization rests upon the prior satisfaction of their physiological, safety, love and self-esteem needs. It is at this level that we may expect the fullest individual creativeness. Since our society provides few outlets

---

[15]Theobald, Robert. *An Alternative Future for America II.* Chicago, The Swallow Press, Inc., 1970, p. 34.

[16]Murphy, James F. "Community Recreation: A Dynamic Process," *California Parks and Recreation* 28:14, April/May, 1972.

for this expression, we may expect the level of frustration and anomie to continue.

One can trace a relationship between the often narrowing and confining structure of leisure service agencies and the level of frustration and degree of discontent of youth. This was noted by the President's Commission on Civil Disorders, whose report stated that recreation facilities and program provisions in the ghetto areas of many of the nation's cities were woefully limited and unsatisfactory.[17] Leisure service offerings are often conceived with only a limited, narrow view of the rather large role they play in community life. Leisure services are often viewed (both by community residents and public officials) as unobligated time provisions—meaning one has usually had to *earn* the right to participate or has met the necessary traditional requirements considered to be appropriate for engaging in recreation and leisure program offerings. The delivery of leisure service is too often limited to those who conform to these rigid specifications: voluntary activity engaged in leisure for its own sake. Such a rigid requirement prevents a great number of people who have not satisfied lower-order needs from experiencing leisure activity. The unemployed, retired or dropout does not qualify for participation according to the preceding definition.

The implication of the *discretionary time* model of leisure means that the community is a static entity which has only one conceptual and pragmatic orientation. It appears that a sense of community will be stimulated more as a result of peoples' engagement in activities that demand interrelationship of efforts. What usually binds a community together is a common state of mind on the part of its members, a sense of interdependence and loyalty; a result of a dynamic on-going developmental process.

This approach to community life moves human exchange from a banal form of indifferent and formal communication to a more meaningful plateau of interchange which allows the provision of leisure service to function as a holistic process. Leisure service personnel naturally become affiliated with allied human service fields, including social work, counseling, community action and health care. Leisure service personnel become oriented to the *art of community development,* in which emphasis is continuously placed upon the overall quality of community life instead of any specialization, project or program.

Urban life requires that a more active and meaningful pattern of interpersonal and intergroup relationships be fostered. The goals are a deeper and more widespread feeling of local pride and generation of more viable community leisure opportunities. Presently many barriers to

---

[17] *Report of the National Advisory Commission on Civil Disorders.* New York, Bantam Books, Inc., 1968, pp. 143-150.

participation such as foreboding community centers, street access routes which are major transportation links, formality in program structure, insensitive leaders, etc. thwart basic aspirations and create conditions which often institute a psychological threat to the participant. Therefore, people have tended to adopt attitudes of helplessness and dependency. By encouraging primary group experiences in which fundamental social units may be developed, leisure service managers not only provide a setting in which leisure may be engaged in and enjoyed, but also help promote the nucleus of a self-sustaining social group.

Murphy states that there are four essential goals a community leisure "encourager" has:[18]

1. to stimulate the community's ability to accomplish things for itself—solve its own problems;
2. to make appropriate use of various outside related human services and resources;
3. to recognize and take effective steps to meet community needs;
4. to recognize leisure service as a holistic entity and community problems as an outgrowth of the total environment.

According to this conceptualization of leisure service delivery systems, they can be viewed as a self-help process by which people develop an increasing motivation and skill to cope with community problems (including the misuse of leisure) and gain a sense of pride in their community. The creation of a positive and viable community environment by leisure service managers is fundamental to satisfying basic human needs.

The Mess of Decision Making

The traditional view of organization theory has placed decision making at the top of the hierarchy. The result is that the managers at the top of the organization often have only the vaguest notions about the nature of their own work and its effect, if any, on the recipients of leisure service. The social reality of most community recreation operations and particularly youth outreach work is easily lost. The groundwork is laid for manufacturing a mythology that aggravates the very problem with which it is seeking to come to grips. It is unfortunate that many supposed well-meaning managers have not had their hearts on the real task of the agency, which is to meet basic human needs and provide opportunities for meaningful leisure expression by people.

The inappropriate methods of communication and service devised and practiced by leisure service bureaucratic hierarchies serve to reduce effectiveness. Carney, Mattick and Callaway have interpreted the "mess of reality" as perceived by street-level workers and how the end result

---

[18] Murphy, Op. cit., p. 14.

is eventually interpreted by the top managerial level in the organization. They state that:

> (1) the worker at the lowest level [the street-club worker, the case-welfare social worker, the recreation instructor , etc.] reports the "mess of reality" as it is reflected in his street-level perception of the situations he is obliged to deal with; (2) his supervisor [the center director, the supervising social worker, the district recreation supervisor, etc.], however, either cannot use, or does not want to hear about, this "mess of reality." He has problems of his own—too much work, not enough manpower, the exigencies of a busy life—which require a different view of reality. He wants to be helpful, but there are limitations on his time and energy that he communicates to the levels above and below him. Thus, at this second level, a "clean-up" process of selection, rationalization and ordering of priorities begins. (3) When the first-level supervisor reports on his work to his supervisor [the executive director of several youth-serving agency units, the senior recreation supervisor, the head of the branch welfare office, etc.], the selective process of communication has, again, refined the "cleaned-up mess of reality"; it is now simpler, more general, and beginning to take on the logical, conceptual form of processed information structured by the internal needs of a bureaucratic hierarchy. (4) By the time that the top level of the organization [the director of parks and recreation, the board of trustees of the youth-serving agency, etc.] receives what is left of the original street-level perception of the "mess of reality," it has undergone a remarkable transformation: the youth-serving agency or park and recreation department has had a "high degree of success," the welfare system has been "adequately serving" its clients, the city administration has been "coping" with crime and disorder, etc. Unfortunately these refined versions of reality are not reflected in the work and experience of the lowest-level worker, who is obliged to confront the same old "mess of reality" and do what he can to bring order out of chaos while seeking the support and help of those above him who have their own version of reality.[19]

Efforts which seek to link the top and the bottom levels of the bureaucratic hierarchy so that the top level is not "victimized" by the selective communication process just described are essential if leisure service expects to provide meaningful service offerings to the community. Bridging the hierarchical levels in organization results in the fullest understanding possible of the "street" situation so as to effect the most meaningful service.

Contemporary organization theory allows for decision-making authority and responsibility to be distributed throughout the organization. Each individual has the right to make decisions commensurate with his position in the organization, which holds him responsible for the effect of his particular decisions. This type of process appears to be more responsive to the people as communication links are established at every level in the hierarachy (center director, supervisor, director). As pointed out by Carney, Mattick, and Callaway, the further up the hierarchy each problem must go for solution, the more time and effort are required and the slower the organization is in responding to the situation.

---

[19] Carney, Frank J., Mattick, Hans W., and Callaway, John D. *Action on the Streets: A Handbook for Inner City Youth Work.* New York, Association Press, 1969, pp. 13-14.

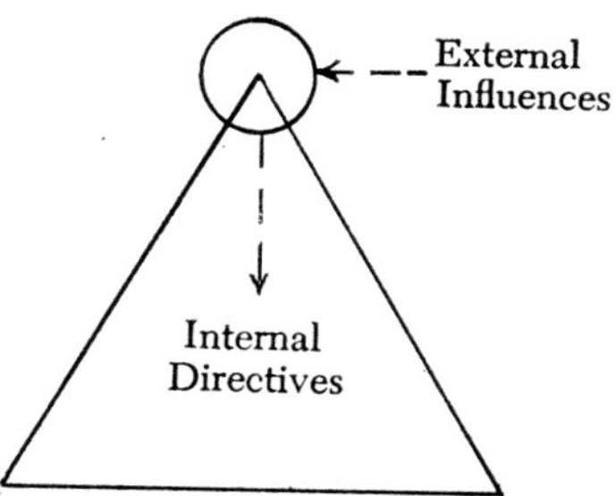

Figure 2-2. Traditional View of Organizational Change (From Hampton, D. R., Summer, C. E., and Webber, R. A. *Organizational Behavior and the Practice of Management.* Glenview, Ill., Scott, Foresman and Company, 1968, p. 646).

Gray has stated that this clustering effect in the decision-making process or *galaxy concept* seems to be an appropriate response because numerous decisions cluster around a central theme and it is not necessary to consult each level of the hierarchy since decision networks form around each major task.

The traditional view of the manager's role emphasizes control and adaptation to ensure continuity and necessary adjustments. The centralized-function structure of organization assumes that the top man is the only one responsive to the outside world, with everyone below responsible to him.

As noted in Figure 2-2 the top man is the center of information flow. He responds to external forces and adjusts internal processes. This view of organizational change is consistent with the Theory X approach espoused by Douglas McGregor.[20]

A question needs to be posed at this point with respect to the state of operation that exists in most leisure service agencies. If the structure of the organization is derived from its relation to the social and physical environment, should the decision-making process emanate from the top down or the bottom up? The type of centralized operation characteristic of most traditional organizations, including leisure service agencies, in which face-to-face contact with the clientele constitutes the "blood and guts" of the operation, appears to be totally inadequate and irrelevant as a means of initiating a responsive service function within communities.

There is another perspective, the behavioral view of organizational change, which states that there are actually multiple channels through which external pressure and information enter the organization.[21] This

[20] McGregor, Douglas. *The Human Side of Enterprise.* New York, McGraw-Hill, 1960.

[21] Hampton, D. R., Summer, C. E., and Webber, R. A. *Organizational Behavior and the Practice of Management.* Glenview, Ill,. Scott, Foresman and Company, 1968, p. 649.

more realistic view of management analyzes the structuring of the operation so that appropriate change decisions are made at all levels within the organization—not solely by the man at the top.

Figure 2-3 shows how the emphasis in the behavioral model of change is on the totality or unity of organization and its internal and external goals. This model corresponds to McGregor's Theory Y. The central principle of Theory Y is that of *integration:* the creation of conditions such that the members of the organization can achieve their own goals best by directing their efforts toward the success of the operation. The principle of integration demands that both the organization's and individual's needs be recognized. It means working together for the success of the organization so that all may share in the resulting rewards of service. The behavioral model of organizational change acknowledges that there must be a tolerance for balance within each part and among the parts that constitute the whole.

This approach to management places the primary emphasis upon the recognition of any legitimate request and need that may be beneficial to the delivery of service. It places the organization within truly legitimate community context and encourages the solicitation of citizen requests for programs and services. Management's modification of the structure, duties or authority will then have greater impact both on the organization and in the community.

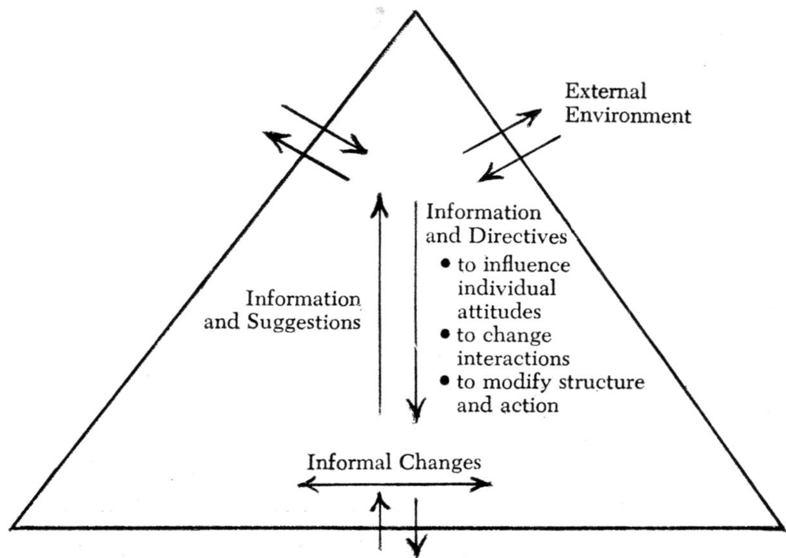

Figure 2-3. Behavioral View of Organizational Change (From Hampton, D. R., Summer, C. E., and Webber, R. A. *Organizational Behavior and the Practice of Management.* Glenview, Ill., Scott, Foresman and Company, 1968, p. 649).

The behavioral view of organizational change comes closest to assuring participants that their basic needs will be recognized and fulfilled. It also creates a climate whereby the structuring of leisure opportunities will be relevant to a given community.

CHAPTER 3

Recreation and Leisure Service: A Social Concern

The primary area of social concern is the impact of technology upon the human and physical environment. While the founders of the playground and recreation movement in America recognized early in the twentieth century that the needs of the underprivileged were paramount in municipally operated recreation programs, they were not much concerned with the quality of the natural environment. However, as noted by Nesbitt, Brown, and Murphy[1] the earliest practitioners had a motivation in which the social ends of human development were central. Recreation and leisure service is not a panacea for all the social ills of our society, but it does contribute to the improvement of the social and physical environment.

THE SOCIAL ENVIRONMENT

The increased complexity of urban life has magnified the conditions which encourage social stress, frustration and isolation. The dissension and violence emanating from poor slum neighborhoods in the early 1960's began to highlight the urgency of the deleterious conditions, and the imperative nature of dissatisfied human needs. Jenkins reported a study of New York City neighborhoods in regard to recreation needs and services. The study indicated a deficiency of group work and recreation facilities in the areas of most need. The study approach embodied the philosophy that priorities in community services should go to persons least able to pay as well as those experiencing maximum pressures involved in neighborhood change or in social disorganization.

The study yielded important data as well as new concepts in the delivery of leisure service. By recognizing individual differences in consumer patterns, a long-held tradition in programming that has seldom been practiced, recreation service could assume that individuals would seek activities of their choice.[2] However, the primary determinant in

[1] Nesbitt, John A., Brown, Paul D. and Murphy, James F. *Recreation Leisure Service for the Disadvantaged: Guidelines to Program Development and Related Readings.* Philadelphia, Lea & Febiger, 1970, p. ix.

[2] Jenkins, Shirley. *Comparative Recreation Needs and Services in New York Neighborhoods.* New York, Community Council of Greater New York, 1963, p. 13.

achieving satisfaction through socially approved activities has usually been equated with one's financial capacity to purchase enjoyment. The need for public and voluntary youth-serving leisure service was considered to be important in the lives of disadvantaged groups, particularly impoverished blacks, Puerto Ricans, and Chicanos. Jenkins found the deprivation in the nation's largest city to be particularly severe in the areas of greatest socioeconomic need. As a general pattern, it was found that the neighborhoods with the highest degree of socioeconomic need and community disorganization rated well below the city average in terms of available public and voluntary agency group work and recreation services and resources.

Additionally, many of the problems associated with segregated housing were reflected in neighborhood recreation center racial composition. The fact that an agency was found to be open to all citizens did not mean that services were used by members of all groups. Black residents comprised a higher percentage of membership in public recreation centers than they did of the population, which reflected a need for subsidized recreation and leisure service for deprived groups.[3]

Public recreation and leisure service is the right of all people; that being constitutionally guaranteed and affirmed by the Supreme Court. On two grounds, that of segregation in one form or another, and through inadequate and inferior provision, it has, in effect, been denied to large masses of the black population as well as to other racial minorities.

One of the most difficult problems facing leisure service has been that of achievement of integrated participation. Whether as a consequence of neighborhood housing patterns, the aggressive or antisocial behavior of some black or brown participants, the withdrawal of whites at various age levels, or, for numerous reasons, the tendency of blacks to avoid activities with white participants, the problem has been found to be a pervasive one.

The amount of neglect and deprivation of ghetto life in America finally resulted in some of the most violent and bloody racial disorders during the summer months of 1967 and 1968. President Johnson appointed a commission, the National Advisory Commission on Civil Disorders, to determine the reasons for the disorders that occurred in 1967.[4] According to the Commission, inadequacy of recreation facilities and leadership was the *fifth* most important cause of the riots. Among the 20 cities that accounted for the 24 most serious disorders, grievances relating to recreation were found in 15 and were ranked of first importance in three, second in one, and third in four cities.

---

[3] Ibid., pp. 150-152.

[4] *Report of the National Advisory Commission on Civil Disorders*. New York, Bantam Books, Inc., 1968.

The Commission examined ghetto grievances and identified those complaints which seemed most causal. Of the 12 most significant grievances, poor and inadequate recreation facilities and leadership ranked fifth behind police practices, unemployment, housing and education. Recreation was regarded as a *more* significant grievance than the ineffectiveness of the political structure, discriminatory administration of justice, inadequate municipal services and inadequate welfare programs. In several cities dissatisfaction over recreation facilities was the proximate cause or issue in a violent outbreak.

The fundamental inequity of opportunity in health, housing, welfare, education and recreation has stirred the more youthful and emotional elements of the ghetto communities to respond to these atrocities in the form of increasingly violent protest action. Public officials, in many cases, have largely failed to serve as catalysts for social change and progress in slum areas. Rigidity has led to a failure by public officials to respond adequately either by ethical or professional standards.

Two studies, one by Kraus[5] of the five boroughs of New York City and 24 suburban communities in New York, New Jersey, and Connecticut, and one by the National League of Cities[6] of recreation in 15 major cities, showed that public recreation and leisure service for blacks and other deprived groups was poorly conceived, extremely inadequate, underfinanced and in demand by inner-city residents. The researchers of these investigations questioned whether egalitarian principles consistent with professional leisure service objectives to serve all people with quality service were applied.

The study by Kraus points out compounded costs of neglecting recreation as an essential component of the cluster of community services necessary for human well-being. These findings are significant because they provide a systematic analysis of black participation in public recreation programs, the extent of program integration and the administrative problems encountered in planning and managing recreation facilities and programs of the residents of urban and suburban communities today.

The study points to the severity of the problem in the following ways:

1. There is a relationship between racial disturbance and inadequate recreation facilities and leadership.
2. Recreation is the right of all people; through segregation and inadequate provision of leisure service, it has been denied to large segments of the urban population.

[5] Kraus, Richard. *Public Recreation and the Negro: A Study of Participation and Administrative Practices.* New York, Center for Urban Education, 1968.

[6] *Recreation in the Nation's Cities: Problems and Approaches.* Washington, D.C., Department of Urban Studies, National League of Cities, 1968.

3. The urban black has a special problem with respect to leisure and its use since there are a comparatively high proportion of unemployed blacks; thus, free time is frustrating and often negatively based.
4. More and improved recreation patterns for blacks—beyond entertainment and athletics—have improved the overall image of blacks.
5. Recreation serves as a "threshold" or entry to other forms of social service in the community setting.

Kraus revealed that little deliberate use is made of leisure service as a means of developing intergroup relationships. This is particularly true in school desegregation programs, in which bused-in children are promptly returned to their home neighborhoods at the end of class and not allowed to participate in after-school recreation activities.

The whole question of the delivery of recreation and leisure service has been scrutinized as a result of surveys and investigations of impoverished conditions in central cities growing out of the civil unrest during the 1960's. Public servants have assumed that all groups of people are equal in their need for recreation and that it is universally a voluntary experience. The fallacy of these concepts is that as an operational set of guidelines they have not worked for various subordinated groups.

The voluntary nature of recreation has been presumed to be a requisite for participation in recreation and leisure service programs. It has rarely been voluntary, however, for blacks, Chicanos, Puerto Ricans and American Indians who have lacked the "appropriate" knowledge, attitudes and skills necessary for engaging in white-structured and white-managed programs. A lack of specialized approaches to recreation and leisure service delivery for subordinated groups has deprived them of the opportunity to participate on a voluntary, willful basis. According to Farina[7] leisure is the state or condition of being free from the urgent demands of lower-level human needs. The physiological, safety, love and belonging, and esteem needs must be satisfied in order for one to become self-actualized, which is the end or goal of leisure. However, if one is plagued by the inability to satify lower-level needs, he is not free to address himself to the attainment of satisfaction of higher-level needs. Needs at lower levels in Maslow's hierarchical ordering are more basic and have greater power than those at high levels. "Hence lower level needs must be relatively well satisfied, on a continuing basis, before the individual is free to concentrate his resources on achieving satisfaction of higher level needs."[8] In Maslow's scheme, an explanation is pro-

[7] Farina, John. "Toward a Philosophy of Leisure," *Convergence* 2:15-18, 1969.
[8] Ibid., p. 15.

vided for the wide range of motivations that may be attributed to people's engagement in leisure.

The National League of Cities study, co-sponsored with the Bureau of Outdoor Recreation and the Department of Interior, found that "in most cities surveyed, officials readily admitted that the needs of all population groups were not being adequately met. Only in recent years have cities begun to recognize an obligation to provide recreation for the handicapped and the deprived."[9] The survey also stated that the inadequate and inappropriate provision of facilities has resulted in resentment by inner-city residents toward administrators of leisure service. One's predisposition to experiencing leisure is conditioned by a number of factors including physical desire, personality and environmental readiness and competence.

Two of the eight findings reached by the National League of Cities that are of particular relevance to the provision of leisure service for deprived citizens are as follows:

1. Residents of deprived urban neighborhoods are almost entirely *dependent* upon public recreation facilities, whereas residents of more affluent neighborhoods have a wide range of recreation alternatives. Adequate recreation programs and facilities are considered a high priority item among the deprived.
2. Residents of urban slum neighborhoods frequently charge that too much effort is directed toward middle and upper income groups, and that recreation planning in urban areas is being performed by persons having no real knowledge of the needs or desires of the deprived. To overcome this charge, planners should encourage the participation of a wide spectrum of the community in the planning process. To be successful, recreation programs must be what the people want, not what the recreation department believes to be best for the people. Increased emphasis on citizen participation can be an essential component for the development of meaningful programs.[10]

Comments appearing in the National League of Cities report noted that municipal recreation development projects and programs have often been activities in which the economically deprived, especially young people, have been unable to participate. This form of planning in depressed areas appears to have been done consistently by persons having no real knowledge of the needs or desires of subordinated racial or ethnic groups.

While many city officials have claimed that the recreation needs of economically disadvantaged persons are essentially the same as those

---

[9] National League of Cities, Op. cit., p. 2.
[10] Ibid., p. 2.

of the rest of the community, studies by Jenkins, Kraus, The President's Commission on Civil Disorders and National League of Cities have documented the dependency of the poor on public, commercial and voluntary group-work recreation facilities. They concluded that the deprived require greater opportunities for recreation than do the advantaged. It was suggested by the National League of Cities report that "the special needs of the poor require more neighborhood recreation facilities in inner-city areas and more person-oriented recreation programs in which supervisors can work with small groups in meaningful interpersonal relationships."[11]

Many leisure service agencies find themselves in a position in which they no longer are meeting the needs of the urban poor. Their life style and milieu often are neglected, unrecognized and even suppressed. Perhaps the biggest area of concern which serves as a barrier to effecting the efficient delivery of leisure service revolves around the issue of citizen involvement. Williams states:

> Citizens, often wanting to have a word or hand in decision making and program determination, feel inadequate when confronted with professional superiority and techniques, a feeling produced not totally from lack of education but more from lack of experience. Civil Service systems fail to recognize the inner-city residents volunteer service of special skills in considering them for employment. Governmental restrictions and arbitrary boundaries for grants and projects eliminate interested communities and neighborhoods from participation. Often, too, agencies find the individual's stay in the community to be temporary, and are wary of involving transient residents in lasting programs and situations. In addition, agencies are often confronted with citizen demands that create hostilities between the two groups.[12]

The issue of self-determination, magnified by the plight of subordinated groups, has become an emotional one which is stimulated in urban communities because of the rigid stance of the "establishment" with regard to social change. It is suggested that the free will of man to be heard has been denied at the various levels of government. As a result, the "establishment" is not only being questioned, but it is being challenged by proponents of local community control. The proponents for decentralization of service, through which decision making is brought closer to the people, argue that there is need for change, but to alter the "establishment" through conventional channels appears to be impossible because, in the eyes of the poor and "have nots," government does not really want to change.

Recreation and leisure service agencies too, have failed to effectively

---

[11] Ibid., p. 17.

[12] Williams, John G. "Modernizing Urban Park and Recreation Systems." Speech delivered at the National Congress for Recreation and Parks, Houston, October 19, 1971.

incorporate the needs and human resources of subordinated groups in the organization and delivery of programs. Williams states:

> There is a definite failure on the agency's part to recognize indigenous human and natural resources, particularly in the case of youth, that could be utilized by the agencies. Too often, lack of financial resources is the excuse given for poor programming, and no attempts are made to overcome this economic limitation.[18]

Baltimore's Bureau of Recreation undertook an investigation in 1970 in an attempt to develop leadership for inner-city residents. The project was co-sponsored by the National Recreation and Park Association and the Office of Economic Opportunity. Two similar facilities located in comparable inner-city areas were provided, one to be operated, staffed and funded as a centralized facility operated by the city Bureau of Recreation; the other facility was turned over to a neighborhood board as the model of a self-determined, decentralized operation. Each facility had a similar budget which was provided by the city plus an additional $15,000 grant from O.E.O. to supplement its program and staff. The two facilities operated for a period of one year and efforts were made to evaluate the effectiveness of the two facilities.

There was not a great deal of difference in the quality of the two programs. The staff in the centralized facility had some advantages in that they had a greater number of years of experience and more formal education and in some instances, the program reflected this difference. However, the decentralized program had much more community support in terms of participation and acceptance due to the involvement of many citizens on the recreation center board and various committees. Additionally, the leadership of the center came from the community and had been selected by the community.

Overall the demonstration project pointed out the possibilities of decentralizing certain functions and programs of park and recreation services and the advantages of involving more citizens in self-determination as it applies to the destiny of their community. The area of professional concern related to establishing a viable relationship with socioculturally disadvantaged clientele is paramount. Certain important steps need to be taken if the park and recreation movement is going to meet the challenge of the urban poor, alienated youth and other frustrated groups. According to Williams there are six areas of critical importance:

1. Professionals will have to examine their philosophy, goals and objectives, principles, standards, techniques, etc., to determine if they are appropriate for inner-city clientele. For best results these

---

[18] Ibid.

changes should be made with sincerity and a desire to change on their own rather than by political force or outside pressures.

2. New techniques need to be found for better communication.
3. Make the inner-city residents more aware of some of the professional problems by involving them in programs and program determination. Involve them more in the process of making government and appropriate legislative bodies aware of the wants and needs of the community.
4. Get Civil Service Commissions, who are often the recruiters, examiners, and certifiers of recreation and park personnel, to re-evaluate and change educational and experience requirements to make them more realistic.
5. There is a need to get educational institutions to redirect training from a work-oriented society to a leisure-based society.
6. Find ways for government to do more research and experimentation with new programming in park and recreation areas.[14]

Because minority groups, youth and other disaffected people find government remote and unresponsive to their needs, decentralized neighborhood units have assumed a new urgency. The National Advisory Commission on Civil Disorders recommended the establishment of neighborhood city halls that would make information about government programs and services available to ghetto residents. This would enable them to make more effective use of such programs and services and increase meaningful community access to an involvement in the planning and implementation of policy affecting their neighborhoods.

There are many subgroups in America, including blacks, Chicanos, youth, senior adults, etc. Because of their diversity and uniqueness, each requires a different response. While leisure service agencies have attempted to meet the differing needs of each group, they have often lumped them all together for purposes of expediency and efficiency when designing programs and facilities. But this approach will not work very successfully any more. According to Altshuler[15] there is a need to treat a group in such a way as to develop its sense of unity, by responding to those particular values, attitudes and interests that are likely to cultivate group pride. When the "lumping" strategy is applied to black people, for example, we may expect it to fail for the following reasons: "(a) white separatism and discrimination, (b) the consequent black sense of being an oppressed, permanent minority, and (c) the excessive size of . . . cities as primary local jurisdictions."[16]

---

[14] Ibid.

[15] Altshuler, Alan A. *Community Control: The Black Demand for Participation in Large American Cities.* New York, Pegasus, 1970, p. 125.

[16] Ibid., p. 126.

Changing Role of Community Leisure Service

Traditionally, most leisure service agencies, like other local and state government services, have operated under a centralized authority which has perpetuated the "chain-link fence" philosophy described in Chapter 2. In contrast to this view, there is a concept of the role of professional recreation personnel as *community catalysts* or *encouragers*. Areas of concern outside his immediate realm will have significant influence on the delivery of leisure service in relation to the whole field of human services, in which health, education, employment and welfare concerns will function in concert with each other. For example, leisure service offerings will be devised to impart basic skills and knowledge which will help welfare recipients cope with consumer problems, provide basic insight and information which can subsequently lead to employment opportunities and improve environmental conditions. In this way, leisure service personnel will adapt their skills and knowledge to fit more realistically with the new functions of recreation and parks necessary in urban life.

It is suggested by Gray and others that in order to adjust to their new role, leisure service managers must become "outreach" workers and advocates for social change who are goal-oriented rather than "isolationists" who are facility-oriented within the protective confines of their chain-link fences. Gray's idea is not new in the delivery of leisure service, although it has recent origins. The rise of protest tactics has made possible dramatic social action to deal with the problems of race, poverty and inferior and inadequate recreation facilities and program offerings that would not otherwise be on the agenda of leisure service agency policy.

The Columbia University gymnasium dispute, which flared up on April 24, 1966, represented a significant change in the role of recreation professional personnel with regard to participation in civil rights protest activity. Since 1957, Columbia University had conducted an outdoor recreation program for ghetto children in Morningside Park, New York. The program was conducted under an agreement with the city parks department. Columbia University decided to construct a gymnasium in Morningside Park, with Columbia subletting to the city the lower portion of the building for community use. The protest demonstration on April 24, 1966 was organized by Thomas Hoving, then Parks Commissioner. Hoving reportedly pledged to do all in his power to prevent construction of the gymnasium. "Hoving is regarded as having helped to mobilize community opposition to the gym . . . The gym became a convenient symbol for all the grievances of the ghetto against the university."[17]

---

[17] *Urban Riots: Violence and Social Change.* Edited by Robert H. Connery, New York, Vintage Books, 1969, p. 129.

This type of action demonstrated a change in the traditional approach undertaken by professional leisure service managers, who largely had kept out of the issues of racial and other social concerns not "directly" related to the delivery of leisure service.

The outgrowth of the Columbia University dispute appears to be an emphasis of the growing separation between theory and practice of egalitarian principles of democratic living and of the increased chance of making egalitarianism (equal opportunity for all people) operational for all Americans less likely with each passing year.

Enforced isolation of blacks, Chicanos, and other subordinated groups within the community setting becomes potentially dangerous because of the way it nourishes white racism at both individual and institutional levels.[18] A pluralistic approach appears to be more conducive to building interracial and intergroup harmony and spirit.

The status of the provision of leisure service for blacks and other subordinated minority groups has remained largely unchanged since the 1920's (when special attempts to meet the needs of blacks were first introduced by the Bureau of Colored Work of the Playground and Recreation Association of America) despite significant social changes due to Supreme Court decisions, legislation and improved service concepts. Blacks are increasingly migrating to central city areas in metropolitan communities. Seventy-four percent of all blacks lived in metropolitan areas in 1970, and some 57.8 percent of the black population compared with 27.5 percent of the white population were living in central cities.[19]

The facilitation of a pluralistic structuring of society in which there are cross-racial friendships, racial interdependence and a strong measure of personal and group autonomy, appears to increase opportunity for beneficial cross-racial evaluation and mutual respect. It represents a desire by many subordinated groups to re-structure their life styles to achieve a fresh and vital sense of community and self-determination.

The Future Course of Race Relations

The future of race relations has no clear picture. The developments which arose in the 1960's were not entirely anticipated. While symptoms were present, most public officials were making apparent appropriate steps to ameliorate the deleterious conditions of slum life and important social legislation and court litigation opened the way to increased black opportunities in the social, political and economic structure of the country. However, there appear to be important indices of identifiable

---

[18] Pettigrew, Thomas F. *Racially Separate or Together?* New York, McGraw-Hill Book Company, 1971, p. 301.

[19] Lerner, William. *Pocket Data Book: USA 1971.* Washington, D.C., U. S. Government Printing Office, 1971, p. 40.

social change which affect the pattern of racial interaction in general, and relate to the provision of public recreation and leisure service for black people.

The future provision of recreation services in urban areas for black people appears to depend upon and will be directly affected by changes in the social structure and by altered life styles which reflect new roles and relationships between people. They include the following:

1. The urbanization and metropolitanization of black people in the six decades since 1910 resulting from technological, political, economic and social changes have brought black people into contact and competition with white society. The population influx of semi-skilled and unskilled blacks to urban areas and a consequent decrease in available land for parks and recreation facilities have lessened recreational opportunities for the black population in the near future.
2. An increasing industrial trend to move from urban to suburban areas has meant less job opportunities for black people. This, coupled with the continuing migration of black people to the cities, has increased the urban unemployment rate.
3. The movement of middle and upper-income persons to the suburbs has influenced the development and placement of recreation facilities near urban fringes where the majority of the white population resides.
4. A diminishing urban tax base for local government income at a time of increased demand for improved health, education, welfare and recreation services has created a compounded need for more service to be delivered to the central cities by public authorities.
5. Federal legislation and Supreme Court decisions have improved the social, economic, and political status of blacks by significantly undermining the legal structure of segregation and inequities of everyday life faced by blacks.

These conditions have influenced the increased concern by public, private, and voluntary recreation officials to locate needed facilities and services in central city areas and have led to participation by black residents in the planning and operating of health, education and welfare services and in the political life of the city. There has also been a corollary movement in this direction in community recreation service.

Poor black youth and adults suffer most from the fact that the great majority of existing recreation areas are located outside inner-cities, and are relatively inaccessible to them. In addition, restrictive state and local policies and expenditure patterns are tending to preserve and prolong these inequities.

Local leadership of recreation and leisure service appears to have been most successful when a comprehensive approach has been incorporated into providing needed services. This principle embraces the belief that leisure service is most meaningful when jobs, education, health and welfare and recreational opportunities are embodied in a single effort to make leisure a positive and constructive reality. The concept is strengthened by decentralizing the control and direction of recreation in the communities affected by the provision of leisure service. It is essential that neighborhood youth and adults become involved in the planning, coordination and administration of the programs.

Examples of community self-help programs which have been successful and are representative of the pluralistic concept of leisure service delivery are as follows:

1. Los Angeles youth have participated in "Direction Sports," which combines education and competitive sports. The program operates out of inner-city neighborhoods several days a week and includes competition in arithmetic skills between two teams, with the winning team applying bonus points toward its score in the touch football game which follows the exercises in educational games.
2. Seattle has initiated "Pitch-In," a special game program for poor youth. "Pitch-In" coordinates all youth activity programs including employment, education and recreation throughout the city. Programs have included creative writing, a debate program, family films, a neighborhood teen newspaper, and a mobile library and bookstore. In addition, film making, street theater, and a downtown beautification project have been parts of the program.
3. The Encampment for Citizenship program, an educational project designed to provide leadership opportunities to young people from a variety of racial and economic backgrounds, has been operating for the past several years. The Encampment program emphasizes learning by participation. Campers are offered a mixture of lectures, films, discussions, "how-to" workshops, part-time service work, and recreation and cultural activities. Workshops held include study of black and Mexican-American heritage, American Indian culture, environment, civil rights and educational reform.
4. The city of Reading, Pennsylvania, has had a "work-reaction" program, which combines employment and recreation. The project enables youth to work during the morning hours and take part in recreation activities during the afternoon. The lunch hour has involved a period for discussion of issues selected by youth.
5. The city of Louisville has developed a community and vocational program for central city youth. "Project WORC"—for work orientation, recreation and culture—the program is primarily aimed at improving the participants' "self-concept." Youth are paired with assistant principals and special teachers to supervise recreation

and other activities for young people. They are also involved in recruiting and hiring youth for school programs.

These and other comprehensive recreation program efforts are designed to directly attack the recurring problems of youth. Self-help programs emphasize the knowledge and skills needed by members of a community so that they may meet many of their own basic needs in terms of food, housing, clothing, education and recreation. Self-help skills are particularly important in depressed urban areas, where a majority of blacks reside, as contrasted with advantaged communities where sufficient wealth exists to purchase desired services.

The perpetuation of the previous patterns of relations in leisure service does not seem to fit with recent history. Black children born in the decades of 1950 and 1960 are relatively free from the principal social controls recognized by their parents and grandparents, from the restraints of an extended kinship system and the acceptance of the inevitability of white supremacy. There has been a dismantling of the formal structure of white supremacy. The black appeals and demands for liberation since 1966 have been for the total elimination of racial oppression and the eradication of the burden of racism that black Americans have borne individually and collectively since the first settlement in America.

Successful re-structuring, particularly of public leisure service programs aimed at paralleling the new thrust of black pride, has been oriented to local community needs and has been organized and administered substantially by the neighborhood residents affected by service. The development of productive cultural enrichment and self-help programs oriented to indigenous neighborhood needs has contributed to the democratization of recreation and enhanced the value of the programs.

Any prediction about the future would have to be cognizant of the preceding five conditions. The tenets of egalitarianism were largely developed by white people in a dominant position in society, and as conceived, do not appear to be tenable in a biracial society. At the same time, separatist demands by black militants also seem to lack sufficient viability in a white-controlled society.

It is contended by some social scientists that broad measures to "institutionalize" the total black experience would increase racial pride, a powerful motivating force. The entire program of projecting positive black models—businessmen, professional people and entertainers—would provide the foundation for unified political action by the black community representatives who speak in its best interests.

Comer states that the development of unique black potential would not be in conflict with egalitarian principles, He thinks it would be in harmony with the total American culture[20]:

[20] Comer, James P. "The Social Power of the Negro," *Scientific American* 216: #4: 27, 1967.

> The idea of creating Negro enterprises and institutions is not intended as a rejection of genuinely concerned white people or as an indictment of all existing organizations. White people of good will with interest, skills and funds are needed and—contrary to the provocative assertions of a few Negroes—are still welcome in the Negro community. The kind of "black power" that is proposed would not promote riots; rather, by providing constructive channels for the energies released by the civil rights movement, it should diminish the violent outbursts directed against the symbols of white power and oppression: the police and the white merchants.
>
> To call for Negro institutions, moreover, is not to argue for segregation or discrimination. . . . The aim is to make these cities places where peple can live decently and reach their highest potential with or without integration.

The racial character of the nation's central cities and suburban population compositions has resulted in concentrations of black and white groups. The emerging pluralistic approach, an interdependent structure, appears to offer the best opportunity of fulfilling egalitarian principles and is the most consistent with democratic ideals.

The inherent contradiction in the traditional democratizing philosophy, based on the dictates of white standards of conduct and premises for participation in the social life of sociey (more typical of homogeneous community structure of the 1920's and 1930's), does not allow for the differentiation of sub-community programs and services. The present existence of segregated black and white neighborhoods requires separate structuring and delivery of public recreation and leisure service in order to meet the varied and unique needs of each community.

Pluralistic or Singular Program Design

There appear to be two reasonable alternatives to the contradictory situation confronting America with respect to race relations:

1. Change the social order to conform more closely to the internalized ideal of the American creed–assimilation–which has not worked practically.
2. Change the thrust of the socializing function of minority participation to conform to the actualities of achieving full citizenship in a pluralistic relationship.

The former alternative appears more difficult to achieve as it would demand radical and most probably violent change in the social order. It also appears that there is reason to doubt whether the present structure of the American society could change rapidly enough to meet the demands of subordinated blacks when it is highly dysfunctional with regard to their needs. The full integration of American blacks into the public sectors of our society on an equal basis has occurred largely through "forced" means. Social equality will require a vast alteration of the attitudes of many white Americans. Total assimilation would involve the disappearance of a separate black sub-community and group identity, which ultimately would lead to the absorption of black genetic strains into the white race. Such a proposal denies the progress blacks have achieved in the past two decades and would not be realistic in light of black Africa's ascendancy to power or of American black identification with black liberation developments.

The latter alternative of resocialization of the black American in terms of his group values and interests as they relate to the actualities of American society would tend to ameliorate black frustration and alienation. Moreover, this resocialization would provide the black community with a legitimate group point of reference from which to pursue its interests. Recreation and leisure services, directed to the sub-community level, would seemingly be more reflective of black needs and interests and would be more in line with present sociopolitical trends.

A pluralistic approach to service seems to be the most attainable method of satisfying the leisure needs and interests of the black community. When recreation service assumes the role of a catalytic agent, sub-community provisions appear to be more tenable and appropriate. Programs would recognize the black community needs, cultural values and would be relevant to the functional requirements of black Americans.

If black Americans are finally to achieve a meaningful share of what American society has to offer, that society itself must evolve into a more just democracy. The black community must become unified and integrated to maximize the interests of the group. As LeMelle and LeMelle put it:

> The achievement of legitimacy for a total black point of reference is the necessary first step toward establishing mutually viable black/white relations in the United States.[21]

The standardization of a city-wide recreation program based on typical or modal community interests and needs is irrelevant to the times and to the demographic and ecological character of the nation's urban communities. Programs must be tailored to the particular needs of the various neighborhoods and districts consistent with the findings in the studies by Jenkins, the National League of Cities, Kraus and the Kerner Commission in order to be adaptable to the particular specialized needs of citizens. Since residents of deprived urban neighborhoods are almost entirely dependent upon public recreation facilities, leisure services are considered a high priority among them.

A society aimed at achieving democratic, egalitarian objectives seemingly must develop means whereby subordinated people, who for years have occupied the bottom of the socioeconomic ladder, have the opportunity to participate meaningfully in the abundance and richness of American society. In addition to providing leisure opportunities for black people, recreation and leisure service must provide assistance in

---

[21] LeMelle Tilden J., and LeMelle, Wilbert J. *The Black College: A Strategy for Relevancy*. New York, Frederick A. Praeger, Publishers, 1969, p. 130.

helping them achieve skills consistent with their subcultural values unimpeded by dominant values and beliefs.

The primary goal of America, as stated by the National Advisory Commission on Civil Disorders, must be a single society in which every citizen is free to live and work according to his capability and desires, not his color. While it still is a long step from the constitutional and legal enactment of civil rights to their implementation, the constitutional basis of these rights has been firmly established and has served as an important lever for exerting pressure for full inclusion of black people.

The demand by blacks is not for the inclusion of blacks as such, but for the elimination of any category defined as inferior in itself. According to Parsons, "The pluralistic solution . . . is neither one of separatism—with or without equality—nor of assimilation, but one of full participation combined with the preservation of identity."[22] The provision of recreation and leisure service in line with a pluralistic approach would support the integration of racial groups without jeopardizing a loss of black identity. It would also be compatible with helping to raise the previously inferior social status of blacks.

The recognition of a black subculture appears to be a positive and meaningful concept in race relations. The incorporation of a pluralistic approach consistent with democratic egalitarian principles but conceived biracially appears to fit the most appropriate sociopolitical trends that have emerged during the last half decade. Mackler and Giddings suggest as follows:

> those persons whose behavior and beliefs do not conform to the dominant American culture patterns are by no means without a culture. . . . So long as our perceptions of the country's race relations problem are stated in terms of the absence of culture rather than of the presence of a different subculture, we will continue to misinterpret our difficulties and their basic dimensions.[23]

The provision of recreation and leisure service which recognizes the validity of the black subculture and incorporates a program consistent with the life style and self-determination of black people appears to be the most relevant approach to the elimination of racism and inappropriately designed recreation facilities and activities.

THE PHYSICAL ENVIRONMENT

The tremendous increase in outdoor recreation demand is primarily a result of an expanding, affluent society. Today more than 70 percent of

---

[22] Parsons, Talcott. "Full Citizenship for the Negro American?" In: *The Negro American.* Edited by Talcott Parsons and Kenneth B. Clark, Boston, Houghton-Mifflin Company, 1966, p. 750.

[23] Mackler, Bernard, and Giddings, Morsely G. "Cultural Deprivation: A Study in Mythology," In: *The Urban R's: Race Relations as the Problem in Urban Education.* Edited by Robert A. Dentler, Bernard Mackler and Mary Ellen Warshauer, New York, Frederick A. Praeger, Publishers, 1967, p. 211.

the nation's population resides in metropolitan areas and the trend toward urbanization is continuing.

> As metropolitan areas expand and interest in recreation grows, a premium is placed on open spaces, those green areas devoid of intensive residential, industrial and commercial development.[24]

Preserving and Improving the Physical Environment

The destruction of the physical enviroment has resulted in man himself being an endangered species. We have made tremendous demands upon our natural resources to accommodate the growing interest in the use of the outdoors for recreation purposes.

> With the growing shortage of open space in metropolitan areas, there is increasing pressure to use publicly owned land for schools, highways, water supply and sewerage systems, hospitals, urban renewal projects, and similar community ventures rather than for open space and parkland.[25]

The population growth has also had a deleterious effect on the natural resources and the environment. Already America has the fourth largest population in the world and each year we increase by a number equal to the population of the whole San Francisco-Oakland urban area and nearly a million more than the entire Washington, D.C. urban area.

The full impact of childbearing occurs not at conception nor even at birth. It steadily mounts as a child grows, becomes educated, seeks employment and recreation opportunity, and finally sets up a separate household and becomes a parent himself.

Our need for parks, playgrounds, wilderness areas, beaches and other recreation areas has never been greater. The combination of population increase, higher incomes, shorter working hours and even greater metropolitization has resulted in a demand for these facilities and the leisure opportunities that existed when there were fewer numbers of people and a less affluent, mobile and urban population. The quality of life requires that an increase in the number of areas and facilities be made *available* and *accessible* to more people.

Kraus notes, however, that the mere provision of recreation areas and facilities does not guarantee satisfactory use by central city residents:

> The failure of disadvantaged persons to take part in outdoor recreation programs may not only be because of their lack of funds and transportation; it may also be related to a different set of tastes and interests. This suggests the need in urban recreation planning to explore perceptively the needs and interests of all

---

[24] "Planning," *Community Action Program for Public Officials: Outdoor Recreation.* Vol. 1, Washington, D.C., National Association of Counties. 1969, p. 1.

[25] Kraus, Richard. *Recreation and Leisure in Modern Society.* New York, Appleton-Century-Crofts, 1971, p. 409.

residents within the city and to analyze the city itself as a total living organism in order to determine what provision should be made for recreation, in terms both of facilities and programs.[26]

Approximately 9 percent of public recreation areas are located in urban areas (much less in central cities where low-income residents reside) while 91 percent are in suburban areas and outlying districts. In effect, low-income residents seldom use parks because they are too costly, too distant from their homes or these people in general have a different attitude about using park facilities.

It is fairly well understood by most sociologists that different ethnic groups vary in income and life style and attach different meanings to neighborhood and community outdoor places as well. It has been observed that poor people and black people have the greatest stake in their particular "turfs." Affluent whites can abandon any particular locale with ease if it becomes uncongenial.[27] It is necessary, therefore, for specific objectives to be formulated in terms of the social functions outdoor recreation serves for specific population groups.

Middle-class property owners who have a highly individualized and diverse life style have no transportation difficulties. Friends are widely dispersed and few physical places have wide-spread common usage. Space outside the dwelling unit, including hallways, streets and open spaces, is public and anonymous. It is perceived as belonging to everyone, and as such belongs to no one. In the more stable and homogeneous working-class neighborhoods, boundaries between dwelling units and public spaces are highly permeable and the people often feel at home on the streets. Streets are not just paths but have become bounded places to which residents feel they belong.[28]

Lee provides an example of the differences in which an outdoor recreation place is used by a section of a community:[29]

Local territorial definitions of place were observed in a small neighborhood park situated in a Chinese district of Pacific City. Community service workers report that the primary users of the park are propertyless low income residents, who use it as a place to join others for conversation, games of chance, or to observe local social life. Higher status residents use the park only as a pathway or a setting for local ceremonies. Territorial use varies both spatially and temporally. From daylight until 7:30 A.M. the park is used as a training ground for the Chinese martial arts. From 8 to 11 A.M. elderly men slowly gather on the upper level to play games and visit. Activity is greatest between 11 A.M. and later after-

---

[26] Ibid., p. 431.

[27] Altshuler, Op. cit., p. 127.

[28] Lee, Robert G. "The Social Definition of Outdoor Recreational Places," In: *Social Behavior, Natural Resources and the Environment*. Edited by William R. Burch, Jr., Neil H. Cheek, Jr. and Lee Taylor, New York, Harper and Row, Publishers, 1972, p. 76.

[29] **Ibid., p. 77.**

noon. Between midmorning and later afternoon mothers bring their small children to play in the children's playground, which is located at the northeast corner of the lower level of the park. When the weather is favorable they are joined in the late morning by elderly women who come to sit in the sun and visit. Adult women seldom use other sections of the park except as a pathway. At noon, Caucasian white collar and construction workers occupy benches throughout the park to eat their lunch. A group with similar spatial orientations, the tourists, use the park as both an attraction and a pathway from midmorning until evening. In the late afternoon and early evening younger Chinese men, who had been working earlier in the day, come to visit and play games. Throughout the day both black and white Skid Row indigents wander about the park, begging from tourists, sleeping, and drinking.

Preserving and Using Parkland

It is generally agreed that the unique features of parks must be preserved and that people must be made aware of them in order to enhance the encounters with parks. Local and state park systems must be expanded, particularly in urban areas where their occurrence has been minimal.

If leisure service managers were to incorporate the concept of *environmental stability,* which implies a continuing process of dynamic homeostasis or self-renewal, they would be more cognizant of the need to implement and maintain a sound environmental policy. It is a tangible concept that would strengthen the present qualitative measures defined by artistic or cultural perception that do not seem to provide a very sound basis for aesthetic judgment. It would provide park supervisors, park rangers, community center directors, etc., with a more reliable method for assessing stress or intrusion of human behavior upon the natural environment or community ecosystem. By judging the irreparable damage automobiles cause to state and national parks, leisure service managers could propose bicycle, monorail, cross-country skiing, canoeing, hiking and other alternative transportation systems.

While it may be easy to incorporate sound environmental policies, it would be difficult for leisure service managers to make judgments about the physical environment. It is interesting to note that a new occupational category is being generated—an *ecolomist.* Such a person would be an invaluable resource for making appropriate environmental judgments as they relate to the provision and maintenance of parks and recreation areas. This new practitioner is knowledgable in land use, urban planning, architecture, landscaping, engineering, transportation and zoning. He must be able to apply this knowledge with the goal of preserving the ecology, minimizing pollution and providing working room, living space and recreational areas to meet the needs of residents of a particular community.

The concept of a "new town" has a particularly meaningful reference to the need to maintain an ecological balance in human settlements.

New towns are planned to provide a balanced population, access to work and to recreational areas, to open spaces and to cultural facilities. "Ideally, there would be a balance of workers and varied occupations, of open space and developed areas, of economic, social and occupational groups."[30]

Open space and park and recreation areas which incorporate greenery not only have aesthetic value but also serve a utilitarian purpose. "Greenbelt areas . . . play a definite role in removing gases and . . . matter from the atmosphere."[31] Trees are also effective in serving as natural air filters. They reduce city noise and provide a thermostat effect on surrounding areas. "In the summer, for example, when city air conditioners are pumping heat into the atmosphere, parks and green spaces help cool the urban environment."[32]

Unfortunately, the modern American has an insatiable appetite for goods and services. This results in the need "for more highways, parking lots, shopping centers and subdivisions, the irrevocable paving of some 1 million acres of open space each year [which] will soon increase to 2 million acres."[33] Scientists are not sure how much longer man can intervene on behalf of nature and expect to continue to have enough oxygen to breathe. However, man continues to survive in the midst of dirty air, traffic congestion, noise, and a lack of privacy and open space.

In the past several years, the urban dweller has been deprived of a number of amenities that in one way or another contribute to the quality of life. "The butterfly, for example. It can't contribute anything to the GNP. But it did contribute the visual diversity of human experience. Now, in many communities across the nation, the butterfly has been practically extirpated by air pollution and pesticides. The vacant lot has been paved, the swimming pool has been filled for a building lot. . . . Small boys . . . these days often come up against unpenetrable chain-link fences."[34]

Recreation needs are satisfied not only by developing parks, beaches, open spaces and other outdoor recreation areas, but by observing sound ecological and conservation practices which help to create an aesthetic environment. Recreation areas and facilities provide leisure opportunities for people to meet their social needs. The need for open space is particularly essential in the nation's central cities where park and recreation areas and facilities lag far behind the outer rings of cities and the suburbs.

---

[30] Fabun, Don. *Dimensions of Change.* Beverly Hills, California, Glencoe Press, 1971, p. 59.

[31] Murray, Linda. "The Rationale is 0," *Open Space Action* 1:13, May-June, 1969.

[32] Ibid., p. 13.

[33] "200 Million: Not Far From a Madding Crowd," *Newsweek,* November 27, 1967, p. 89.

[34] Ibid., p. 90.

> To the slum child of Harlem and Chicago's South Side, the conservation epic, the wilderness, the great outdoors are unfamiliar phrases of little meaning. In the central portions of Boston and New York City there are countless children and adults who have never walked on wet sand or tasted the salt of the nearby sea. There are children in the midwest cities of Chicago, St. Louis, and Kansas City who have never seen corn growing in fertile fields. For a great many people of northern California cities the redwoods could just as well be on the moon. In some cities, children look out of their bedroom windows upon foul rivers, masses of railroad cars, or abandoned industrial sites. To them, the beauty of the great outdoors is only a story book tale of another time and another place.[35]

This view is substantiated by a report called "Recreation Problems in the Urban Impacted Areas of California." An urban impacted area is defined as a segment of a city which exhibits an abnormal concentration of various social maladies: high unemployment, high underemployment, low incomes, high rates of dropping out from school, low educational attainment, high rates of family instability, high rates of public health programs, high rates of juvenile delinquency, substandard housing, substantial governmental services, etc. The report stated that while over half of the residents of urban impacted areas use local parks or recreation centers, residents over 50 years of age and those with incomes below $4,000 use them much less. These impacted urban areas are found all across America. The size of the impacted areas and the variety and complexity of the social ills to which residents of these areas fall prey underscore the lack of adequate leisure opportunities available to low-income and older residents.[36] The paucity of space and facilities as well as an impoverished physical environment serve as barriers to satisfactory leisure experiences.

The beauties of nature, which most Americans take for granted, are largely unknown to the ghetto dweller, the invalid or blind person. The sounds, sights and aromas of the ghetto aren't those of birds singing, a woodland stream, a field of flowers or a virgin forest. "Rather, as Richie Havens tells it in a popular folk song, 'Choked cities yell and rage in fumes and gas.' "[37]

Kraus[38] undertook a study to determine the impact of physical blight and urban congestion, rise in crime and other social pathologies, budgetary limitations, intergroup tensions, and growing demands for local control of community services upon park and recreation departments in the United States. The cities surveyed had a population of 150,000 or more.

---

[35] Jensen, Clayne R. *Outdoor Recreation in America.* Minneapolis, Burgess Publishing Company, 1970, p. 19.

[36] "Recreation Problems in the Urban Impacted Areas of California." Sacramento, Department of Parks and Recreation, 1970.

[37] Tucker, Sterling, "Nature and the Ghetto Dweller," In: *Man and Nature in the City.* Washington, D.C., U.S. Government Printing Office, 1969, p. 47.

[38] Kraus, Richard. *Urban Parks and Recreation: Challenge of the 1970's.* New York, Community Council of Greater New York, 1972.

Kraus found that if leisure service agencies are to justify continued support, they must shift their priorities in the direction of making significant social contributions to urban life.

Kraus also learned that some 47 percent of the urban leisure service agencies surveyed had some program in ecology. "They are sponsoring conservation programs, nature education centers, community clean-up drives and waste recycling campaigns, and are spearheading the antipollution and environmental protection efforts of civic organizations and task forces."[39] Many administrators indicated that the concern for environmental issues is now being considered more fully with respect to their own planning and management of park and other outdoor recreation resources than in the past. Kraus writes that it is the leisure service agencies themselves that have frequently caused serious ecological damage.

> Often natural areas are invaded for the construction of recreation facilities or access routes. In addition, recreational use is often responsible for marked deterioration of the environment. Careless practices by hikers, campers or snowmobiles may do serious damage both to vegetation and wildlife. Boating may cause pollution of lakes and waterways. Mass events in city parks or other natural areas almost inevitably result in extensive littering, requiring costly clean-up efforts.[40]

It was found that cultural centers, marinas and water sports facilities have been constructed primarily to meet middle- and upper-class leisure interests while inner-city-oriented facilities such as vest-pocket parks, portable pools and mobile program units have been emphasized by many urban communities. In general, the trend of many leisure service agencies is to construct smaller recreation facilities to meet local neighborhood needs rather than large complexes to serve broad geographical areas.

Based on the findings of the study, Kraus recommended the following guidelines for policy with respect to facility development and ecology and environmental concerns:

Facility Development

1. Facilities must be planned and developed with the full cooperation of community residents. Whenever possible, they should meet varied needs. Community centers should be planned to serve aging persons, handicapped persons, and pre-school children during the morning hours and children, youth and adults during the afternoon and evening hours. To make full use of centers and to justify their construction today, multi-use centers (which may include

[39] Ibid., p. 6.
[40] Ibid., p. 37.

other municipal offices or social services such as legal assistance, drug abuse centers, medical and dental services, or family counseling) should be considered whenever possible.

2. For reasons of safety in today's urban setting, local recreation facilities and playgrounds or small parks and centers should be planned with extremely convenient access and as close as possible to where large numbers of people congregate or travel. In low-income areas, it is desirable that they be attached to, or part of housing projects or public schools to permit joint sponsorship and multiple uses.
3. Neighborhood playgrounds should be designed to accommodate "demand goods"—that is, have the potential for a variety of interesting activities that draw participants. This may mean that they have built-in tables for quiet games, multi-use blacktop areas, small amphitheaters, barbecue areas for family or neighborhood picnics, multi-purpose meeting rooms, and night lighting.

Ecology and Environmental Concerns

1. Park and recreation departments should directly sponsor a variety of ecology-oriented activities such as waste recycling programs, anti-pollution and anti-litter campaigns, conservation education courses, nature centers, bicycling and walking tours through natural areas and closing park roads to auto traffic on given days. Efforts should be made to involve large numbers of young people as participants and volunteers in such programs in order to build a solid base of support for environmental protection.
2. Park and recreation authorities should, both individually and through their departments, assume leadership in promoting community programs to preserve green spaces (including nature preserves, marshes, wildlife sanctuaries, tidelands areas, or simply open space) and generally prevent pollution and protect vegetation and wildlife. They should help to mobilize individuals and organizations with similar concerns into team efforts and, when this can be done without compromising their position as civil employees, promote needed social action or legislative drives to protect the environment.[41]

Planning a Competent Leisure Environment

It is clearly important that sound planning be undertaken to accurately assess the characteristics and leisure preferences of a given population. There are some population profile indices which the National Association

[41] Ibid., pp. 13-15.

of Counties noted that will affect recreation demand and should be taken in account: size of population, income, education, mobility and age.[42]

Population—Increases in population should be noted at the local level since this has tremendous impact on available resources.

Income—National surveys indicate that the sharpest rise in recreation participation occurs when individuals earn $3,000-$7,000. Participation continues to climb with median family income in the $7,000-$10,000 range, and then declines. When a community's median income range falls in any of these categories an increase in recreation demand should be noted.

Education—It has been generally determined that the higher a person's education level the greater will be his rate of participation in recreation. It is also possible to note particular activity preferences with educational levels.

Mobility—The use of cars, bicycles, boats, etc., influences recreation participation. The mobility factor can be measured, for example, by determining the number of registered passenger cars and the number of residents of driving age.

Age—The younger the population grouping the more likely will be the demand on recreation facilities for competitive sports and group activities. The grouping between 25 to 64 years of age demands family facilities and activities such as picnicking, swimming, boating and arts and crafts. The population grouping over 65 years of age participate more in passive recreation and group activities such as arts and crafts programs, hobbies and bridge.

A profile may be made of each community to note the total number of residents, overall population density, distribution by age and occupation, education, and income levels, amount of free time and travel habits or mobility. Other important factors which must be ascertained are the number of persons physically handicapped, mentally ill, retarded or socioeconomically deprived and their special recreation needs. A population profile may be made for each neighborhood so that areas of greatest immediate need may be assessed quickly and action taken to facilitate outdoor recreation opportunity.

It is essential that leisure service managers develop a plan by which quantitative and qualitative recreation values are determined by exercising management responsibility. Whether we like it or not recreationers are inadvertently destroying, through overuse, the natural and physical environment. Interestingly enough, the real resource problems may not be how to predict future increases in use patterns, but how certain

---

[42] National Association of Counties, Op. cit., pp. 7-9.

leisure service management policies and procedures can limit, or even decrease, recreation use-intensity.[43]

The quality of recreation experience depends largely on the *quality of the leisure environment.* It is imperative that resource recreation planners and managers design and implement sound mechanisms so that patterns of use of recreation areas and facilities do not have a deleterious impact upon the natural environment.

Raymond F. Dasmann of The Conservation Foundation has half-seriously called for new approaches to national park management. He stated:

> Each year the park that builds or improves the fewest roads to accommodate the least number of people will get the highest marks. Prizes should be given for the number of new campgrounds that were not built, for the numbers of people accommodated outside the boundaries of Yellowstone and Yosemite and not in Yosemite Valley or Yellowstone Village. Quality of national park experience for those people proved capable of appreciating a national park might be a substitute for the measurement of number of visitor days.[44]

Dasmann's appeal to more qualitative considerations in the use of the out of doors is in the direction of excellence of park experience rather than quantity of park use. And recreation is a vital environmental consideration and is no longer a secondary use of natural resources.

> Recreation programs and policies can be a *major* force in shaping our environment. All of the actions that pollute the land, such as suburban sprawl, are problems because, in the final analysis, they interfere with the enjoyment of the outdoors. The same . . . is true of water pollution. Technological processes assure us of clean drinking water, but the heart of people's concern that we clean up rivers, lakes, and harbors is the fact that people demand the right to enjoy these resources.[45]

Leisure service managers must be cognizant of the fact that a safe and clean environment is necessary for people to be free to express their creative and physical capabilities. Recreation and leisure service needs to join the nationwide campaign and assume an increasingly aggressive posture to assure that the natural and physical environment will support and encourage leisure expression.

The preservation of outdoor areas is necessary for people's mental health. Brightbill stated that there is an essential need to educate people

---

[43] Schafer, Elwood L., Jr., and Moeller, George. "Predicting Quantitative and Qualitative Values of Recreation Participation," In: *The First Recreation Symposium Proceedings.* Upper Darby, Pa., Northeast Forest Experiment Station, Forest Service, 1971, p. 16.

[44] Dasmann, Raymond F. "National Parks and the Problems of our Environment." Speech delivered at the Environmental Management Seminar, Mather Training Center, National Park Service, Harpers Ferry, West Virginia, February 19, 1969.

[45] Rasmussen, William M. "Recreation and our Environment," *California Parks and Recreation* 11:11, December, 1969.

for the proper use of our natural resources not only because our physical survival is at stake, "but our outlook, our spirit, and our peace of mind are interwoven with the physical environment."[46] It was Brightbill who also stated that "leisure and living, let alone preparing for them, mean nothing if the natural environment is fouled."[47]

Do leisure service personnel have a voice when a highway intrudes into a park or when a wilderness area is converted into a commercial outpost or when open space is converted into subdivisions for a housing project? Do we have any stake in the future of man's existence? By preserving our natural environment do we enhance the potential for leisure expression and satisfaction? The improvement of the quality of life remains the *basic purpose* of recreation. The pursuit of leisure *must* be in harmony with both the social and physical environment. It seems the leisure service field, let alone people's happiness and state of mind, are at stake and inextricably bound up with the quality of the physical environment.

---

[46] Brightbill, Charles K. *Educating for Leisure-Centered Living.* Harrisburg, Pa., The Stackpole Book Company, 1966, p. 33.

[47] Ibid., p. 180.

CHAPTER 4

Basis for the Leisure Service Delivery System

The traditional role of recreation and leisure service has been altered in recent years. As Kraus points out, leisure service agencies have increasingly recognized:

> a crucial need to provide socially-oriented programs and services, rather than permit recreation to maintain the identity of a "fun" program without meaningful goals. Thus, a growing number of park and recreation authorities are attempting to mobilize all elements in their communities in joint recreation efforts, to combat urban blight and other problems of the inner city, and to strive consciously to make cities more livable for all social classes.[1]

Social protest became volatile and common in the 1960's and now has spilled over into the 1970's. According to Kenneth Boulding:

> Social protest arises when there is strongly felt dissatisfaction with existing programs and policies of government or other organizations, on the part of those who feel themselves affected by these policies but who are unable to express their dissent through regular and legitimate channels, and who feel unable to exercise the weight to which they think they are entitled in the decision-making process.[2]

The statement by Boulding underscores some of the elements that were present during the 60's and early 70's which have served to accelerate progress toward goals set by blacks, women and youth. Recreation and leisure service has been affected as a result of urban violence, civil disorder and youth demands. New methods for assessing leisure needs have been generated as a result of these occurrences and some changes have been instituted to provide a meaningful solution to pressing social problems. The riots and other forms of disorder and growing alienation among young people have pointed rather directly to the need for increased and improved methods of leisure service delivery in order to meet the needs of the growing number of disenchanted people.

---

[1] Kraus, Richard. *Urban Parks and Recreation: Challenge of the 1970's.* New York, Community Council of Greater New York, 1972, pp. 8-9.

[2] Boulding, Kenneth. "Towards a Theory of Protest," In: *The Age of Protest.* Edited by Walt Anderson, Pacific Palisades, California, Goodyear Publishing Company, 1969, p. vi.

The investigation of several large urban community park and recreation systems by Kraus revealed the changing role of leisure service in the form of social service and public responsibility. According to Kraus leisure service agencies recognize that:

> the major urban problems of the 1960's and 1970's—crime and vandalism, economic constriction, physical blight, racial militance, and flight of the white middle class to the suburbs—have all made parks less usable and reduced their base of popular support. And they recognize the corollary of this development, that unless park and recreation departments can contribute effectively to the healthy redevelopment of cities, they are likely to decline still further in support.[3]

While it appears that leisure service delivery systems are increasingly oriented to the concerns of the socially and economically disadvantaged, and have assumed the reputation of being "welfare" operations, such a unitary concept is inappropriate. Leisure service agencies must recognize that although it is imperative to improve upon their efforts to disadvantaged groups, leisure opportunities must be stimulated for every social class rather than just the poor. The vitality of city life is essential to the maintenance of America, and leisure service operations contribute to the beauty and pleasure of city living. By disengaging its efforts to serve all people, recreation and leisure service undermines the *balance* and *vitality* of community life. It is essential that leisure service be viewed as an equal partner within the total framework of community life. It should endeavor to exert pressure within the local power structure and seek to influence the physical, human and institutional priorities of city life.

Toward a Relevant Philosophy of Leisure

As the leisure service delivery system must be viewed in a holistic sense, as outlined in the Introduction to this text, so too must the various states of human development and facets of institutional life. According to a publication by the Institute of Design, Illinois Institute of Technology, there is a need for integrating man's life style and insuring more freedom to structure his own time to suit himself and still be a productive member of society, as illustrated in Figure 4-1.

> Instead of suffering the sequential and inevitable terminal states of human development—play, education, work and retirement the leisure age man will be able to exist in a more free, permissive time reference. He will hopefully be able to "naturally follow his instincts" in regard to when he wants to play or work or relax. Retirement as an idea in the past was only intended for the disabled and aged, however, the idea of retiring from the mainstream of events or to exist periodically in a sort of psycho-social "moratorium," to "drop out," to ponder and reflect upon what one is doing should be possible at any time.[4]

---

[3] Kraus, Op. cit., p. 68.

[4] Institute of Design. *Leisure: A Study of Man and Leisure in the Environment.* Chicago, Illinois Institute of Technology, Institute of Design Communications Center, 1970, p. 54.

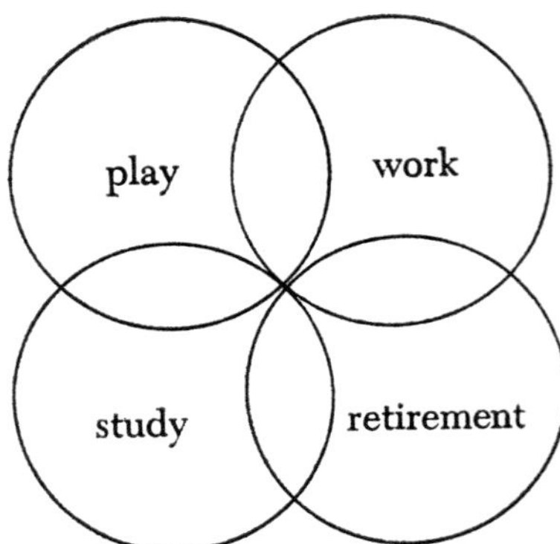

Figure 4-1. Time for the Leisure Age. (From "Time for the Leisure Age," In *Leisure: A Study of Man and Leisure in the Environment.* Chicago, Illinois Institute of Technology, Institute of Design Communications Center, 1970, p. 54.)

It is suggested by this study design report that our present comprehension of time and its effects on our life patterns and on day-to-day activity is limited. "Only by controlling and adjusting our time can we begin to consider it a 'free time.' In terms of future guidelines there seems to be sufficient evidence pointing toward a unified approach to leisure in the context of time."[5]

The amount of human fragmentation in American technological society pervades all aspects of life. The large, impersonal bureaucracies, extreme social mobility, growing affluence and constant social change have made it difficult for the individual to perceive the reality of the world around him, let alone be able to function in it. It is recognized that a sense of community, the moral fabric which binds people together as a social unit, has lost much of its ability to respond to human needs and desires in a personal way. It has been determined by many sociologists that an inability of societal members to relate to others beyond one's own neighborhood or "place" is destructive to a sense of identity. This is so because a sense of community requires the ability to effect relatedness among a variety of people, social functions, institutions, events and stages of life. A potential solution to human fragmentation and isolation from the mainstream of life appears to require a reintegration of institutional functions—i.e., school, work, education and leisure—as depicted in Figure 4-2.

The inability of man to comprehend life outside his own limited social sphere has seemingly contributed to the growing number of alienated people in this country. It is rare when we are free or unihibited to enjoy a "pure" experience,

[5] Ibid., p. 54.

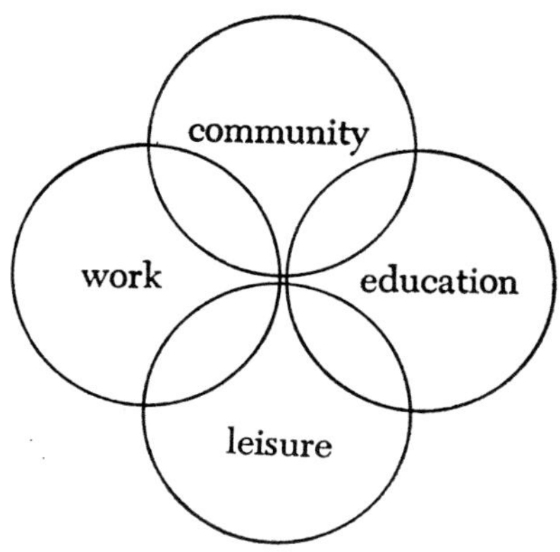

Figure 4-2. Integration of Institutional Functions.

> where we are lost in complete thought or relaxation, or have an opportunity to laugh, to howl and groan until we feel drained, or feel we have been uplifted by something we have learned. It seems that given the freedom to do so we would like to turn on and off these sensations at will, to demand serenity when we are tired and need rest, to orchestrate the madness of a howling comedy—to feel vital in all our life experiences.[6]

As noted earlier in this text, it is necessary to view leisure service within an ecological context in which all of the components of the delivery system—social and physical environment, participants, and leisure service organizations—mutually modify and complement each other. The mutual competence of ourselves, the environment, social processes and leisure service organizations to interact and our ability to select, to plunge into or to retreat and to change our actions are essential to a satisfactory leisure experience.

It has been noted by Toffler[7] that leisure can serve as a basis for an entire life style and will increasingly become more important as society shifts from a work orientation toward greater involvement in leisure. Roberts states that while the rhythm of life in advanced industrial economies has been traditionally based around the organization of work, for many people "leisure has now become such a central and dominant part of their lives that it is their behavior and attitudes towards work that are determined by their leisure."[8]

It is suggested by the comments of Toffler, Roberts, the Illinois Institute of Technology study and others that the bureaucratization of leisure approaches commercialization. Private time spent in leisure is often re-

---

[6] Ibid., pp. 69-70.
[7] Toffler, Alvin. *Future Shock.* New York, Bantam Books, Inc., 1971, pp. 284-302.
[8] Roberts, Kenneth. *Leisure.* London, Longman Group Limited, 1970, p. 25.

duced, leisure is too organized, man is deprived of the possibility to choose and he stops being the master of *his* leisure: so much is offered to him that his creative and inventive powers become superfluous.

One cannot always apply only utilitarian principles and demand that leisure always contribute something useful to man or society. Man and his whole life, including leisure, would then be subjected to the interests of production, in which he represents a working force, or to the interests of politics. "Man desires, needs, and has a right to pursue even those activities whose only end is he himself. If he is free to choose, he is naturally inclined to the more attractive forms of life, to recreation and entertainment."[9]

Planning for Leisure

"Doing your own thing" has reflected and represented a tremendous threat to most leisure service agencies which have been unable to anticipate and plan adequately for a number of people, particularly youth, who seek to express themselves in a manner which runs counter to the normal flow of programming practices. It is obvious that instead of a reduction of nonconformists, we may expect to see more unconventional leisure behavior in the future.

Toffler suggests that the more fragmented or differentiated the society and the greater the number of life styles it promotes, the more likely it is for one to retain a negative attitude about the values and styles of life of the dominant group. However, advanced technological societies ideally promote freedom and create more opportunities for self-realization. Therefore, there is more freedom to move in and out of these niches and more opportunity to create one's own.

The organization of leisure opportunities is primarily geared to the dominant life pattern and is fixed to coincide with the hours when the majority of the population will be free. However, not everybody fits in with society's dominant pattern of life. It is difficult for such "outsiders" as the unemployed, hippies, retired, physically disabled and housewives, whose life schedules deviate from the normal rhythm of life, to participate in the leisure opportunities typically provided. It therefore becomes essential that leisure service managers seek to provide opportunities for all people in a community with reference to their beliefs, values, expectations and life styles. As Roberts puts it,

> Enjoying leisure in modern society is conditional upon having a job because, without work, a person's normal rhythm of life and his approach to the daily routine is undermined, and participation in normal forms of recreation and social relationships becomes impossible.[10]

---

[9] Kotasek, Jiri, et al. "Leisure—A Field of Action for Adult Education," *Convergence* 2:24, 1969.

[10] Roberts, Op. cit., p. 13.

Leisure service personnel need to realize that opportunities should be provided which will not render people psychologically incapable of participating and which will not curtail their own personal life rhythms. The role of leisure service managers must then be not one of maximizing some life styles and values (those associated with the dominant group) and minimizing others (associated with hippies, housewives, unemployed, physical disabled and retired people) but of achieving an *integration of both sets of life styles and values.* Our goal in the future may well be the incorporation of a planned and controlled laissez-faire doctrine, which would "not try to direct people's energies into channels specified in advance. We should aim instead to nourish the individual's potentialities so that each, according to his capacity, could find his own solution."[11]

The traditional leisure service delivery approach assumes that the average citizen is unable to invent new uses of leisure. It is therefore necessary for a professional elite to discover relevant criteria and implement ways of providing leisure opportunities that always meet the moral aims of the community. It has been suggested by Parker that those responsible for instituting the leisure requirements of the community need to develop policies which will "provide leisure facilities for the 'type of people' who need them; the other to stimulate an awareness of the possibilities of leisure-like behavior in a variety of situations."[12]

Measuring the Effectiveness of Local Leisure Service

Leisure service today is marked by a lack of precision and effectiveness. The plethora of problems—vandalism, poor budgets, inadequate staffs, citizen hostility and indifference—are partly manifestations of the haphazard way in which service is delivered. A large part of this difficulty has been caused by the inability of leisure service agencies to define their goals and objectives adequately and the methods by which they attempt to measure the effectiveness of programs designed to implement agency objectives.

Hatry and Dunn state:

> Traditional measurement practices generally focus on matters such as acreage, facilities and personnel. While these are useful, alone they will not indicate the degrees to which recreation services are meeting the needs and desires of the public.[13]

Gray suggests that if one were to characterize recreation and park operations today the largest single element would be tradition. While

---

[11] Parker, Stanley. *The Future of Work and Leisure.* New York, Praeger Publishers, Inc., 1971, p. 139.

[12] Ibid., p. 142.

[13] Hatry, Harry and Dunn, Diana. *Measuring the Effectiveness of Local Services: Recreation.* Washington, D.C., The Urban Institute, 1971, p. 5.

tradition in itself is not a damaging factor, the degree to which leisure service agencies have become stagnant and intolerant of change has resulted in their loss of meaningful contact with a number of participant groups. Several critics have suggested that we offer a general program of activities for a poorly defined clientele, with few positive results. We have stated our goals so often in such general terms that they are almost meaningless. Because of their lack of clear scope, they offer little or no guide to our operations, are next to useless in decision making and are of little help in evaluating outcomes.

The goal of leisure experience should be absolute congruence between the satisfaction sought and the satisfaction obtained. Lack of congruence is usually quite obvious. Gray has suggested that recreation activities which fail to produce a reasonable level of satisfaction are marked by poor participation, short tenure, antisocial behavior, apathy, etc. They typically generate little excitement and the programs are of short duration.

Gray has proposed application of a systems concept to be used by leisure service agencies to determine more accurately their ability to provide detailed information about people and the social and physical environment. Hatry and Dunn[14] suggest that data on measures of effectiveness collected systematically and regularly are needed to help:

a. Provide current information on how recreation services are meeting public needs.
b. Provide a baseline from which future progress can be measured.
c. Estimate the future effectiveness of current types of programs.
d. Determine budgets for recreation-related programs.
e. Prepare community plans involving land or facilities, including capital improvement requests.
f. Provide annual status reports of the effectiveness of the community's services.
g. Deal with public questions as they arise throughout the year.

Hatry and Dunn[15] suggest that new measurements of effectiveness be initiated to evaluate more adequately the response to leisure service delivery. They would supplement the traditional emphasis which has utilized descriptive indices which are more representative of the resources of the agencies. Because agencies tend to overlook *outputs* (effects), they do not adequately reveal how well leisure services are meeting the needs and desires of the public. New measurement devices include:

a. *Total attendance and participant-hours or days for each major activity or facility during a given time period;*

[14] Ibid., pp. 11-12.
[15] Ibid., pp. 16-37.

b. *Number and percent of different participants and nonparticipants for each major recreation service during a given time period;*
c. *Number and percent of persons living within and not within X minutes or Y miles of a specific type of recreation facility or activity;*
d. *Crowded indices*: including number of persons turned away or deterred from using a facility because of crowdedness during a given time period;
e. *Variety indices*: including number of different activities, facilities or features available at specific points in time;
f. *Safety indices*: number and rates of accidents, injuries and criminal "attacks" for a given time period;
g. *Index of overall perceived satisfaction of citizens;*
h. *Index of physical atrtactiveness of recreation areas and facilities;*
i. *Delinquency and crime indices*: juvenile delinquency and crime rates affected by recreation programs;
j. *Incidence of illness affected by recreation service;* and
k. *Economic impact indices*: changes in business income, job opportunities and property values due to recreation services.

Inasmuch as each of the preceding indices represents only the relative status of leisure service's impact upon various community conditions, it is paramount that each be applied specifically to different groups in the community as each cultural, ethnic or class grouping is affected to different degrees by leisure service. Hatry and Dunn state:

> The needs of various groups should be explicitly considered before deciding on . . . [agency] action. The values of the measures of effectiveness that pertain to each population group should be identified.[16]

Every community is unique and it is important that leisure service agencies be cognizant of the significance of the attachment and mutual feeling of belonging of residents of each neighborhood. By properly determining the nature of each neighborhood's composition, resources and other pertinent social attributes, leisure service managers can more adequately assess the distinctive aspects and form of leisure opportunity that may be successfully blended into the style of people's lives. According to Roberts each community has a subculture of informally defined behavior expectations which govern the roles and relationships between residents.

> The types of behavior that are considered proper, and the types of social contact that members of the community ought to have with one another, are defined by the norms of the sub-culture, and leisure is one aspect of the inhabitants' lives that is affected by the existence of these norms.[17]

---

[16] Ibid., p. 38.
[17] Roberts, Op. cit., p. 52.

It should be emphasized that there are common elements in leisure which are prevalent throughout society, but the various neighborhood subcultures take the form of variations within a common framework. Roberts states that when members of specific communities venture outside their own areas to engage in leisure programs offered by the wider society, individuals carry with them the norms they have acquired within the subcultures to which they belong.[18]

New Basis for Planning

The meaningless and poorly conceived objectives and methods developed by some agencies have often been inappropriate for the clientele being served. Also, as will be noted later in the text, some of the traditional standards utilized by the leisure service delivery system lack validity and precision. Additionally, as stated by Kraus:

> the application of a uniform set of standards to all cities does not take into account their differences with respect to population makeup, availability of open space, recreational needs and interests, financial capability, topography, and similar factors . . . In [larger] . . . cities, populations are often so mixed in terms of racial or religious background, age, and socioeconomic class that the assumption that each 'neighborhood' needs a uniform set of play lots, playgrounds, and small parks has little validity.[19]

Optimum utilization of potential recreation resources is not being achieved in most cities in the nation.[20] The National League of Cities reported that many publicly owned facilities are underused because they are not available in the evening or on the weekends or they are not relevant to the needs of the community.

Several new approaches have been developed by city planners and leisure service managers which have incorporated criteria of social need as the basis for planning leisure services in communities. This contemporary approach revolves around the identification and definition of needs and problems before the development of services. The use of the method of social and resource index of need differs from the traditional leisure service approach in which a packaged program is offered and people encouraged to accept it.

By realistically assessing community needs, program priorities now may be determined which reflect the philosophy, goals and objectives of the agency. The philosophy of the agency provides a set of values and beliefs which are reflected in the agency's professional approach to ser-

---

[18] Ibid., p. 55.

[19] Kraus, Richard. *Recreation and Leisure in Modern Society.* New York, Appleton-Century-Crofts, 1971, p. 440.

[20] *Recreation in the Nation's Cities: Problems and Approaches.* Washington, D.C., Department of Urban Studies, National League of Cities, 1968.

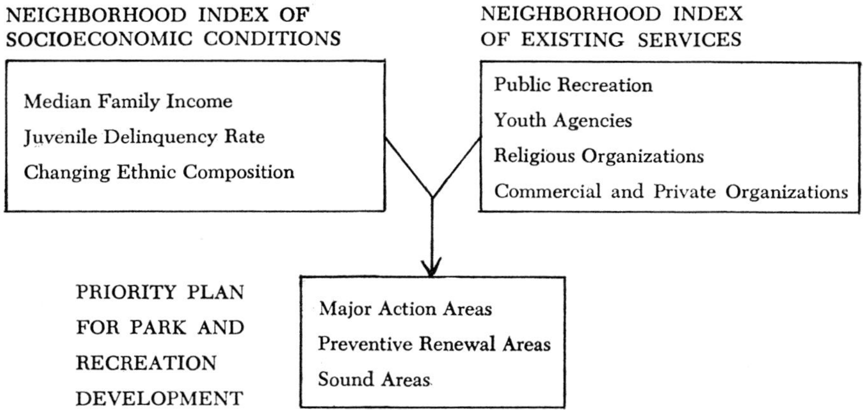

Figure 4-3. Priority Plan for Park and Recreation Development.

vice.[21] The criteria defined for program priorities should reflect the agency's philosophy about the value of leisure as an essential human need and about the special functions which it views as its particular mission in the community.

As already noted in Chapter 3, the Community Council of Greater New York undertook an analysis of the 74 neighborhoods of New York. They compared each neighborhood's resources with those elsewhere in the city.[22] They analyzed the comparative need for leisure service in each neighborhood by using three socioeconomic factors as criteria: (a) median family income, (b) juvenile delinquency rates, and (c) changing ethnic composition.

The study revealed that nine of the city's 74 neighborhoods contained 53 percent of the total park and outdoor recreation acreage in the city. In contrast, 45 of the city's neighborhoods, particularly the rundown and poorer sections, had only 10 percent of the recreation space allotment. The results were illuminating because it provided leisure service personnel with a more realistic method for estimating and interpreting the effects of various aspects of community life upon the delivery of leisure service. It was concluded that the neighborhoods with the greatest amount of social pathology and community disorganization were, for the most part, receiving fewer public and voluntary group leisure services. This process is illustrated in Figure 4-3 to show how measures of

[21] Carter, Genevieve W. "Better Ways of Establishing Program Priorities." Speech delivered at California State Conference of Settlements and Neighborhood Centers, April 30, 1960.

[22] Jenkins, Shirley. *Comparative Recreation Needs and Services in New York Neighborhoods.* New York, Research Department, Community Council of Greater New York, 1963.

social pathology and community disorganization can indicate the "levels" of priority of need for leisure service.

The index of socioeconomic conditions is related to each neighborhood and its existing services and functions as a basis for estimating comparative need in the respective local areas. A study undertaken by the New York City Planning Commission delved more specifically into the city's social maladies. The commission was able to determine the areas in greatest need of recreation and park development. The method of labeling priority areas is indicated in Figure 4-3. The three types of areas determined were as follows:

a. *Major Action Areas*—where problems of poverty, deteriorated housing, disease and crime are the worst and where leisure services are generally the poorest.
b. *Preventive Renewal Areas*—densely populated neighborhoods generally located in the path of outward migration from major action areas.
c. *Sound Areas*—where social problems tend to be minimal and leisure opportunity relatively adequate. The highest priority for leisure service was assigned major action areas, with preventive renewal areas and sound areas next in order of allocation of human and physical resources.[23]

In 1966, following the Watts riot, a study was conducted in Los Angeles which developed a method for determining a comparative priority need for local leisure services, as depicted in Figure 4-4. The study, conducted by Staley, assumed the following:

a. There are measurable social characteristics and reaction resources which indicate comparative need for recreation by neighborhood.
b. All citizens have important *basic needs* for recreation services, but due to different socioeconomic characteristics and interests, they have differing needs for recreation services.
c. Priorities in community-subsidized recreation services should go to those experiencing maximum social pressures of density of population, low income, number of youth, and evidence of social disorganization.[24]

A comparison is made between the resources index and neighborhood need and then a comparative recreation service index can be determined. The measurement indices of neighborhood recreation resources and social needs indicate that it is essential that leisure services be tailored to yield

[23] Reichstein, Steven, and Douglas, Neiland. *Recreation Facilities in New York City: A Method of Assigning Budgetary Priority.* New York, Department of Planning, 1968.

[24] Staley, Edwin J. "Determining Neighborhood Recreation Priorities: An Instrument," *Journal of Leisure Research* 1:69-74, Winter, 1969.

NEIGHBORHOOD RECREATION RESOURCES

1. Number of full and part time professional staff hours per 1,000 population per year
2. Acreage of neighborhood recreation centers per 1,000 population and/or population/acreage standard
3. Number of recreation centers with staff per 10,000 population

RECREATION NEEDS

1. Youth population 5-19 years of age
2. Delinquency petitions per 1,000 youth
3. Population density per square mile
4. Median family income

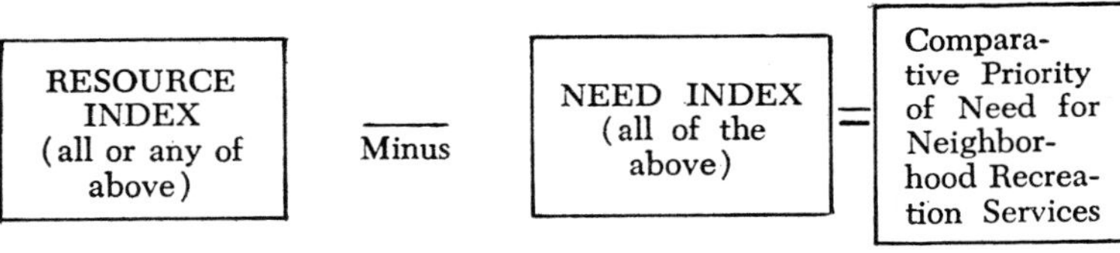

Figure 4-4. Formula Used to Determine Comparative Priority of Need for Neighborhood Recreation Services (From Staley, Edwin J. "Determining Comparative Priority of Need for Neighborhood Recreation Services: An Instrument," *Journal of Leisure Research* 1:71, Winter, 1969).

program offerings more suited to the relative social and physical characteristics of each neighborhood.

Local leadership of recreation and leisure service appears to have been most successful when they have incorporated a comprehensive approach to providing needed opportunities for leisure expression. This principle embraces the belief that leisure service is *most* meaningful when jobs, education, health and welfare and recreation opportunities are embodied in a single effort to make leisure a positive and constructive reality.

The concept is strengthened by decentralization of the planning, organization, direction, control and evaluation functions in communities affected by the delivery of leisure service. It is essential that neighborhood youth and adults, as representatives of the constituency of the community, become involved in the management of programs.

A pluralistic approach to leisure service seems to be the most effective method of satisfying the needs of the various subcultural groups. When leisure service assumes the role of a catalyst, subcommunity provisions appear to be more tenable. A pluralistic leisure service configuration as it applies to dominant-minority relations and subcultural enclaves requires that allowances for cultural and physiognomic traits be acceptable to the larger society and that members of the subordinate groups (blacks, Chicanos, hippies, etc.) are accorded equality and respect for their differences.

Leisure service managers might even assume the role of *advocates* for their leisure clients by serving as liaisons between leisure consumers and service producers. The movement toward decentralized participation places the principle of participant involvement in a practical perspective. Involvement may range anywhere from advice to total community control, depending upon the community.

The new politics inspired by the inadequacies of centralized bureaucratic control of economic, political and social services has been strengthened considerably by the power of youth protests, civil rights militancy and the involvement of the poor in the War on Poverty.

Besides these external forces, the rapidity of social change requires greater flexibility, which is possible only if primary service organizations such as schools, leisure service agencies, and health care centers are responsive to the needs of people on the grass-roots level. Until the leisure service delivery system is responsive to high priority needs on the neighborhood level, the distance between citizens and such human service organizations can be expected to widen and contribute to social disorder and growing alienation among citizens.

CHAPTER 5

A Conceptualization of Leisure Service

In Baltimore, Maryland, a recreation center director sits in a loosely defined circle of pre-school children and tells a story about turtles. Fifty miles away, in the Washington, D.C. area, the owner of a ceramics studio works up the clay which will be used by her afternoon students. Inside Yellowstone National Park, a crew of summer park aides cleans up a campground area and makes necessary repairs on tables and fire pits. Many miles west of the park, an employee of the California Department of Fish and Game finishes his task of planting catchable trout in the north fork of the Yuba River. In Albuquerque, New Mexico, 32 boys of elementary school age are receiving judo instruction from a young Boys' Club physical director. Across the nation, a former classmate of his is working with a small group of patients at Bellevue General Hospital in New York in a drama program. And, within a mile of the hospital, a park planner makes an on-site inspection of a "vest-pocket park" which is under construction.

All of these people are engaged in a common task—the provision of leisure services. To put it another way, they are all working to provide opportunities for people to engage in leisure, or recreation, behavior. Some, such as the Boys' Club instructor and the center director, are involved directly and immediately with participants. Others, such as the park planner and the summer park aides, work more with the physical environments and resources which will be used by participants. Nonetheless, they are all related to the delivery of leisure services.

The list of examples could be expanded endlessly to cover all phases of public, private and commercial recreation and at all levels, from local to national.

Each of the individuals mentioned above is part of a delivery system. For example, the Yellowstone campground is one of many in the park; and, the park is one of many sites administered by the National Park Service. At each site, and in the various sub-units within each site, opportunities are provided for people to engage in leisure behavior. Similarly, the center providing the pre-school program is one of many administered by the Baltimore Bureau of Recreation. Both the National Park Service and the Baltimore Bureau of Recreation have objectives, articulated or inferred, which define the kinds of opportunities they wish to provide for the overall agency and for the various sub-units.

In Yellowstone, the intent of the interpretive center staff is different than the purposes of the personnel responsible for campground maintenance. The overall mission of the superintendent of Yellowstone will be somewhat different than the one pursued by the superintendents of Cape Cod National Seashore, Arches National Monument or Lake Mead National Recreation Area. True, the general objectives of preserving the resources and the heritage and providing for the enjoyment of people will be common purposes. The nature of participation, however, will differ somewhat from site to site, and, therefore, the specific purposes of each superintendent and staff will differ. In Baltimore, the center staff works at different specific objectives than the personnel of the sports unit, or the drama staff even though the common intent is to provide opportunities for enjoyable leisure experiences.

To provide these opportunities, each agency commits its resources of legal authority, finances, personnel, physical facilities and natural and developed land and water areas. The resources are organized and managed, with appropriate planning, with the intent to provide the kinds of objectives which the agency has for the particular unit, facility, site or program. Hopefully, the intent or objectives of the agency are defined cooperatively and with the involvement of the public which is to be served. However, whatever the process by which the objectives are defined, *the basic purpose of any recreation agency is to provide opportunities for people, individually and collectively, to engage in leisure behavior.* This complex of opportunities might be spoken of as a program. In this sense the term program has broader meaning than the more traditional definition which includes only organized activities provided rather directly to participants. Provision of instruction in judo is part of the program of the Boys' Club, provision of a campground environment which encourages and permits camping and certain other related activities is part of the program of the National Park Service and provision of catchable trout is part of the program of the California Department of Fish and Game.

In providing programs (opportunities) for its participating public, the agency is delivering leisure services. The public is in direct contact with some of the services. The pre-schoolers and their parents are in an immediate relationship with the center director and with the physical environment of the center. However, the pre-school program also is the result of other energies and resources not directly experienced by the youngsters and their mothers. A custodial staff keeps the center attractive and ready for use; an area supervisor supports the activities of the director; and a central administration sets the financial framework for the center's operation. These efforts also are part of the leisure service delivery system.

Every recreation agency presents a complex of opportunities for the public which it hopes to serve. For some agencies, the range of opportunities is very broad and diversified; for others, it is highly specific. The number of services offered by a typical tax-supported recreation and park department in a large municipality and the specialized services of a commercial ceramic studio are illustrative of the contrast. *The philosophical commitment of the agency, articulated or not and planned or unplanned, influences the nature of the opportunities which are provided.* At least two major continuums exist, along each of which any agency's position may fall.

Direct Service Versus Enabling Service

Some agencies are committed to providing direct service to their public. That is, their efforts are to deliver the opportunities they offer so that people can participate in them immediately and directly. When the varied assortment of Albuquerque boys arrived for the judo class, it was ready to go. The facility was in order and properly equipped, and the instructor was present and prepared. Conditions were appropriate for the boys' experiences to begin. They had nothing to do but engage in the activity which was provided.

The pre-school program and the ceramic class probably also illustrate a direct service approach. However, under different conditions, the pre-school activity could grow out of an enabling approach. Let us assume that there was no program in Baltimore for pre-school children three months ago. A group of mothers approached the center director and asked about the possibility of getting such a program established; they were told that the Bureau of Recreation would help them if they wanted to pursue the idea. With the assistance of the center staff, they developed the kind of a program they wanted and they recruited and employed an instructor for the program. The Bureau provided the facility, publicized the program, and handled financial arrangements (collection of fees, payment of instructor, etc.). In this situation, the participants created the opportunity with the help and support of the agency. The agency enabled the program, but they did not deliver it "ready-made."

The direct service approach determines or makes some assumptions about peoples' recreation desires and interests; the resources are then provided, ready to be used. The enabling approach serves as a catalyst, and helps people to implement their desires and interests. It assists people in planning and obtaining needed resources; in some cases, it provides the resources, which might include organizational skills, training, equipment, and areas and facilities.

The continuum, then, is from providing opportunities which permit direct and immediate participation to providing services which enable people to develop their own opportunities. Some agencies tend to operate rather consistently on one end of the continuum or the other; others vary their approach, depending upon the specific programs with which they are involved. For example, a department may offer activities for elementary school children on a direct service basis, and meet their responsibilities for adult sports through an enabling approach. When a combination of approaches is used by one agency, the criterion for adopting an enabling position on any particular activity frequently is the assumed capability of the participants. Do they have the capacity to become involved in providing their own opportunities?

Some agencies have taken the position that becoming involved in developing your own leisure opportunities is, in fact, a recreation experience itself. The contention is that the values and enjoyments received by the people who do so are generally comparable to those received by participation in direct service opportunities. There seems to be much logical support for this contention.

Cafeteria Approach Versus Prescription Approach[1]

A second continuum along which an agency will position itself is related to objectives. Some agencies set a rather general framework of objectives. They may strive, for example, to provide wholesome recreation opportunities for all ages; or, they may attempt to provide the resources for people to use their leisure time constructively. These objectives may be defined in writing; frequently they are not. In either case, the basic intent is to offer a range of activities and opportunities to the public which is to be served. The expectation is that people will pick and choose, "cafeteria-style," from among the possibilities offered. Except for the general framework, there is no direct attempt to control the specific values which the individual receives from participation. The typical municipal recreation and park department operates at this end of the continuum. Wide ranges of opportunities which are intended to appeal to different ages, different interests and different levels of skill are offered. The environments within which the opportunities are provided are structured so as to minimize or eliminate hazards to the health, safety and welfare of participants; care is taken to avoid encouraging or permitting activities which are contrary to the major social values and expectations of the public served, and the experiences which result from participation are assumed to be constructive. It is intended that participants will benefit, sometimes similarly, but often in ways unique to each person. No systematic effort is made to bring about particular benefits.

An opposing approach is to work consciously for the development of

---

[1] The concept of a "cafeteria approach" is taken from a lecture given at California State University, San Jose, by Mr. Al Taylor, on October 17, 1961. Mr. Taylor was Community Relations Consultant, Oakland Recreation Department at the time.

certain defined benefits and values which result from taking part in the opportunities provided by the agency. Agencies operating at this end of the continuum often have an ethic or a creed which serves as a basis for their operation. Or, they work in an institutionalized setting. An illustration of the former would be the various councils of the Boy Scouts of America, which foster behaviors and values consistent with the Scout Oath. Hospitals and treatment centers would illustrate institutional settings in which recreation therapists seek certain specified benefits for the patients and clients with whom they work.

Redl and Wineman,[2] writing from the perspective of treatment homes for disturbed children, provide a very good discussion of several objectives which might be sought as specific outcomes of recreation programming and which serve to illustrate this approach: the enhancement of the educative process, socialization of participants, facilitation of diagnostic and cathartic processes, counteracting destructive behavior, etc.

In this "prescription" approach, agencies define rather specific objectives to be achieved. If this is done, agency personnel have a clear responsibility also to develop evaluative techniques for determining the degree to which objectives have been achieved.

As with the direct service/enabling service continuum, some agencies will utilize a combination of approaches, depending upon clientele and specific programs. For example, a veteran's administration hospital may offer a "cafeteria-approach" to activities for short-term, convalescing patients in which the objectives are simply to reduce boredom and enrich the normal hospital routine. However, activities provided on the neuropsychiatric ward of the same hospital may be designed to contribute to specific objectives developed by a medical team for individual patients.

The leisure services provided by any agency encourage a variety of recreation behaviors. The following are illustrative.

Socializing Behaviors

Some recreation behavior is centered around the process of relating to other people in a social sense. Examples would be dancing, dating, going to parties, visiting friends, etc. In these activities, we are in the company of people we like, and we relate to each other with a minimal consciousness of social role. That is, we usually relate to people as people, in social situations, rather than as instructor to student, clerk to customer, physician to patient, etc.

---

[2] Redl, Fritz, and Wineman, David. *Controls from Within: Techniques for the Treatment of the Aggressive Child.* New York: The Free Press, 1952, pp. 79-87.

Associative Behaviors[3]

Another type of behavior encouraged by recreation agencies is people getting together around common interests: car clubs, stamp collecting groups, gem and mineral societies, etc. Frequently this kind of behavior includes developing an organizational structure, holding meetings and electing officers in addition to actually participating in the common interest (rebuilding cars, collecting stamps, and doing lapidary work).

Acquisitive Behaviors

Some recreation participation is manifested in collecting things: old bottles, matchbook covers, dolls, toy soldiers, antique furniture, etc. This often leads to associative behaviors as well; the bottle collector frequently joins a club and finds added enjoyment of his interests in the company of the other collectors.

Competitive Behaviors

This category includes the whole range of sports and games. Competitive behavior usually occurs within the context of a set of rules or procedures which define what may and may not be done. Also, there is an opponent, either actual or implied. In gin rummy, the opponents are actual (the other players); in solitaire, the opponent is implied. The essence of the activity is to outscore, or in some other symbolic way, defeat the opponent. In all cases, some type of skills, and often strategies, are involved.

The diversity of sports and games is immense. Included are team sports, individual and dual sports, low-organized games, table games and many others. In some sense, pursuits such as fishing and ballooning are sports; in these cases, the opponents are the fish and the laws of gravity.

Testing Behaviors

Closely akin to sports and games are testing kinds of behaviors. Here, our skills are tested against some criterion or some environmental condition. In small-bore rifle competition, the marksman not only aspires to shoot better than his opponents; he also may have in mind the criterion of a perfect score and he may mentally test his performance against this standard. The mountain climber frequently stakes his life on his skill as well as on his equipment. At a much less hazardous and less spectacular level, the crossword puzzle buff also tests his skill.

---

[3] Kaplan, Max. *Leisure in America.* New York, John Wiley and Sons, Inc., 1960; pp. 171-188. Kaplan provides an excellent description of both sociability and association as uses of leisure.

Risk-taking Behavior

Many recreation pursuits clearly involve considerable risk. In sport parachuting, the jumper assumes a life or death risk with each jump. Obviously, the participant, in measuring the risks, assumes that he has a reasonable chance for success, and safety.[4] The great popularity of gambling casinos in Reno and Las Vegas rests, in part, on the attractions of risk-taking, with a different loss or gain at stake.

Explorative Behaviors

A fairly large percentage of the motorists on the nation's highways at any time are engaging in what might be called explorative behavior. Sightseeing, travel, scuba diving, spelunking, hiking, and other activities allow the participant to discover new environments or to rediscover the finds of past adventures. For the amateur entomologist, the explorations might be with the microscope, or, for the hobby archeologist, in the sifted dirt of an exposed hillside. For many people, reading can be an exploration.

Vicarious Experiencing

Reading also is an illustration of vicarious experience. Television viewing, movie attendance and spectator sports might also be classed in this category.

Sensory Stimulation

In another vein, most of what might be grouped under vicarious experiencing could also be labelled sensory stimulation. And, in a much broader sense, all recreation behavior involves sensory stimulation to some degree. However, some experiences seem more dependent upon this factor than others. The enjoyment of sexual activity, consumption of alcohol, drug use, visual experiences such as light shows and certain types of music are at least partially based on either sensory stimulation or sensory manipulation.

Physical Expression

Another facet of behavior which also seems to involve some sensory elements is physical expression. There is a joy, often, in the simple act of running or jumping. Frequently, skills and movement will be involved, as in diving, skiing and the many dance forms.

---

[4] For an interesting discussion of the whole notion of risk-taking, see *Why Men Take Chances*. Edited by Samuel Klausner, New York, Anchor Books, 1968.

Creative Behavior

All of the arts, including dance, are also related to expression in a creative sense, usually through some medium—clay, paint, the spoken and written word, musical instruments, the camera, and countless other elements.

Appreciative Behavior

Creative behavior is participatory. That is, people do things; they paint, they sculpt, they write, they act, etc. The outcomes or results of such activity often are observed and enjoyed by others. The settings are concert halls, museums, art shows, living rooms with stereo sets, etc. Appreciative behavior also is participatory; and in some cases it may be creative, as when two people viewing the same abstract painting enjoy a different experience. However, in appreciative behavior the participant usually responds to the product, or result of the creative process, rather than interacting directly with the material as happens in the case of the artist.

Variety-seeking Behavior

Much of what we do in our free time probably involves an element of change from life's normal routines; the city dweller goes to the mountains, the accountant plays tennis, the personnel director goes on solitary hikes in the woods, etc.

Anticipatory and Recollective Behaviors

Jensen[5] and others suggest that the recreation experience includes an anticipatory phase and a reminiscent phase in addition to the actual participation. The former includes looking forward to the experience, planning, getting any needed equipment ready, etc. The latter includes talking about the experience, seeing photos and slides, showing souvenirs to friends, etc. While these two dimensions are part of the total experience, they also might be viewed as recreation behaviors definable in and of themselves.

The preceding behaviors are not mutually exclusive. For example, mountain climbing may involve risk-taking, testing of self and equipment, appreciation of scenery, association with members of a climbing club and physical expression.

As indicated earlier, the resources of any recreation agency ultimately are devoted to providing opportunities for one or more of the behaviors just enumerated to occur. The opportunities may encourage either highly skilled behavior or behavior which requires little skill. The com-

[5] Jensen, Clayne R. *Outdoor Recreation in America: Trends, Problems and Opportunities.* Minneapolis, Burgess Publishing Company, 1970, p. 14.

parison between swimming lessons for a beginner and scuba diving classes is illustrative. Some opportunities will involve more or less "one-shot" behaviors, such as a trip to Europe. Others provide for very frequent participation, as is found in teen drop-in centers and on playgrounds. Similarly, time and distance considerations are factors when the opportunities provided by the National Park Service, for example, are compared with the opportunities provided by municipal recreation and park departments. The national parks are structured so as to accommodate most readily vacation types of uses. Car camping, backpacking and related pursuits usually require more than an afternoon's worth of free time; and the parks usually are located some distance from most users, so travel time is also involved. On the other hand, one can drop down to the swim center located at the local high school for a quick swim any summer day, after work and before supper. The opportunities encourage many other differences in behavior: individual or group participation; the amount of equipment required; the intensity of participation (as in tournament bowling versus a bowling date for a young single couple), and others.

The basic method used by agencies to structure opportunities which encourage different kinds of recreation behaviors is the creation and/or manipulation of physical and human environments. Let us say, for example, that the San Francisco Recreation and Park Department wants to provide opportunities for residents of the city to play golf. Obviously, the department will do such things as acquire land and develop a golf course, or golf courses. They will employ personnel to maintain the course and keep it in an attractive condition. They also will employ personnel who will offer lessons; who will regulate play so that it proceeds efficiently; who will offer other services such as food and drink, equipment sales, etc. Further, they will train and supervise these employees so that appropriate service is provided. The department probably will make the public aware of the golfing opportunities it has available by means of the various mass media.

All of these activities involve the creation and/or manipulation of physical and human environments. Planners, landscape architects, construction foreman, park leadmen, gardeners, custodians and other similar individuals are immediately concerned with the creation and manipulation of physical environments; and so are the center director and the judo instructor. When the judo instructor arranges the mats, makes sure the showers are clean and ready for use and puts a display up on the club bulletin board, he is manipulating the physical environment. He does so with the reasonable expectation that certain kinds of behavior will be elicited from the boys. He also manipulates the human environment, of which he is a part. He directly influences the actions of the boys through communication, leadership and teaching activities. And the group itself serves as an influencing element. The executive director and the program director of the club also are concerned about the human environment; they engage in such activities as recruiting qualified leadership for club programs, providing in-service training programs for personnel, providing supportive supervision, setting appropriate rules of conduct which create and maintain a desirable interpersonal climate among participants, etc.

The human environment includes agency staff and participants, and the physical environment includes natural resources, developed land and water areas, facilities, equipment and supplies. These two environments, physical and human, are somewhat inseparable. One affects the other, and they act upon the participant as a combined influence. For example, the way in which a leader responds to the group with which he is working is influenced by the facility in which he is operating. The same art instructor will behave somewhat differently in a well-equipped studio as opposed to a poorly equipped one. On the other hand, an imaginative instructor can make much better use of an inadequate facility than can a leader who is less well qualified.

Leisure services, then, are those activities which, through the creation and/or manipulation of human and physical environments, provide opportunities for the expression of a wide variety of recreation behaviors. Included are all activities which are directly related to creating and manipulating environments, and those which support the direct operations. Budget management, legal counsel and policy definition are illustrative of the latter. Specifically, the process involves planning, organizing, staffing, directing and controlling.

In broad dimension, the leisure service delivery system is based on the agency's commitment to provide opportunities which encourage and facilitate selected kinds of recreation behaviors; the specific nature of these behaviors depends upon the objectives of the particular agency and upon the human and physical resources which are available.

The effective delivery system is one which recognizes the needs, interests and characteristics of the public it seeks to serve. Typically, it is developed on the basis of some initial and tentative assumptions about potential participants, defined largely on a group basis. It then moves toward individualization and modification of the service as participants, and their uniquenesses, are actually encountered. For example, let us assume that we wish to develop leisure services for older adults. Even without any direct contact with the group we hope to reach, we can estimate with reasonable confidence some of their needs, interests and characteristics. If we involve some older adults in the planning stages, as we should, we can be even more confident in the accuracy of our estimates. However, we cannot fully confirm our plans until we are in actual contact with the participants. At that point, and in a continuing manner, we need to look for and effect modifications which will make the leisure services more relevant to the particular group to be served. It is clear that if we are to accomplish this, we must know something about the participants we wish to serve.

CHAPTER 6

The Recipient of Service: The Participant

If you were asked to think about the most recent recreation activity in which you engaged, it is probable that you could describe it in reasonable detail. You could tell where it happened, when it happened and what you did. You might be able to offer a reason why you engaged in that particular activity at that particular time. Chances are that your description would define the beginning of the experience and the termination of it: "We went fishing early Saturday morning and came home Sunday about noon," or, "I played basketball between my one o'clock class and my chemistry lab at four." From your point of view, your participation was an experience, and you derived certain satisfactions, frustrations and feelings from it.

To other people who watched you participate, your activity might be seen as a behavioral sequence. That is, they might observe what you did as a unit of behavior, or a series of behaviors. They might infer something about your motivations for doing what you did, about values and benefits as well as detrimental conditions which resulted from your activity and about the various factors which might be influencing the nature of your participation.

Recreation and park personnel have a responsibility to develop some basic understandings about the people for whom they provide leisure services. It seems self-evident that we can be effective only if we do develop such understandings. However, many of our understandings will be based on inferences. The leader does not know directly why an individual played basketball rather than pinochle unless he is informed by the participant. Similarly, the leader cannot say for certain what will attract a participant's attention and energies tomorrow after class or after work. However, he can make some guesses in both cases. That is, he can guess why the individual played basketball and, if certain conditions prevail (weather, the presence of friends, the stability of his health, etc.), what he probably will do tomorrow. The more the leader knows about people—people of the same age, sex, education, etc.—the better his guess should be. Better yet, the more the leader knows about the participant personally, in his own uniqueness, the more accurate his inferences should be. In part, this is true because he can best understand the participant's behavior from his perspective. It may appear to the leader that the participant's reasons for playing basketball are to get exercise and to enjoy competition. If the leader has some responsibility for structuring the activity in which an individual engages, he probably will do what he can to enhance the individual's chances for meeting those objectives. The leader may put considerable emphasis on score-keeping; he may set the activity up with 10-minute time periods rather than 6-minute ones. However, if the participant's objectives in playing are largely social and if he basically just wants to enjoy the friendship of his teammates, the leader's efforts may be counterproductive. The leader will not have really understood the participant's recreation behavior.

In this sense, the attitudes of the individual participant are the key factors in understanding behavior. A leader may see an overnight camping trip in the Black Hills as a marvelous opportunity to enjoy nature. Someone else might see it as a frightening intrusion into the unknown. An individual's behavior, obviously, will reflect his perceptions, not those of another person. An individual's fear of surfing might seem unrealistic to an advocate of the activity, but from his own point of view, his reluctance to participate makes sense; from another person's perspective it may not. *However removed from reality they may be, the perceptions of the participant (or nonparticipant) are the basis for his or her behavior; and, they are the keys to understanding the behavior we observe.* Naturally, we cannot see or feel things exactly as the participant does, but, the nearer we can come to this, the more confidence we can have in our inferences.

Participation also is best understood as the relationship between an individual and his immediate environment. Recreation behavior takes place in a setting which includes physical, and often, human elements. Tennis usually takes place on an asphalt, lawn, cement or dirt court. The court is marked with appropriate lines, and divided by a net. Typically it is surrounded by a fairly high fence. These are the physical features. The scene is not complete, however. There must be people, an opponent or opponents and a partner, for play to proceed in the usual fashion. The nature of any given player's behavior probably will vary according to the nature of the physical and human environment. A poorly surfaced court will produce different responses from a player than one which is in excellent condition. Further, the presence of spectators may cause different behavior than would be observed if only the players were in attendance. Either the presence or absence of spectators or the condition of the court might influence an advanced player differently than a beginner and a timid personality differently than a "grandstander."

Usually, more is involved than a unilateral relationship. More typically, the individual is influenced by the environment, and in turn, he or she influences the setting within which the recreation behavior takes place. Take the tennis example as an illustration. Assume that an advanced player is playing against a less experienced player on a court which has an inferior surface. This situation may produce several changes. The less experienced player may rise to the keener competition and play better than she normally does; the advanced player may let down, mentally, and play less well. Both may become irritated with the condition of the court and agree to certain temporary rule changes to accommodate the poor surface (unusual bounces will be played over; serves will be taken from and into the same court rather than using alternate courts, etc.). Many other illustrations could be drawn to show that as one element or aspect of the setting changes, it influences other elements or aspects. *In a sense, the individual participant and the environment within which his recreation behavior occurs represent an ecological unit.* An awareness of the various changing interrelationships between the physical and human elements which make up the unit will contribute significantly to understanding the recreation behavior involved.

In any setting, the individual participates as a totality. Again, we might use the tennis illustration. Obviously there are movement skills involved: the serve, the forehand volley, the backhand, the lob, the smash, etc. There also are knowledges: how to score, legal and illegal procedures, matters of etiquette and expected courtesies, etc. And, there are feelings: attitudes about winning and losing, responses to well or poorly executed plays, the feelings about the presence or absence of spectators, etc. Moreover, any particular action might illustrate a similar content. The lob involves the ability to execute the movement in the sense of the physical skill, the knowledge of when to use it and the feeling of confidence which encourages its use when the appropriate time occurs. *These three areas—cognitive (knowledge), affective (feeling) and motor (skill performance)—seem to be a part of most recreation experiences and behavior.* Some activities emphasize one or two; except for the physical involvement of the eyes, movie viewing tends to fall in the affective and cognitive domains. Listening to music without dancing or overexertive toe-tapping likewise involves these two areas. Throwing a pot on a ceramic wheel or running a competitive two-mile race involve all three domains; just running for exercise probably is limited, for most people, to the motor and affective areas. A failure to recognize this totality of the recreation experience serves to distract from an adequate understanding of behavior.

For all practical purposes recreation behavior is goal-directed. *That is, people engage in recreation to meet certain goals.* While these goals tend to be rather individualistic, most people indicate that enjoyment, fun or satisfaction are their main reasons for participating. While this contention is valid, it is somewhat too general to be operationally useful to recreation and park personnel. If an individual said to a leader, "Please plan an experience for me which will be enjoyable," the leader might have some difficulty doing so. On the other hand, if he also would tell the leader that he enjoys being with other people, that it gives him great pleasure to feel a sense of accomplishment, or that he likes to do familiar things, or new things, the leader will have a better idea of how to provide an enjoyable experience for him. It seems reasonable to suggest that enjoyment can be defined more precisely. For many it involves companionship, affection, being with others. Or, it can involve accomplishment, recognition, a sense of doing well. For some, enjoyment comes through acquiring things; others find satisfaction in the expression of power, over people (as in club offices, etc.) or over things (as in conquering a mountain). Altruistic endeavors, such as volunteer work, also are a source enjoyment for some people. The list of what makes for enjoyment is a list of motivating forces. Different theorists have expressed these in different ways: needs, wishes, drives, motives, goals, etc.

There is considerable divergence among writers about the specific nature of motivation. However, there seems to be fairly widespread acceptance of the notion that several motivating factors can be defined which are common to most people; at least most people in Western society today. A list from Krech, Crutchfield and Ballachey[1] is illustrative. They discuss five forces which they label major social wants: affiliation, acquisitive, prestige, altruistic and curiosity. Other lists are similar; some shorter, some longer. The want or need for affiliation and companionship and the want or need for achievement or prestige seem to be mentioned most frequently. It should be relatively apparent that recreation behavior often provides many opportunities for satisfying these two needs or wants. A painting well done, a successful drama production, a skilled serve in handball, a par game of golf and a model airplane which draws appreciative comments from friends all contribute to a sense of achievement and self-worth. The art class, the stage crew, the fellow handball players, the golf foursome and other model enthusiasts are all potential contributors to feelings of belonging and affiliation.

Companionship and, indirectly, achievement are elements in Maslow's[2] scheme. As indicated in Chapter 2, Maslow felt that needs operate in something of a hierarchical fashion. Physiological needs and safety needs are at the bottom of the scale; these must be satisfied before the higher level needs become operative. Love, belonging, and companionship

---

[1] Krech, David, Crutchfield, Richard S., and Ballachey, Egerton L. *Individual in Society.* New York, McGraw-Hill Book Company, Inc., 1962, pp. 89-99.

[2] Maslow, Abraham H. "A Theory of Human Motivation," *Psychological Review,* 50:370-396, July, 1943.

needs are next, followed by self-esteem needs. Self-esteem seems directly related to achievement; it becomes an influencing factor only when love and belonging needs are rather consistently met. The highest level of need is the one for self-actualization or the need to express fully one's capacities and capabilities. Again, belonging and self-esteem probably are the most common factors which motivate recreation behavior.

No matter what the specific factor influencing each individual at any given time, we can assume that participants are striving to meet some personal objective. And, whether or not they continue to engage in the particular activity depends in part on their perceptions of success or failure. Typically success will lead to continued participation; consistent failure usually results in a rejection of the activity. For example, a physicist may say she takes tennis lessons for enjoyment. Further conversation leads us to conclude that she plays mainly to meet, and be with, other people. The basic motivation is companionship. Let us assume that this particular tennis class is made up largely of people who leave immediately after the lessons, and who seem very little interested in socializing or even being friendly. The chances are good that our physicist will discontinue the class, even though she may be learning new skills and improving her game. Three factors are at work in this situation: What are her objectives? At what level of performance will these objectives be satisfied? How does she perceive or evaluate her performance? These questions are basic to understanding her behavior.

Let us say that achievement rather than companionship is the general motivation for enrolling in the tennis class. There are several levels to which our physicist may aspire. She may be satisfied if she does well enough not to look foolish in front of the remainder of the class, or she may be satisfied only if she is the top student and wins the intraclass ladder tournament. What is crucial is *what does she aspire to do, and how does she feel about her performance?*

Another notion which may contribute to understanding recreation behavior is the concept of conflicting motives. It is possible for two motivating forces to act in opposition. The physicist may be enrolled in the tennis lessons and suddenly have the opportunity to attend a foreign film series on the same evening. If she has a deep interest in foreign films, she may be in a conflict situation. In this case, she may want to engage in both activities, but the overlapping time schedule prevents her from doing so. A different kind of conflict could occur if she wanted to take the tennis lessons, but was reluctant to be on the courts during the heat of the day when the lessons were scheduled. In this latter situation, the same activity contains both attractive and repelling elements. Classic examples would be a neophyte sport parachutist standing at the plane's door and an adolescent at his first dance. The parachutist is faced with the potential exhilaration and achievement of the jump as well as the fear that his equipment or his technique may fail. The adolescent struggles with a conflict between his heterosexual interests and his fear of looking foolish in front of friends.

The goals or objectives most people seek in recreation tend to be immediate ones. Satisfaction usually comes directly and at the time of participation. However, some people may be motivated by more distant goals as well as the immediate ones. Practice on the putting green may be seen as a way to develop skill for later competition; in addition, it provides fun while the golfer is practicing. Running may be used by the skier to keep in condition during the off season, but he may also enjoy the activity itself.

Of course, recreation behavior often is motivated by multiple goals. The ceramics class may provide for companionship as well as a sense of achievement. Similarly, almost any activity has potential for contributing to the satisfaction of more than one goal.

Obviously, different people are motivated by different specific goals, even though there may be common general needs and wishes. One individual may satisfy his wish for achievement by playing the guitar and racing sports cars and another may seek recognition in square dancing and oil painting. Why?

The reasons for different individual expressions of recreation behavior are interrelated and exceedingly complex. However, one useful approach which contributes to understanding is to examine the influence of several variables, or individual differences. Differences such as age, sex, income, race, occupation, education, health, marital and family status and personality all have potential for influencing recreation behavior.

In many ways all pre-school children are similar. Among other things, they have relatively short attention spans, they tend to be quite active and they have not yet developed the capacity for learning highly coordinated motor skills. However, there is wide variation among them, even at the same chronological age. Some remain absorbed in activities for relatively long periods of time, some seem more quiet than others and some develop hand-eye coordination considerably earlier than their age-mates. When we talk of four-year-olds, we can describe some of the characteristics of average four-year-olds, but we must recognize that many children will differ from our description of typical characteristics. It is much the same with other individual differences. For example, some characteristics typically associated with persons of low income or with higher educational attainment can be defined, but any one poor person or any one college graduate might exhibit characteristics quite different from what would be found in the larger percentage of such persons.

Women are alike in some ways, but certainly not in most ways. The average construction worker differs in some respects from the average lawyer; but they also may have more similarities than differences when compared as individuals. Growing up as a black person in America is a different experience than growing up as a white one. We can describe some potential influences of race on recreation behavior, but none of them may be operative for any one specific black child or adult.

Nonetheless an awareness of typical characteristics does contribute to an understanding of recreation behavior. As suggested in Chapter 5, we usually use these typical characteristics as initial assumptions when we plan leisure services. Suppose a leader is asked to plan a program for a group of teen-agers with whom he has had no prior contact. His initial step probably will be to make some assumptions about the group based on what he knows about the typical interests and behaviors of adolescents. If he does, the leader is guessing that the group will include many people who are similar to the average teen-ager. This is an appropriate approach, if he tests his assumptions at the point he has the opportunity for actual contact with the people. They may be quite different from what the leader guessed; but until he can relate to them directly, his best bet is to plan on the basis of what is known about teen-agers generally.

It is similar with other ages and with other potentially influencing factors. *The basic approach to planning leisure services for any given group (young, old, poor, rich, etc.) is to assume that the characteristics which influence their recreation behavior are similar to those of typical members of the group until the leader has the opportunity to confirm, deny or modify his assumptions.* Once a leader begins working with the group, it is imperative that he be sensitive to the particular individual uniquenesses and differences which might be present.

We spoke earlier of the idea that the participant engages in recreation behavior as a total being; he is involved in most activities physically, intellectually and emotionally. Similarly, he brings to the experience a variety of potentially influential characteristics which operate interrelatedy. A middle-income, American Indian female who is employed as a reading consultant on a rural county school superintendent's staff is a totality. Her financial status does not operate as an influencer independently of her sex identity, her racial heritage or her occupational role. The overall influence of these conditions is a result of the fact that they occur and operate together. One may be a more potent influencer; but even so, it does not exist in isolation of the other factors.

Nonetheless, it is possible to identify types of influences that such factors as income, health, age, sex, race, occupation and education exert on recreation behavior. A few examples will illustrate.

Age

The influences of age are biological, psychological and, to some degree, cultural. A four-year-old rarely, if ever, plays handball. He usually does not have sufficient hand-eye coordination to do so. This is a result of his physical development. He probably has not yet developed the social concept of team play used in doubles competition; this is a psychological factor. Also, he gets very little encouragement from society to engage in such an activity, a cultural condition; in our culture boys usually do not play handball until they are older. In addition, handball courts usually are not neighborhood facilities. More often they are located at a high school or community center which may be some distance from our four-year-old's house. Pre-school children tend to play quite close to home; as yet, they are relatively dependent and they are more or less closely supervised. Again, these are cultural factors, which probably grow out of a parent's recognition of the child's physical and psychological development.

An older adult has a good concept of team play and of cooperation and competition. However, the biological factors of declining energy and physical strength may preclude handball as an activity. It is even possible that a senior citizen's friends discourage him from handball because it is seen as a young man's game. If so, a cultural factor is at work.

Sex

Cultural factors probably are most pronounced in the area of sex identity. Relatively few men engage in sewing as a recreation pursuit although clearly, they have the physical and intellectual capacity for it. Most have no interest in doing so, and interest is a psychological factor. However, the origin of this lack of interest probably is cultural. In our society, sewing as a hobby usually is considered a feminine activity.

Times are changing, and today there is much more acceptance of participation by one sex in activities which are identified with the opposite sex. This seems especially true of women taking part in formerly all-male pursuits such as mountain climbing, surfing, hunting and team sports.

Income Level

Obviously, the amount of money which is possessed by an individual influences his or her recreation behaviors. For example, it takes money to buy golf equipment and appropriate apparel and to pay green fees. We are much less likely to see poor people playing golf than more affluent individuals.

This is only part of the influence of income, however. The poor person usually has a more limited background of exposure and experience; he probably has not had the opportunity to develop needed skills, and it is quite possible that he does not view golf as an appropriate or available activity. Poor health and medical problems are common among the poor; these may hinder his participation, if the other factors do not. Also, he may reject any activity such as golf as symbolic of the life which he feels he cannot attain. His frustration and the resulting hostility and alienation may influence not only his selection of activities, but also his willingness or unwillingness to participate in any program offered by a traditional recreation agency. Further, if Maslow's scheme is correct, he may be so preoccupied with survival and safety needs that he has no motivation to engage in an activity such as golf. As with age, these influences are a combination of biological, psychological and cultural factors.

Racial and National Identity

Does the condition of being Japanese or Mexican-American influence recreation behavior? It may.

One likely way in which race or nationality may serve as an influence is in terms of the preservation of cultural heritage. If an individual desires to maintain his Mexican identity, he may choose activities which help to do so. Perhaps he enjoys cooking authentic Mexican food or listening to folk music which originated in Mexico. Maybe he will take part in a dance class which emphasizes Mexican dance forms.

These kinds of motivations, in part, have resulted in black art festivals in neighborhood schools, dramatic activities at Jewish community centers, Oktoberfests at halls owned or rented by German clubs, and Japanese brush painting classes in the social halls of Buddhist temples.

Another possible influence of race is related to segregation. Some of the most blatant examples of discrimination have occurred at recreation facilities, notably swimming pools and beaches. The situation has improved greatly since the 1954 Supreme Court decision which held segregation in public facilities to be unconstitutional; however, discrimination no doubt still exists in more subtle forms. If a person has been denied access to a recreation activity because of his race, he may never develop the appropriate skills, or, more important perhaps, the interest in participating. As an example, blacks who had no access to tennis facilities as youths and young adults probably have no interest in playing in their middle years. At least, this is a likely possibility. They haven't the skills, and therefore, the possibility for satifaction is lessened. On the other hand, many younger members of minority races now engage in a wide variety of activities which formerly were the almost exclusive domain of white participants.

Marital and Family Status

The family is an important determiner of recreation interests. Indeed, the home is the first recreation center, in a sense, and parents are the child's first recreation leaders. The home environment makes heavy influences on the child's interests through the examples, exposures and implements (toys, books, etc.) provided by the parents.

Just as the parent influences the child's recreation behavior, the presence of children has potential for affecting the parents' choices of behaviors. The young, childless couple has considerably more freedom in what they do than does the young couple with a set of twin two-year-olds. The family with two teen-agers faces a different set of circumstances in planning a two-week vacation than does an older couple whose children have left home.

Marriage also results in some changes in an individual's recreation patterns, as any husband who forgets to come home from bowling at the promised hour of midnight knows; or as any wife recognizes as she sits in a remote fishing cabin rather than at the plush resort area she had in mind as a vacation spot.

Education and Occupation

The potential influence of education is related to occupation and to income as well. Generally, the higher one's education level, the greater the chance for a well-paying job.

There appears to be another dimension to the influence of education. Increased education usually leads to a broader background of experiences, including those in recreation. The student at all levels is exposed to activities, events and knowledges which have potential as personal recreation interests. The more education an individual has, at least up to the B.A. or B.S. degree level, the greater the chances for exposures and opportunities to occur.

An interesting notion related to occupation is the possibility that cultural expectations function in relation to certain work statuses as they do with respect to sex identity. For example, members of higher-prestige occupations may be inclined to engage in activities which, in some ways, symbolize their occupational position. In any given community, if the dentists tend to play bridge, a new dentist starting practice in the town may be encouraged by colleagues to join a bridge group because "it is the thing to do." A plumber may not feel comfortable at the local country club, even though his income is greater than that of many of the regular members. He doesn't think it is the thing for him to do, his friends don't think it is appropriate for him and the members of the country club might not encourage him even if they have the opportunity to do so.

A clearer influence of occupation is the factor of free time. The plumber may have considerable free time, particularly if he is not self-employed. He may work a seven-hour day, five days a week, and he probably will get at least a two-week vacation every year. His physician may be lucky to get away from his practice for one week during the summer, and he may rarely enjoy a Sunday without being called to the hospital for emergencies and baby deliveries. Naturally, the amount of time an individual has influences what he can do. Different activities have different time requirements; watching television involves a different commitment of time than does a trip to Europe.

Health

Health has been mentioned in the previous examples. It is apparent that one's health encourages or prohibits certain activities. A man with a cardiac condition is an unlikely candidate for a mountain climbing group. An overweight woman probably will not choose a badminton class at the YWCA unless she has losing weight as a direct objective. On the other hand, a middle-aged adult who has been conditioning himself by a gradual program of hiking and jogging may be a very good prospect for a wilderness backpack trip, or some other similarly demanding physical activity.

Personality

All of the preceding factors, and many others, come together in personality. And personality probably is the most significant determinant of recreation behavior. Our interests, values and capabilities are part of our personalities. Indeed, our personalities are what we are. When we engage in recreation behavior, we express our personalities.

The difficulty related to personality is that it is not very useful, operationally, to recreation and park personnel who wish to plan for leisure services. Suppose we have a group of people assembled in a community center. It will be fairly easy for us to determine how many are male and how many are female. Also, we can make some reasonably accurate guesses about ages. If we ask, we can get information about racial identity, marital and family status, occupation, education and even health. The answers we get will have some common meaning for us. However, if we ask each to describe his or her personality, we will get a myriad of responses which will not be especially useful. We might give them all one or more of the many personality inventories which are available, but this is not a very practical possibility at this time. It would be difficult to do, in terms of time and costs, and most people probably would object to taking such tests except in school or medical settings.

An idea related to personality is that of life style. Life style, as the term suggests, is how we live. It includes such things as what actions, objects and ideas we value; whether or not we are aggressive or timid in our relations with others; whether or not we tend to be conservative or liberal in our acceptance of change; whether we are independent or reliant on other people; how confident we are in making decisions; and a host of other ways of behaving which would be more or less predictable if anyone knew enough about us. The recreational choices we make probably reflect, to some degree, our life styles. Like personality, these are difficult to define, operationally, and they are highly unique and individualistic.

The preceding discussion, of course, is not a comprehensive description of the influences of each factor mentioned. It is intended to provide an awareness of the types of individual variations which may contribute to differences in recreation behavior.[3]

Consideration of individual differences leads to what might be called an opportunity complex. Every person lives his or her recreation life within the framework of certain opportunities; some people have many opportunities to engage in recreation behavior and others have relatively few. Age can be one of the factors which restricts opportunities. The very young and the very old have less mobility than individuals in between the two age extremes; as a result they have fewer opportunities. The four-year-old is not permitted from home unless he is accompanied by an adult, and the aged person may not have sufficient energy or money to get beyond the immediate environment of his apartment.

The availability of money also helps to set the boundaries of our opportunity complexes. Obviously the rich can choose from among a much wider range of alternatives than can the poor. An older, poor person will have even more restricted choices. Opportunity complexes differ in terms of the range of alternatives which are possible. A person who lives in New York will have a different set of opportunities than one who lives in a small rural town. The notion of any individual's opportunity complex is useful to an understanding of recreation behavior, even though it is far from a precise tool or a well-defined concept.

The primary contention of this chapter is that *recreation is a segment of behavior.* It is influenced by the environment within which it occurs, and by the characteristics of the individual participant. Since the basic

---

[3] For further discussion of the influence of factors such as sex, occupation and education, see Mueller, Eva, and Gurin, Gerald. *Participation in Outdoor Recreation: Factors Affecting Demand Among American Adults.* ORRRC Report No. 20, Washington, D.C., 1962. Age as an influence is dealt with in many sources; one of these is Miller, Norman P., and Robinson, Duane, M. *The Leisure Age.* Belmont, California, Wadsworth Publishing Company, Chapter 11, 1963. Two very useful articles appear in *Recreation and Leisure Service for the Disadvantaged: Guidelines to Program Development and Related Readings.* Edited by John A. Nesbitt, Paul D. Brown, and James F. Murphy, Philadelphia, Lea & Febiger, 1970, pp. 166-174, 348-353. One is "Recreation Leadership with Socioculturally Handicapped Clientele" by Vel Moore. It describes characteristics of the poor. The second is "The Inner-city Clientele: What Are They Like?" by Clarence McKee. He gives attention to racial heritage and identity as influencing factors.

responsibility of recreation and park personnel is to provide opportunities for recreation behavior to occur, it seems only reasonable that we have an unavoidable responsibility to learn as much about the behavior as we possibly can. Only in so doing can we be effective in delivering appropriate leisure services.

CHAPTER 7

Standards and Guidelines for the Effective Delivery of Leisure Service

Goals and Objectives: Definitions and Examples

All leisure service agencies, public or private, large or small, should establish goals and objectives and operate under policies that will aid in successfully meeting those goals and objectives. As pointed out in a program evaluation report of the San Francisco Recreation and Park Department, "it is essential in any consideration of goals and objectives to have a clearcut understanding of the concepts." The following definitions are offered as guidelines within the report:

> *Goals:* A goal is a statement of broad direction, purpose, or intent based on the identified needs of the community. A goal is general and timeless; that is, it is not concerned with a specific achievement with a specified time period.
> *Objectives:* An objective is a desired accomplishment which can be measured within a given timeframe. Achievement of the objective advances the system toward a corresponding goal. Accordingly, objectives must be developed that support and contribute to the achievement of the established goals.[1]

The report offers criteria for formulation of goals and long-range objectives for the San Francisco Recreation and Park Department. The criteria for goals and long-range objectives as submitted in the report and presented below are general in nature and can serve as examples for those instrumental in the establishment of goals and objectives for leisure service agencies.

Criteria

> *Goals must be long range:* By their remoteness, they ensure that provision is made for tomorrow's needs rather than merely the expediencies of today.
> *Goals must be idealistic and visionary:* Progress starts with ideas, some of which frequently seem unattainable and even theoretical in nature.
> *Goals must be challenging:* They should arouse enthusiasm and stimulate involvement and support. Daniel H. Burnham once said, ". . . make no small plans; they have no magic to stir men's blood and probably will not be realized. Make big plans; aim high in hope and work, remembering that a noble, logical diagram once recorded will never die, but long after we are gone will be a living thing, asserting itself with ever-increasing insistency. Remember that our sons and grandsons will do things that would stagger us."

[1] Used by permission of Planning Research Corporation. *Program Evaluation, San Francisco Recreation and Park Department.* Los Angeles, California, 1971, pp. 19-21.

Goals should be locally oriented: Only local residents can and should determine what kind of a city they want and what kind and quality of a recreation system they should have.

Long Range Objectives

1. Provide comprehensive active and passive recreation opportunities for all age groups, equitably distributed throughout the City of San Francisco.
2. Minister to San Francisco's unique neighborhood requirements in providing recreation services.
3. Establish a long range development program enabling timely expansion and preservation of park areas and facilities to meet future requirements.
4. Provide qualified and sufficiently well trained leadership under overall professional guidance at all recreational facilities.
5. Provide safe and secure park settings and reduce violence and unrest in recreation areas.
6. Establish sufficient funding and resources to provide optimal recreational use of all Recreation and Park Department parks and facilities.[2]

The Cupertino Plan

Kraus has pointed out that "since the once widely accepted view of recreation as an activity carried on for its own sake and without extensive purpose, is no longer important enough to justify substantial public support, it is necessary to conceive and plan for the delivery of recreation as a vital community service."[3] Because of this fact, many committees recently established to determine goals for local communities throughout the country have included broad goals for park and recreation agencies within their reports. After almost two years of study, the Cupertino, California Citizen's Goals Committee included the following goals within their report:

1. To encourage the development of recreation facilities and programs which can enhance the enjoyment of life for every age group.
2. To provide areas of green within reach of every resident for rest and relaxation.
3. To press for the development of adjacent and regional park facilities.
4. To provide for hiking and equestrian trails in the foothills.[4]

The Cupertino Parks and Recreation Commission adopted policies designed to aid in the achievement of each of the four goals. The Commission adopted twelve additional goals in an attempt to further outline the services of their department to the public. These goals were as follows:

1. Provide a comprehensive, year-round recreation program of high quality, available to all, regardless of race, creed, ethnic or socio-economic background, sex or age.
2. Develop an attractive, diversified park system comprising imaginatively designed indoor and outdoor areas and facilities to meet the varying interests of the residents.

---

[2] Ibid., pp. 20-29.

[3] Kraus, Richard. *Recreation and Leisure in Modern Society.* New York, Appleton-Century-Crofts, 1971, p. 431.

[4] Used by permission of Butler, Merle O. "City of Cupertino, Parks and Recreation Master Plan." Unpublished document. Cupertino, California, 1972, p. 10.

3. Maintain the parks system in accordance with high standards so as to contribute to the beauty, charm and attraction of the city.
4. Cooperate with the school districts in the joint planning, design, development and operation of areas and facilities for the mutual good of both recreation and educational programs.
5. To utilize land and water resources in cooperation with both public and private agencies for the maximum development of recreation programs and services.
6. Encourage individuals and organizations to provide volunteer leadership in expanding recreation programs to meet the needs of children and adults.
7. Cooperate with schools, churches, parents and juvenile workers in combatting youth delinquency and behavioral problems, with the emphasis on prevention.
8. Develop an understanding of the special needs of youth and plan wholesome recreation programs with their help, enthusiasm, and talent to meet their needs.
9. Encourage population stability and preserve values by helping make Cupertino an exciting place in which to live and raise a family.
10. Provide opportunities for the development of leisure skills and attitudes with children to insure their ability to live full lives as adults and parents.
11. Provide opportunities for people to meet and enjoy recreation in groups, thus forming new friendships in Cupertino.
12. Maintain high standards in leadership, facilities, and equipment consistent with the concepts generally associated with Cupertino.[5]

The Cupertino Parks and Recreation Commission determined that in addition to adopting goals designed for their local community, it was necessary to review standards, goals, principles and policies that had been suggested by regional, state and national committees, commissions and agencies for adoption at the local level. Twenty-four of 33 policies outlined in the January, 1972 Parks, Recreation and Open Space Report of the Planning Policy Committee of Santa Clara County, California were directed toward local programs. These policies are listed below:

1. Cities should make every effort to locate neighborhood parks in developing areas and to create green and open spaces in older neighborhoods, such as plazas, creative parks, etc.
2. In already built-up areas, cities should cooperate with school districts to make maximum recreation use of school facilities.
3. Whenever possible new neighborhood parks should be located adjacent to elementary schools to make possible joint use of school facilities.
4. Cities should provide community parks in newly developing areas on the basis of one park of 20 acres or so for each high school service area.
5. Whenever possible community parks should be located to adjoin high schools or junior high schools for joint use of the school's recreation facilities.
6. In acquiring future mountain park areas, consideration should be given both to the natural beauty of the area and its capacity to accommodate necessary recreation or ancillary facilities.
7. The County and cities should make every effort to protect the roadside (scenic corridor) of scenic roads in the County by Scenic Highway Zoning.
8. The Skyline which has been planned as a protected roadway with frequent parks adjoining it should be implemented as soon as possible. Consideration should be given to establishing other chains of parks connected by a scenic road.

[5] Ibid., p. 11-12.

9. Cities should provide swimming pools in all or most community parks and wading facilities in neighborhood parks when appropriate.
10. Trails should be encouraged along publicly owned rights of way to increase walking opportunities in a pleasant and safe natural environment, such as streamsides. Legislation should be enacted for the right of condemnation for walking, hiking, riding and bicycling trails.
11. Regular planting should be made of all available water areas in the County suitable for sustaining fish.
12. Large expanses of natural or open landscaped areas in all parks with clusters of trees for shade should be provided.
13. Hiking and riding trails should be provided in large natural areas with a variety of terrain inviting to hikers seeking change from the urban environment. Legislation should be enacted for the right of condemnation for walking, hiking, riding and bicycle trails.
14. Special consideration should be given to the provision of facilities for the activities of "outdoor spectator sports," "camping," "power boating," "bicycling" and "golf." Provision should be made to encourage the private sector to enter the field of outdoor recreation. For example, tax relief, not based on gross income, may attract business, and thereby relieve the public agencies.
15. A countywide system of "Bicycle Routes" should be established, signed and protected, which would employ existing roads emphasizing continuity and safety.
16. Innovative approaches should be taken to use expressway rights of way for development of separated bike paths to help relieve vehicular congestion. Every effort should be made to connect existing centers of activity, employment, and places of residence.
17. There should be a countywide system of separated "Bike Paths" utilizing greenway utility easements and rights of way which could link schools, parks, churches, etc. as well as flood control streamside easements and rights of way, the levees of the South Bay, skyline mountain ridges, and scenic highways. Legislation should be enacted for the right of condemnation for walking, hiking, riding, and bicycle trails.
18. In planning parks, an effort should be made to remove deterrents by:
    a. Supplying swimming, hiking, fishing, camping, and picnicking facilities in greater quantity and within a reasonable distance of population centers.
    b. Encouraging provision for and use of public transportation.
    c. Providing recreation programs to teach skills required for golfing, tennis, swimming, and water skiing.
    d. Providing rental or loan equipment for boating, camping, water skiing, and golfing. Keep fees for these activities to a minimum.
    e. Encourage industry to stagger days off to give greater recreational opportunities to a greater number of people for the available facilities.
19. Maximum use should be made of water features created in all parks. Similarly maximum use of water recreation potential of waters in the county should be made.
20. The county and local jurisdictions should protect their water features from urban encroachment by the use of flood plain zoning in cooperation with the Flood Control District, and by zoning restrictions on building on the edge of water courses. Strong measures must be taken to abate pollution.
21. Primary attention should be given in park planning and management in all parks for the preservation of natural beauty and integrity of the land. Landscape design should support this concept.
22. When the unit cost of a recreation facility requested by a special interest group is excessively high, such a facility should not be provided by a public agency, except under consideration of charging fees.
23. In the early years of establishment of a park system, emphasis should be placed on acquisition. As a guide, 75% of available funds should be devoted to acquisition and 25% to development.

24. Urban growth should be staged, so as to utilize first those areas already committed to urbanization by existing utility extensions. In these staged growth areas, open space should be planned in advance of development to provide for increased population growth.[6]

In addition to recognizing the policies of the Planning Policy Committee of the Santa Clara County, the Cupertino Parks and Recreation Master Plan includes the following principles established by the State of California Park and Recreation Commission which relate to the broad aspects of physical planning for recreation areas and facilities.

1. *Opportunities for all.* A recreation and park system should provide recreation opportunities for all, regardless of race, creed, color, age, or economic status.
2. *Analysis of facilities, needs and trends.* Planning for recreation parks and facilities should be based initially upon comprehensive and thorough evaluation of existing public facilities, present and future needs, and trends; thereafter periodic review, re-evaluation and revision of long-range plans should follow.
3. *Analysis of private facilities.* Facilities and services provided by private agencies and institutions and commercial recreation enterprises to meet leisure needs of the population should be carefully evaluated by the public recreation agency and cooperating jurisdictions before plans for new recreation parks and facilities are prepared so that a proper relationship between private and public facilities may be established and duplication may be avoided.
4. *Public cooperation.* Planning for recreation parks and facilities should be undertaken with full cooperation of the citizens, so that the recreation system may reflect their thinking concerning the needs and interests of all groups.
5. *Unified system.* Recreation parks and facilities for a city, county, special district or metropolitan district should be planned as related parts of a unified, well-balanced system to serve the entire area of jurisdiction.
6. *Integration in general plan.* The recreation plan, showing both existing and proposed recreation parks and facilities, should be integrated with all other sections of the general or master plan for the locality.
7. *Related areas.* Planning for recreation parks and facilities should encompass areas beyond a city, county, or other jurisdiction that are related to it.
8. *Central location.* Each recreation center or recreation park should be centrally located within the area it is planned to serve and should be provided with safe and convenient access for all residents of the area.
9. *Flexibility and adaptability.* Within a particular park the location, size and design of activity areas and facilities should be regarded as flexible, so as to be adaptable to changes in the population served and in the recreation program offered to meet changing needs.
10. *Beauty and efficiency.* Beauty and functional efficiency should complement each other in recreation parks and facilities and should be equally important goals of planning.
11. *Advance acquisition of sites.* Land for recreation parks and facilities should be acquired or reserved well in advance of the development of an area, in the same manner as it is reserved for other public purposes.
12. *Achieving space standards.* Space standards for recreation parks should be met and the land acquired even if the limited financial resources of a recreation agency oblige it to delay complete development.

---

[6]Ibid., p. 12-15.

13. *Suitability of sites.* Selection or acceptance of sites should be based on their suitability for the intended purpose, as indicated in the over-all plan for the recreation system.
14. *Perpetuity of use.* Recreation parks should be lands dedicated and held inviolate in perpetuity, protected by law against diversion to nonrecreation purposes and against invasion by inappropriate uses.[7]

Space and facility standards as recommended by the National Recreation and Park Association will be discussed later in this chapter. These standards, used together with the various goals, guidelines and principles determined at the local, regional and state levels, will enable the Cupertino Parks and Recreation Department to:

1. Develop a comprehensive plan of park and recreation areas and assist in a systematic approach to land acquisition.
2. Determine what and how many recreation areas and facilities are needed to best serve the people and where these areas and facilities should be provided.
3. Justify to political bodies the acquisition and development of park and recreation lands and facilities and to determine priorities.
4. Assist in evaluating the effectiveness of the park and recreation system.[8]

The Cupertino Plan serves as one example of the establishment of goals and objectives for recreation at the local level. There is no doubt that the existence of a good leisure service program at the local level enhances the total livability of the community. A well planned recreation program, then, is vital to every citizen within every community and the degree of success of each program can be determined only when outcomes are measured against pre-determined goals and objectives.

Goals, Objectives and Values

Goals and objectives of leisure service agencies must be consistent and compatible with basic human psychological needs. Those responsible for determining the goals and objectives for leisure service agencies, regardless of the type, size or location of the agency, should be aware of the values which may be considered as forming the fundamental or basic goal of recreation. The following values result from recreative expression and activity.

1. *Emotional and physical health*—the development of a sound body and mind through wholesome, vigorous, and creative activities.
2. *Character development*—building character through rich, satisfying, and creative leisure living patterns focused toward socially desirable attitudes, habits, and values.
3. *Widening interests*—opening new interests that provide satisfying outlets for individual growth and development.
4. *Citizenship*—developing through recreational associations of people a respect for the worth and dignity of individuals and faith in democratic action.

---

[7] Ibid., p. 15-16.
[8] Ibid., p. 17.

5. *Skills*—development of skills in the arts of leisure-time living that raise the level of the refinement, culture, and happiness of people.
6. *Social living*—developing and strengthening social relationships within the family and the community through close group associations and activity conditions.
7. *Economic value*—strengthening the morale and economic efficiency of the community through expanding leisure-time interests and improved social living conditions.
8. *Community stability*—developing community stability by providing an environment that is conducive to wholesome family living and community life.[9]

Standards: Established Recommendations

For many years, the most widely accepted recreation space standard called for a municipality to provide one acre of recreation land per 100 population. Recognizing the fact that counties, districts, metropolitan authorities and state and federal agencies may join municipalities in providing recreation land, the National Recreation Association has presented the following acreage standards:

Table 7-1. Space Standards Recommended by National Recreation Association, 1965[10]

Near-at-hand areas:	
Neighborhood recreation parks	2.5 acres per 1,000 population
District recreation parks	2.5 acres per 1,000 population
Within an hour's travel:	
Large urban parks	5 acres per 1,000 population
Large extra-urban parks	15 acres per 1,000 population
Total acreage provided by local governments per 1,000 of expected population:	25 acres
Areas provided by state government:	65 acres
Total recreation area provided by local and state governments per 1,000 ultimate population:	90 acres

The four broad categories (see Table 7-1) of recreation land can be broken into specific and definable units. When county, regional, state and national recreation land recommendations are also reviewed, similarities and contrasts can easily be seen. Table 7-2 illustrates important features of various outdoor recreation areas.

[9] Planning Research Corporation, Op. cit., p. 21-22.
[10] Kraus, Op. cit., p. 437.

Table 7-2. Important Features of Outdoor Recreation Areas

Name	*Description and Characteristics*	*Participants Served*	*Effective Service Distance*	*Recommended Acreage*	*Other Requirements*	*Recommended Managing Agency*
Tot Lot	Small area; climbing structures for children and benches for parents should be provided.	Pre-school children	Each block or super-block	Five thousand to 10,000 (sq. ft.)	Enclosed by fence and gate; tanbark, turf or sand under apparatus; trees, shrubs, shelter	Municipal park and recreation department
Neighborhood Playground	Includes play lot area, multipurpose area, field games area, quiet activities area, landscaping; should be adjoining elementary school.	Children of the area	Within ½ mile from each home	Five to 10	Should be away from heavy street traffic, railroads and industrial sites	Municipal park and recreation department
Neighborhood Park	Relatively small area which provides for passive and active recreation opportunities for all age groups.	All age groups	Within ½ mile from each home	Approximately 10	Landscaping, shelter building with storage area, restrooms	Municipal park and recreation department
Playfield	Provides facilities that make possible diversified recreation opportunities for young people and adults; athletic fields are provided.	Teens, young adults, adults (section may be developed for small children)	Within 1 mile from each home	Approximately 25	Recreation center building; off-street parking	Municipal park and recreation department
Community Park	Serves several neighborhoods; provides indoor and outdoor recreation facilities designed to meet a wide range of participant interests.	Primarily teens, young adults and adults	Approximately 1 mile from each home. However, it is more important to recognize an approximate service population of	At least 35 to 40	Served by public transportation; off-street parking provided; recreation center building staffed by full-time professionals	Municipal park and recreation department

Name	*Description and Characteristics*	*Participants Served*	*Effective Service Distance*	*Recommended Acreage*	*Other Requirements*	*Recommended Managing Agency*
City Park	Serves neighborhoods and communities within a city; intensively developed; provides special facilities which may be needed by all residents of the city; scenic areas and picnic and play facilities should be provided.	All residents of the city	Easily accessible to an approximate service population of 20,000	Seven to 50	In larger cities, small parks should be supplemented by one or more large parks which will also be intensively developed, and provide special facilities; such parks should allow for the development of natural features	Municipal park and recreation department
Reservation or Preserve	Forest preserve maintained primarily in its natural state.	All residents within a city, county, state, or even multistate area	Development near large metropolitan area is essential; however, a reservation may be located several miles from the city limits	One thousand or more	Sections should be available for such activities as fishing, horseback riding, camping, hiking, picnicking, nature study	Municipal, county, state, or federal recreation, park or open space agency
County Park	Planned to accommodate large groups; facilities provided for such activities as day camping, horseback riding, hiking, picnicking, swimming; generally natural in landscape and character, less intensively developed than city parks.	Residents of a county	Easily accessible by private or public transportation to all residents of a county	Five hundred to 2,000	Opportunities for all-day visits should be provided	County recreation and park department

Table 7-2. Important Features of Outdoor Recreation Areas (Continued)

Name	*Description and Characteristics*	*Participants Served*	*Effective Service Distance*	*Recommended Acreage*	*Other Requirements*	*Recommended Managing Agency*
Regional Park	Generally large area, but less intensively developed than city or county parks; scenic in character; opportunities for camping, hiking, boating, swimming, fishing should be provided; undeveloped wild land should be available.	Residents of a multi-city region or multi-county region	Can be several miles from potential users; overnight accommodations should be available to allow for two- or three-day visits	Five thousand to 50,000 acres	Should be accessible by private and limited public transportation	Regional park system
State Park	Should emphasize unique and important geological, historical and natural features typical of the state; should foster such recreation interests as picnicking, camping, swimming, boating.	Groups and families are prominent users	No more than 2 to 3 hours of travel time for each resident	Minimum of 1,000; should be determined by topography and desired use factors	Should offer natural scenery of unusual beauty; should provide for statewide historical interests; should offer natural scientific values such as rare combinations of trees, plants and wild life	State recreation and park department
National Park	Should provide for nationally significant geological, biological, archeological or historical interests; must be preserved in natural condition; all facilities built and maintained in keeping with the natural surroundings.	Residents of a nation; international visitors	Persons may travel long distances to national parks	Specific size is irrelevant	Must provide abundance of natural beauty and resources	National Park Service, Department of Interior

Meyer and Brightbill have recommended the following standards for specialized recreation facilities:

> *Golf Courses.* There should be one hole of publicly-owned golf courses for each 3000 of the population, where private courses are also present. Where there is no private course in or immediately adjacent to a city, public provision for golf should be sharply increased.
>
> *Swimming Pools.* Such facilities should be sufficient to serve three to five per cent of the population at one time. The minimum standard is 27 square feet of water surface per swimmer, with deck space provided on a ratio of two square feet of deck area for each square foot of water area.
>
> *Athletic Field or Stadium.* This facility is intended for specialized sports, and is usually located at the high school. The athletic field usually provides a football field, running track, and space for field events. This area should be floodlighted for evening use. Including parking space and seating accommodations, 10 to 20 acres may be required for this facility.
>
> *Baseball Diamonds and Softball Diamonds.* There should be at least one baseball diamond and one softball diamond per 3000 of the population.
>
> *Public Tennis Courts.* There should be one tennis court for each 2000 people. Tennis courts should be built in batteries of two or more courts per location.
>
> *Recreation Building.* The public provision of indoor recreation facilities should include consideration of the availability and use of indoor public school facilities. Where such school facilities are available, public provision of other indoor recreation facilities can be less extensive. The following facilities should be *available* for indoor recreation purposes, regardless of where they are provided:
>
> A multiple-use room for each 4000 or less.
> A gymnasium for each 10,000 of the population or less.
> An auditorium or assembly hall for each 20,000 or less.
> A social room or playroom for each 10,000 or less.
> An informal reading and quiet game room for each 10,000 or less.
> An indoor game room for each 10,000 or less.
> An arts and crafts room for each 10,000 or less.
> An indoor swimming pool for each 50,000 or less.[11]

Standards: Variables

In Chapter 3, we stated that population profile indexes can affect recreation demand. The National Association of Counties determined that size of the population, income, education, mobility and age are variables which should be taken into account. Sessoms noted that research findings of the Outdoor Recreation Resources Review Commission's National Recreation Survey, which were corroborated by independent studies, indicate that there are at least eight factors which condition recreation patterns.

1. *Age*—The amount and type of recreation one pursues is related to his age. The older he becomes the fewer and more passive are his pursuits.
2. *Income*—The number of recreation pursuits of an individual is related to his income. The higher the income, the more numerous are his pursuits.

---

[11] Meyer, Harold D., and Brightbill, Charles K. *Community Recreation: A Guide To Its Organization.* 3rd Ed., Englewood Cliffs, N. J.: Prentice Hall, Inc., 1964, p. 404.

3. *Education*—Education affects recreation participation in much the same way as does income. The higher one's educational attainment, the more numerous are his pursuits.
4. *Occupation*—The number and variety of leisure activities are related to occupation and occupation prestige. The higher a person's occupational prestige, the more varied and active are his pursuits.
5. *Residence*—Suburbanites are more active and pursue a greater variety of recreation pursuits than do urban dwellers, who in turn have a more active participation rate than do those who live in rural areas.
6. *Mobility*—Outings tend to be week-end (overnight) or all-day excursions. The outing destination is usually a public, non-urban area within a three-hour drive from the point of departure. Lakes, seashores, and other natural scenic areas are usually the destinations for people on day outings.
7. *Opportunities for Activity*—Increasing the number of recreation facilities within a given area may create a geometric increase in recreation participation. When the facilities are provided, people use them; in fact, their presence may create a demand.
8. *Natural Character*—Leisure patterns, leisure items, leisure facilities are often used as status symbols. Thorstein Veblen, for example, characterized the leisure class as one which made an outward display of its wealth through leisure experience (conspicuous consumption, conspicuous display).[12]

Sessoms goes further to point out that recent trends have indicated clearly that all standards are relevant only to the time in which they are prepared. Picnic areas, for example, are not needed as much in subdivisions where families cook out in their yards as they are in areas which are a two-and-one-half-hour ride from these homes. Tot lots and playgrounds are not as necessary in upper-income regions as they are in urban, lower-income regions. Greenbelts and open spaces are more important in densely-populated areas than in spacious, well-landscaped subdivisions.

Socioeconomic conditions such as population density and geographical characteristics also must be considered when planning a recreation area. The arbitrary drawing of a circle with a specific radius and the enumeration of so many facilities and acres per 1,000 of population in planning for the provision of recreation is as antiquated a planning concept as is the gridiron street pattern for proper subdivision traffic control.[13]

Standards: Principles

Since variables exist which may cause a leisure service agency to alter its course in its attempts to meet established area and facility space standards, common sense guidelines pertaining to this topic would seem to be needed. Guidelines should be based on the recognized fact that the recreation expression occurring during leisure is an essential part of living. A public leisure service agency should be committed to the provision of recreation opportunities for all residents, regardless of sex,

[12] Sessoms, H. Douglas. "New Bases For Recreational Planning," *Parks and Recreation* January, 1965, p. 17.
[13] Ibid., p. 17.

age, creed, color or economic status. The following statements of principles, which relate to area and facility standards, were prepared for the National Recreation Association's National Committee on Recreation Standards by Robert W. Crawford, Commissioner of Recreation in Philadelphia, Pennsylvania:

1. A recreation system requires properly distributed areas and facilities.
2. A recreation system requires areas and facilities that are diversified in physical character, type, size and degree of development.
3. The different types and sizes of areas are determined by the basic kinds of recreation service they are designed to provide, while the distribution and degree of development of areas are determined by the density and composition of the population to be served.
4. Each recreation area or facility should be located on usable land which is topographically appropriate to, and suitable for, the purpose for which it is intended.
5. Each recreation area or facility should be centrally located within the area it is intended to serve and should afford safe and convenient access for those it is intended to serve.
6. Each recreation area or facility should include facilities that will offer recreational opportunities for all age groups it is intended to serve.
7. Whenever possible, appropriate recreation areas and facilities should be located near, or adjoining, public schools, libraries, or community agencies of a recreational group or informal educational nature.
8. In addition to the actual space required for the recreation activities to be provided, considerations must be given to the space required for safety, aesthetic or scenic values and service functions (parking, circulation of patrons, concessions, rest rooms, etc.).[14]

Standards: Guidelines

Meyer and Brightbill have listed a number of questions that, when answered, can help leisure service agency personnel determine the adequacy of their recreation facilities. It would seem that these questions are the *keys* to the provision of effective and efficient recreation facilities.

1. Are the facilities planned, located, and laid out, or modified and oriented, for functional recreation use? Are they geared to program needs?
2. Is the recreation facilities planning integrated with comprehensive city planning?
3. Does the facilities planning consider long-range as well as immediate recreation needs? Is there included a schedule of priorities for acquiring property and improving it?
4. Are standards applied intelligently? Is space sufficient?
5. Are the facilities accessible to those who use them?
6. Are they planned to keep to a minimum costs of construction, improvement, and maintenance?
7. Are the facilities aesthetically attractive and comfortable?
8. Are supervision, control, and leadership made easy?
9. Are the facilities designed for multiple use?
10. Can maximum use be obtained around the clock and calendar?
11. Are the health and safety of the users protected?
12. Does pedestrian and vehicle traffic flow freely and are adequate accommodations provided without hazard?

---

[14]Crawford, Robert. "Space Standard Principles," *Recreation* 51:33, 1963.

13. Are natural resources used to the best advantage?
14. Are the facilities planned and operated so as not to constitute a nuisance to adjacent property owners?
15. Do the facilities lend themselves to maintaining cleanliness and proper sanitation?
16. Are the "service" facilities well arranged?
17. Are acoustical conditions good?
18. Are crowding of facilities and over-use of equipment avoided?[15]

It was stated in Chapter 4 that leisure service agencies tend to overlook the *effects* of their offerings upon participants. Gray[16] notes that different people experience physical and social conditions in various ways. It is imperative, therefore, that facilities and programs be designed with the particular clientele in mind. Hutchinson has stated:

> The significance of the recreation experience depends upon how the individual organizes the total situation: the activity itself, the interchange of ideas, the relationships of social living, the immediate results of the activity and the potential future outcomes.[17]

Therefore, it is important that recreation participation *must* be evaluated in terms of outcomes, according to the consequential effects experiences have upon the individual participant. In other words "the persons planning programs and parks must know intimately the culture, wishes, social patterns, and life styles of the people who are to use them; the park or program must fit those conditions."[18] It is within this context that the leisure service manager must seek to provide opportunities for the people in a community, styling recreation facilities according their particular beliefs, values, expectations and life styles.

---

[15] Meyer, Harold D., and Brightbill, Charles K. *Community Recreation: A Guide To Its Organization.* 4th Ed., Englewood Cliffs, N. J.: Prentice Hall, Inc., 1969, p. 408-409.

[16] Gray, David. "Exploring Inner Space," Speech delivered before Region III of the California Park and Recreation Society, Long Beach, California, May 18, 1972.

[17] Hutchinson, John L. *Principles of Recreation.* New York, The Ronald Press Company, 1951, p. 6.

[18] Gray, Op. cit.

CHAPTER 8

Planning for the Leisure Service Delivery System

Role of Planning

Planning is the first step in the management process. The other four functions of management are dependent upon the planning function. Managers, supervisors or individuals in the leisure service field who organize, staff, direct and control to accomplish goals will do so according to methods that are the result of the planning process. Quite obviously then, the first step in this process will be selection of the agency's or organization's goals and objectives as well as determination of the method or methods of reaching them. Generally, planning is considered as establishing the best methods of accomplishing work. As Koontz and O'Donnell put it, "Planning is deciding in advance what to do, how to do it, when to do it, and who is to do it."[1] It puts in motion our goals and objectives from a point of beginning to what is to be accomplished. Along with the other managerial functions of organizing, staffing, directing and controlling, it is designed to accomplish the predetermined organizational objectives.

Planning and controlling are dependent upon each other. A manager has nothing to measure, evaluate or control unless he has a plan with which to compare his results. The effectiveness of the planning process is determined by how well he understands the whole management process and can relate it to the other individual managerial functions.

Many times supervisors plan without realizing the relationships and the parts of the planning process. Generally, this type of planning is unsystematic and not well considered. Obviously, the manager or supervisor of a park and recreation system who approaches his planning with understanding, precision and thoroughness will do a much better job and, in turn, will be more assured of desirable results.

Planning should take place at all levels in an organization, from the top administrator to the lowest maintenance man. Each must plan to carry out his work. The scope, the depth and the detailing of their plans will differ, but the process is the same. Without it, the individual will

[1] Koontz, H., and O'Donnell, C. *Principles of Management.* 5th Ed., New York, McGraw-Hill Book Company, 1972, p. 113.

drift aimlessly, wasting much time and accomplishing very little. The process can be likened to an automobile trip. Unless the driver knows where he wants to go and plans how he will get there, where he will stop for gas, where he will eat, etc., he will waste much motion as he goes down the road, getting lost, stopping at restaurants during the busiest hour, etc. Similarly, the manager must plan well so as to make the most of his equipment, manpower, money, material, time and space.

Types of Plans

There are several types of plans that the manager uses in putting into action his programs and moving his organization forward. The first of these plans is called goals and objectives. They are the ends toward which activity is aimed.[2]

Goals and Objectives

This chapter will consider goals broader than objectives. Many objectives will be directed toward the establishment of goals, which is the first step in planning. In previous chapters, various standards and principles of the park and recreation profession have been presented. These principles and standards generally go together in the establishment of a philosophy for the leisure service field.

In the establishment of an agency, department or organization, be it public or private, somewhere there is the authority by which it was established. Generally, as a part of establishing the authority for creating the department, a broad goal that is the purpose for which the agency, organization or department came into being will be stated. In the case of a public park and recreation department, it might be "to provide all citizens of the community an opportunity to engage in a wholesome recreation program during their leisure for the betterment of the individual and the total community." As a result of this broad goal, the agency or department then affirms more specific objectives from the establishing authority.

Generally, these goals are the outgrowth of the guiding principles of the profession. Such a list is commonly found in many textbooks described as planning principles or standards for public park and recreation agencies. An example is found in George D. Butler's *Introduction to Community Recreation* as follows:

1. Provide equality of opportunity for all.
2. Serve all ages.
3. Provide equally for both sexes.
4. Provide opportunities for co-recreation.
5. Encourage family recreation.

---

[2] Ibid., p. 116.

6. Provide a wide range of individual choices in different types of activities.
7. Include relaxing as well as active forms of recreation.
8. Offer possibilities for varying degrees of skill and ability.
9. Provide activities of a progressive nature.
10. Carry over the leisure-time skills and interests developed in the schools.
11. Include activities that will persist at the adult level.
12. Continue throughout the year.
13. Provide activities for different periods of free time.
14. Represent cooperative planning.
15. Encourage individuals and groups to provide their own activities.
16. Be related to other local programs.
17. Furnish outlets for satisfying group activity.
18. Recognize the different tastes and interests of the individual.
19. Provide outlets for creative expression.
20. Serve the specific interests and needs of the people in different neighborhoods.
21. Provide for the ill and handicapped.
22. Afford opportunities for developing good citizenship.
23. Utilize fully all existing properties.
24. Make possible the wisest use of available resources.
25. Place recreation opportunities within the financial abilities of all the people.
26. Conform to recognized program standards.
27. Assure safe and healthful conditions for recreation activity.
28. Be subject to continuous evaluation.
29. Provide opportunity for contact with nature.
30. Utilize the potential volunteer services of individuals and groups.[3]

Recently Los Angeles County's overall goals and objectives were established and adopted by the County Board of Supervisors as follows:

1. To provide a comprehensive regional recreation area system and regional recreation programs to service the specialized leisure needs of the residents of Los Angeles County.
2. To guide and direct the provision of adequate local recreation programs, facilities, and beautification projects to service residents of unincorporated territories of Los Angeles County.
3. To provide specialized services to all communities within Los Angeles County which will augment or improve the standards of service in the total park and recreation field.
4. To provide specialized services within the particular expertise of personnel and physical resources of the department to other agencies as required.[4]

Goals of park and recreation systems are often set forth in master plans which call for the accomplishment of major capital programs as well as operating programs over a period of several years. Some communities have five-year capital improvement programs that specifically outline what is to be accomplished in terms of land acquisition and facility construction on a systematic and regulated basis. Generally, such programs call for referendums totally dependent upon the approval of the voters for their passage. Overall goals and objectives for departments, as previously mentioned, can vary considerably from department to

---

[3] Butler, George D. *Introduction to Community Recreation.* 4th Ed., McGraw-Hill Book Company, 1967, p. 260-264.

[4] "Direction and Guidance for the Nation's Largest Regional Park System," *Communique* 1:No. 5:7, November, 1970.

department, depending upon the emphasis of the department. In too many instances, however, one is amazed to find departments that do not have stated goals and objectives.

If a department or agency does not have written goals and objectives, the top administrator can generally state a few general ones, but how realistic they are and whether their achievement is really sought vigorously is another matter. An example of a departmental goal might be the expanding and strengthening of in-service training for all employees.

These overall departmental goals should be achieved through specific objectives which are more quantifiable, meaning that they are distinguishable in terms of their attainment. It is necessary to have the overall goals as stated, but achievement of them will most likely be reached in stages. An example of this would be the overall expanding and strengthening of in-service training. The quantifiable objectives which are more obtainable would be as follows:

1. A six-week first aid course for new leaders starting January 15.
2. Six-week course for park attendants in preventative maintenance of lawn mowers starting May 1.
3. A 12-week course in program planning for center directors starting October 15.

These objectives are specific, realistic and obtainable and lead to the accomplishment of the overall goal of expanding and strengthening of in-service training.

Similarly, the overall departmental goal of development of a sound evaluation program will be accomplished by the intermediate quantifiable objectives:

1. Having all participants fill out a questionnaire indicating their likes and dislikes of all craft classes at the conclusion of the fall classes.
2. Employing a research and evaluation program of the effectiveness of summer playground programs.
3. Hiring an agricultural consultant to determine the proper fertilizing techniques employed on eight random park areas.

The development of a sound evaluation program can also help a department determine its effectiveness in the implementation of its program and utilization of its money and manpower. The expansion of joint funding and use of park and school facilities can serve the purpose of better utilization of public land and of public funds.

The overall goal of the expansion of joint funding and use of park and school facilities will be accomplished by the intermediate quantifiable objectives as follows:

1. Joint planning, construction and development of the Hilton Park School site and the hiring of an architect by July 1.
2. The opening of a recreation center in the new Westwood Junior High School this fall.

3. The operation of five summer playground programs or school playgrounds next summer.

Each quantifiable objective is directed toward the accomplishment of the overall goal, but without these quantifiable objectives and their specific implementation according to a specific time schedule and plan, the overall goal might never be accomplished. In too many cases, overall goals are just words mouthed by administrators which never become a reality.

Any organization is comprised of many components that contribute to the overall accomplishment of its goals. Likewise, all goals are accomplished through obtainable intermediate objectives.

In the chain of command under the municipal park and recreation director, there will be a park function and a recreation function. Each of these, in turn, should have their overall goals implemented by quantifiable objectives obtainable within weeks and months. Likewise, through the districts and finally in individual facilities such as recreation centers and parks, the same procedure should be followed. These objectives and goals should be stated in writing, with a timetable for implementation and an indication of when they have been accomplished. Such objectives and goals should be constantly before the employers so that they can know toward what they are working.

It is only through this effort from the top to the bottom of an organization that real accomplishment will be made. In addition to being quantifiable, goals and objectives should be measurable so that the person in charge can determine if he really achieved them. Also, quantifiable and measurable goals and objectives give employees a sense of satisfaction and gratification when they can feel the pride of a job well done.

Goals and objectives should be realistic so that individuals, be they at the upper or lower echelon of the organization, can see possibilities and achievement of success quickly. Goals and objectives that are beyond the capacity and capability of employees soon end in frustration. No goals and objectives at all can result in employees appearing to be busy, but actually achieving very little or nothing.

Many organizations which have very fine overall goals never achieve them because the goals are not broken down into obtainable, measurable, realistic objectives that are accomplished by the lower-level employees. On other occasions, organizations fail because the lower-level employee never sees how his small objective fits into the overall goals of the organization, resulting in his feeling useless and nonproductive.

Goal and objective setting is a very important part of planning. It requires practice, work and constant revision, but its results are well worth the effort. Good and effective planning will go a long way to assure success in the other management functions.

Policies

Another type of plan is policy making. Probably more than any other single form of plan, policies are misunderstood by employees. They are thought of in very negative terms as a way used by top-level managers to prohibit employees from doing anything enjoyable, whereas on closer scrutiny, policies can be considered as plans. They are general statements or understandings which guide and assist the employees in the decision-making process as they apply to subordinates.[5] Policies are enduring and permanent. Goals, as mentioned earlier, are the end at which planning is directed, while the policy guides decisions toward the implementation of these ends. Policies are forms of plans that help obtain the overall goals and objectives of the organization. They should always be in the best interest of the organization. When thought of in this way, they tend to be perceived in less negative ways by employees. Very often they come into being as a result of individuals misusing certain privileges within the organization, whereby they get the negative connotation so when they are implemented they are abuses. In many cases, however, policies are implemented in advance to assure the accomplishment of goals or objectives. The Baltimore Bureau of Recreation's policy on center hours of operation is an example. See Table 8-1.

The hours of operation of recreation centers should be during that time of the day when the public to be served is available to use such facilities. The hours of operation of recreation centers should reflect a similar period of time when participants are available rather than the normal working hours of park and recreation employees that would direct these recreation centers. Most people work eight hours a day between 8 A.M. and 5 P.M. and the children would be in school. As a result, the policy for hours of operation for most recreation centers would be between 2 P.M. and 10 P.M., so that the policy would read: "Recreation centers will open and operate between the hours of 2 P.M. and 10 P.M. daily, Monday through Friday, and from 10 A.M. to 6 P.M. on Saturdays." This policy would assure that centers are open when the public is out of school and work to utilize them, and it would not reflect what might be convenient for the employees who operate these centers. This policy is then in the best interest of the public.

Most policies are interpreted through the exercise of initiative as well as discretion. Sometimes it becomes necessary to deviate from the policy when it is in the best interest of the organization and the individuals that the organization serves. An example of this would be in a community with a great number of senior citizens. The hours of operation of recreation centers should be changed to accommodate the senior citizens

---

[5] Jucius, M. J., and Schlender, W. E. *Elements of Managerial Action.* Rev. Ed., Homewood, Ill., Richard D. Irwin, Inc., 1965, p. 146-164.

Table 8-1. Baltimore Bureau of Recreation: Center Hours of Operation

A. *WINTER*

1. During the school months of the year, centers will be open every afternoon and evening, Monday through Friday, if practicable. The hours for full-time personnel should be as consistently the same as is possible, i.e., 2-6 and 6:40-10 P.M.
2. If a center is scheduled to be open to the public at 3 P.M., make certain that it is opened promptly. In the evening, activities should begin promptly at 7. The time from 6:40 to 7 is for organization and preparation for evening program. The time from 2 to 3 in the afternoon is for clerical work, organization, and preparation.

B. *SUMMER*

1. Summer hours depend upon the size of the area, the facilities, the staff available, etc.
2. During the lunch and supper periods, if a staggered schedule can be arranged, centers and playgrounds should remain open.

C. *POLICY*

1. It is a fundamental policy of the Bureau that centers and playgrounds shall not be left without staff during the hours open to the public. Infrequent exceptions may be made with the approval of the District Supervisor for certain district or City-Wide events. *No center may be closed without special permission.*
2. If the Director or leader-in-charge needs to be absent from the center for shopping or community visiting, he should advise his District Supervisor *ahead of time* and also advise his staff. He should indicate on his time report, "Shopping for children's party" or whatever the purpose of his absence from the center. Leaders, before making any community contact or visit, should secure permission from the Center Director.
3. If a center has only one person on staff and that person must make an *emergency* visit prior to the opening hour, he should leave a note on the door stating his destination and the time he will return.
4. Office visits (to get requisitions signed, pick up equipment and supplies, financial office transactions, etc.), except by special appointment, are to be confined to the hours of 1 to 2:00 P.M. on Mondays and Thursdays.

who would be more interested in participating in activities during the hours of 10 A.M. to 4 P.M. Therefore, discretion should be used in deviating from the general policy of hours of operation of 2 P.M. to 10 P.M.

Generally, when policies are altered, it is appropriate that those deviating from them inform their superiors with an explanation. In the case of hours of operation, which are ongoing and constant, it should probably even be done in writing with approval to make it permanent and ongoing.

Another example of a policy is the number of overtime hours that an employee can work during any given pay period. The policy might read: "No employee will work more than 10 hours of paid overtime in any given pay period. All overtime will need prior approval of the district supervisor." Such policies generally are to safeguard from abuses of overtime. During emergency situations, supervisors and managers can use discretion in deviating from minimal overtime policy. Again, deviation should be brought to the attention of superiors, or if time permits, approval can be obtained in advance. Many departments and agencies establish policy manuals that list policies in writing for all concerned.

It is a good practice to have such manuals so that they can be used as a reference periodically when questions arise. Many manuals give interpretations and examples that are often helpful. On other occasions, manuals have gone to the extreme of listing so many policies that they become confusing to the employee, detracting from his incentive to the point that he is afraid to initiate a new program or try anything different for fear he might violate some policy.

Whatever form manuals take, they are best prepared so that they can be changed and updated regularly. How extensive policy manuals are should be determined by the intellectual capacity and training of the employees toward whom they are directed. Quite obviously, individuals who have had professional training in the leisure service field can soon come to resent page after page of a policy manual that tells them how to do everything. Generally, manuals should provide basic information, be kept current and issued only when they help in the overall accomplishment of goals of the agency.

Policies should reflect the goals and objectives of the organization in the implementation of its plans. They are a guide to thinking. It is important for them to be constant, yet flexible so they can be varied somewhat when it would be in the best interest of the organization. As a result they should be distinguishable from rules and regulations, which are more strict and must be obeyed. (Both rules and regulations will be discussed later.)

As has been mentioned earlier, policies should be in writing whenever possible. They should be communicated to all concerned so that they are understood. This can best be accomplished by involving individuals who will be affected by policies in their formulation when practical and possible. Policies should be controlled in terms of keeping them to a minimum.

Procedures

Procedures can also be considered plans in that they give employees details for handling many activities. They are a guide to some form of action rather than a guide to thinking. They tell the individual how to perform a job.[6] Oftentimes a policy will set the stage for certain thinking in an organization and a procedure will be necessary to imple-

[6] Koontz and O'Donnell, Op. cit., p. 120-121.

ment certain parts of the policy. But more generally, procedures are important unto themselves in that they give the employee a course of action. An example of a procedure might be an explanation of how to complete a requisition for equipment. The procedure might be listed on the reverse side of the requisition itself, giving detailed instructions on how to fill out the requisition. It should include such information as to how many copies of the requisition are necessary, how to place the quantity of items to be requisitioned, the necessary nomenclature or description of the equipment, how the requisition is routed through the agency, who gets which copies, etc. The procedure will help the unfamiliar employee in making sure that he supplies the information correctly and submits it properly.

Another procedure might deal with the disposal of governmental property, outlining how it must be accounted for when it is declared surplus, how it can be disposed of, what records need to be kept on it, etc. Again, the procedure is there to guide the actions of the employee so that he

Table 8-2. Administrative Order: Metropolitan Dade County, Florida

DISPOSAL OF COUNTY PERSONAL PROPERTY	
AUTHORITY	Chapter 274, Florida Statutes Section 4.02 of the Metropolitan Dade County Charter.
POLICY	Disposal of all county personal property is the responsibility of the Finance Director, who will maintain complete inventory records of all personal property and who will dispose of all surplus personal property in accordance with state law.
PROCEDURE Initiating Action	A department head having personal property he desires to dispose of will send to the Finance Director a memorandum giving full description of the property and the reason for declaring it surplus. The Finance Department will notify the requesting department as to which surplus depot the property should be sent.
Transportation of Property	The department making the request will forward the property to the designated depot. Arrangements for transporting the property may be made with the Office Services Division of the Finance Department.
Renovation	The Finance Director will have the property inspected to determine if it is more economical to dispose of the property or to renovate it for further use. If renovation is desirable, it will be the responsibility of the Public Works Department, upon notification by the Finance Director, to perform the necessary work.
Disposal	If the Finance Director determines that the county can no longer economically use the property he will dispose of it in accordance with Chapter 274, Florida Statutes, and make the necessary inventory adjustments.
	This administrative order is hereby submitted to the Board of County Commissioners of Dade County, Florida.

is assured of using the proper method. Often procedures protect employee interests so that one does not make a mistake that could be embarrassing to him or cause him to be negligent in his work. Again, as in the case of policies, it is best for procedures to be in writing and easily available for reference.

Oftentimes, departments combine policies and procedures into one manual (see Table 8-2). Again, however, the tendency is for such manuals to become too voluminous, complicated and hard to handle, discouraging employees from using them and defeating the purpose for which they were intended. The level of the employee with which one is dealing, to a great extent, should determine the type of procedure and policy manuals that are desirable.

It is rather unrealistic to think that a manual of policies or procedures or a combination of both could be adequately written and directed to everyone in a larger organization. In this case, separate manuals should be prepared and directed at the level of employee who will use them. Finally, there might be a supervisory manual of policies, and in addition, a manual of policies and procedures for lower-level employees. This would tend to limit the material presented to a specific audience.

Rules and Regulations

Rules and regulations, although very seldom considered as such, can be plans in that they are a cause for required action and like other plans are chosen from among alternatives.[7] Usually, they are the most basic type of plans in that they permit practically no deviation. Rules insist that a very definite action be taken or not taken with respect to the circumstances. In some ways they are much like a procedure in that they demand action, but not necessarily in any time sequence.

There are times when rules are a part of the implementation of a procedure. Rules, quite obviously, differ from policies in that they allow no judgment or discretion in their application. Most often, departments of parks and recreation have rules that govern the public in the use of facilities, but also there are many rules and regulations that govern the employee. An example of an employee rule would be that full-time, permanent employees will work a minimum of forty hours a week except in the case of paid holidays, sick leave or other excused absence. Personnel rules have no value judgments. It is a fact that the employee must show on his time sheet 40 hours of work. These rules are plans in that they demand 40 hours a week of employees to assure the accomplishment of goals and objectives.

In larger organizations in which there is no daily minute-by-minute supervision and in which employees are scattered in many directions

---

[7] Ibid., p. 121.

without rules, many employees might work less than the required hours and thus the accomplishment of the organization's goals and objectives might not be met.

Examples of rules that govern participants' use of facilities in a park and recreation department might be: "No drinking of alcoholic beverages is allowed on any park property" or "Parks close at 12:00 P.M." Generally, such park rules and regulations are adopted by some form of ordinance established by the city or county commission or the board of recreation and parks. Such ordinances give the police or other law enforcement agencies authority to arrest and take police action in the enforcement of rules and regulations.

Rules and regulations are plans in that they carry out the goals and objectives of the department by insisting upon a certain action or prohibiting another action which is not in the best interest of the public. Rules can seem to be negative, but their basis is generally in the interest of the general public whereby the few who would become obnoxious, out of place or disruptive can be controlled and excluded in the interest of the majority.

It is essential that park rules and regulations be in writing, and that copies be made available to all law enforcement agencies and distributed to the public. Certain rules and regulations are often printed on the back of permits, thus making the user aware of them. Many departments have condensed the rules to pocket-size form so that the law enforcement officer can keep them in his glove compartment or carry them on his person. Experience has indicated that the enforcement of rules and regulations is much more likely when the rule and regulation can be cited when an arrest is made. Therefore, rules and regulations which are often violated should be posted in visible locations in parks and facilities so that the public, park managers, center directors or police officers can refer readily to them.

Caution should be exercised against posting of too many rules saying "don't do this," "stop that," "this is prohibited." Additionally, they are unattractive and unsightly and they detract from the general pleasure of facility participants. Rules should be kept constant and up-to-date. Poor rules and regulations that are unenforceable and meaningless should be eliminated. The fewer rules necessary, the more understandable and acceptable they will be.

Programs

Programs are plans in that they are a composite and conglomeration of policies, procedures, rules, assignments and tasks all put together in an effort to carry out a given assignment. Such programs are generally supported by budgets, personnel, equipment and other factors in an effort to achieve specified goals or objectives. Some programs are simple and attainable in a short period of time, while others are complex but still attainable over a longer period. A program consists of a group of recreation activities offered during a season or period of the year for the benefit of the participants. Included are activities of arts and crafts, music, dramatics, sports, games, etc.

Work type of programs carry out the completion of a marina, construction of a recreation center, ballfield or an entire park. A program has all the necessary elements to carry it through to completion. Programs are the results of planning and are a form of a plan in themselves in that they are established to accomplish or meet a goal or objective of an agency.

Budgets

A budget is a financial plan expressed in dollars and cents. It outlines, in terms of money, goals to be accomplished. Sometimes it is expressed in dollars, other times in man hours or other units generally associated with dollars. There are operating budgets as well as capital improvement budgets, but in either case, their entire purpose is to accomplish the goals of the agency. Budgets become control devices in that they generally are approved by the commission, board or council authorizing the agency or department program for a given period, generally one year. Insofar as they are approved by the commission or board to make them legal and binding, they require specific actions for which the agency is held accountable. As a result, budgets should be well planned and include supportive background for justification. Once adopted, they should be followed with as little change as possible. Budgets are prepared in various forms and in varying details, depending upon the given form of government under which they are funded.

The Planning Technique

Now that we have discussed types of plans and their purposes, it is important to outline the planning technique itself.[8] Most of the planning processes take place after goals and objectives have been set. *It is then necessary* for the manager to put his plans into action. Many times the planning process is directed at solving a given problem. During the planning process, the first step is the *proper identification* of the problem, and the solution to the problem becomes the goal or objective. Organizations whose goals and objectives are too idealistic and broad are never very effective in that they seem to be unable to establish the intermediate objectives which are necessary to achieve the larger ones. Or, in the case of solving a problem which is directed at achieving re-

[8] McFarland, Dalton E. *Management Principles and Practices.* New York, The MacMillan Company, 1958, p. 89-90.

sults, if the manager can never directly identify the problem or goal, employees will never be able to accomplish anything specific. The more exact and precise the objectives are, the more precisely they can be set forth in the planning process.

Likewise, if one can really pinpoint his problem or goal, he can begin to formulate a solution. The example we used before, of developing a sound in-service training program to make employees more effective in the implementation of programs, was a broad and admirable goal. We found that to accomplish this goal and to plan further, we needed to break it down into more manageable portions and therefore establish an objective of a six-week first aid course, a six-week preventative maintenance course for lawn mowers and a twelve-week program planning course for center directors. In so doing, the planning becomes more of a reality. We then begin to set deadlines. Next we think in terms of personnel to teach specific courses and seek the necessary components to implement and achieve our goal.

Prior to setting obtainable objectives or stating the problem we had to consider many other things. We felt that there was a need for training. We came to the conclusion that our leaders needed more information, more skills and more insight into their jobs for such is the first step in the planning process. This was all based on the second step in planning referred to as *forecasting*. Our premise was that our leaders needed more training. This was based on information that we had from past records which showed that often in the case of injuries and accidents, our leaders didn't know what to do and that larger number of breakdowns occurred in our lawn mower operation than was acceptable.

We also forecast that we were going to have more children in the forthcoming summer program since school was not in session. We could also forecast that the grass would be growing more in the summertime with the sunshine and the heat and would result in our premise that we should prepare for these situations.

Our next step was that of determining *alternative courses of action.* How could we best set up these training courses? Should we conduct them ourselves with our most skilled personnel; bring in someone from Red Cross or a maintenance equipment company? Or we could send our employees to school at the local junior college and try other alternatives as well.

The next step was to evaluate alternatives in the light of our premises and goals. We stated earlier that we wanted all leaders to know first aid methods; therefore, based on this premise, it would appear that it would be rather expensive to send them to school. The fact that our own leaders might not be as equipped, capable and competent to teach first aid would indicate that to bring in someone from the Red Cross would be the best of the alternatives. In the case of the maintenance men, a better solution might be to send them to the junior college insofar as there are fewer of them. This brings us to our next step: *the selection of a course of action.*

At this point, the plan is adopted and the decision is made. Obviously, we are well on the way to obtaining our goal of in-service training for employees. Quite obviously, we will follow the progress of the program with interest and should we see need for change or a way to improve the program, we will *formulate derivative plans.*

In the case of the first aid course, we should have our supervisory personnel do follow-up on the job instruction. Likewise, we might have to set up an on-the-job follow-up for the maintenance men. In both cases, we want to assure the implementation of what the course taught. The planning process as presented in this section has been outlined briefly, but the essentials are there.

The more one understands the planning procedure, expands upon it and improves upon it, the better his planning will be—resulting in the more accurate and quicker accomplishment of goals and objectives with minimal wasting of time, effort and energy, all to the betterment of the organization.

There are four general ideas that are important in planning.[9] These are as follows:

1. To offset uncertainty of chance in the planning process.
2. To focus attention on goals and objectives.
3. To gain economy in the operation.
4. To facilitate control.

The last phase is important in that one cannot measure or check accomplishments without having objectives against which to measure them to see if they were obtained.

Some of the problems in planning result from lack of accuracy in premising and forecasting as well as lack of flexibility. In today's society, with so many changes occurring so rapidly in the community, our plans are often outdated before they can be implemented.

The changes in the political climate as well as technological change, combined with the lack of funds to carry out our plans, detract and curtail the energy required to carry out proper plans. Even with such limitations and drawbacks, one cannot neglect planning as an important management function. It cannot be left to chance. It should take place at all levels of an organization, generally starting from the top and working its way down to the lowest level of the organization. The planning should be organized and it should be well defined.

As has been stated many times, long-range planning should be included and integrated with a short-range plan. Plans are generally more

---

[9] Koontz and O'Donnell, Op. cit., p. 123-124.

acceptable when people have been a part of the planning process and when the plans are well communicated up and down the chain of command.

Decision Making

Decision making is another step in the planning process. Generally, it is considered the final step except in the cases where derivative or minor adjustments have to be made in plans.[10] Decision making is the actual selection from among the alternative courses of action and, for all practical purposes, is the goal of planning. Not to be minimized, however, is the ability to develop alternatives insofar as one has a much better chance of making a good decision if he has good choices from which to select. The good alternatives usually become more and more apparent so that the forthcoming decision often becomes obvious, but without good alternatives, many managers have found themselves stymied and ineffective.

There are several ways to produce a large number of alternatives. When time permits, brainstorming is a good technique. A number of people familiar with the goals and objectives of the organization should be involved. The ideas are thrown out in large number regardless of their validity and value. They are examined and combined to yield several alternative courses of action. Another method is the use of resource people who have had much experience in the area to suggest alternative solutions.

Selecting from among proposed alternatives is generally done in three ways:[11] (1) from experience, (2) experimentation and (3) research and analysis. Experience is the most often used procedure for producing alternatives and for selecting from among them. Experience has provided us with the best technique to do a job. If something has been successful in the past, it is usually assumed that it will work in the future. We can sometimes alter the technique slightly to make it applicable to a new situation.

When making decisions based on experience, one should evaluate these decisions against challenges in the future. As conditions and times change, our past experiences might not be applicable unless they are modified. Nevertheless, a large percentage of our decisions are based on past experience. This process works effectively when differences, time and experiences are carefully analyzed, measured and evaluated rather than followed blindly. Experience can be a very useful tool in good decision making.

---

[10] Gutenberg, A. W., and Richman, E. *Dynamics of Management.* Scranton, Pa., International Textbook Co., 1968, p. 469-473.

[11] Koontz and O'Donnell, Op. cit., p. 180.

Table 8-3. *PERT Chart with Critical Path for A Typical Park Development Project (No Large Building Construction)*

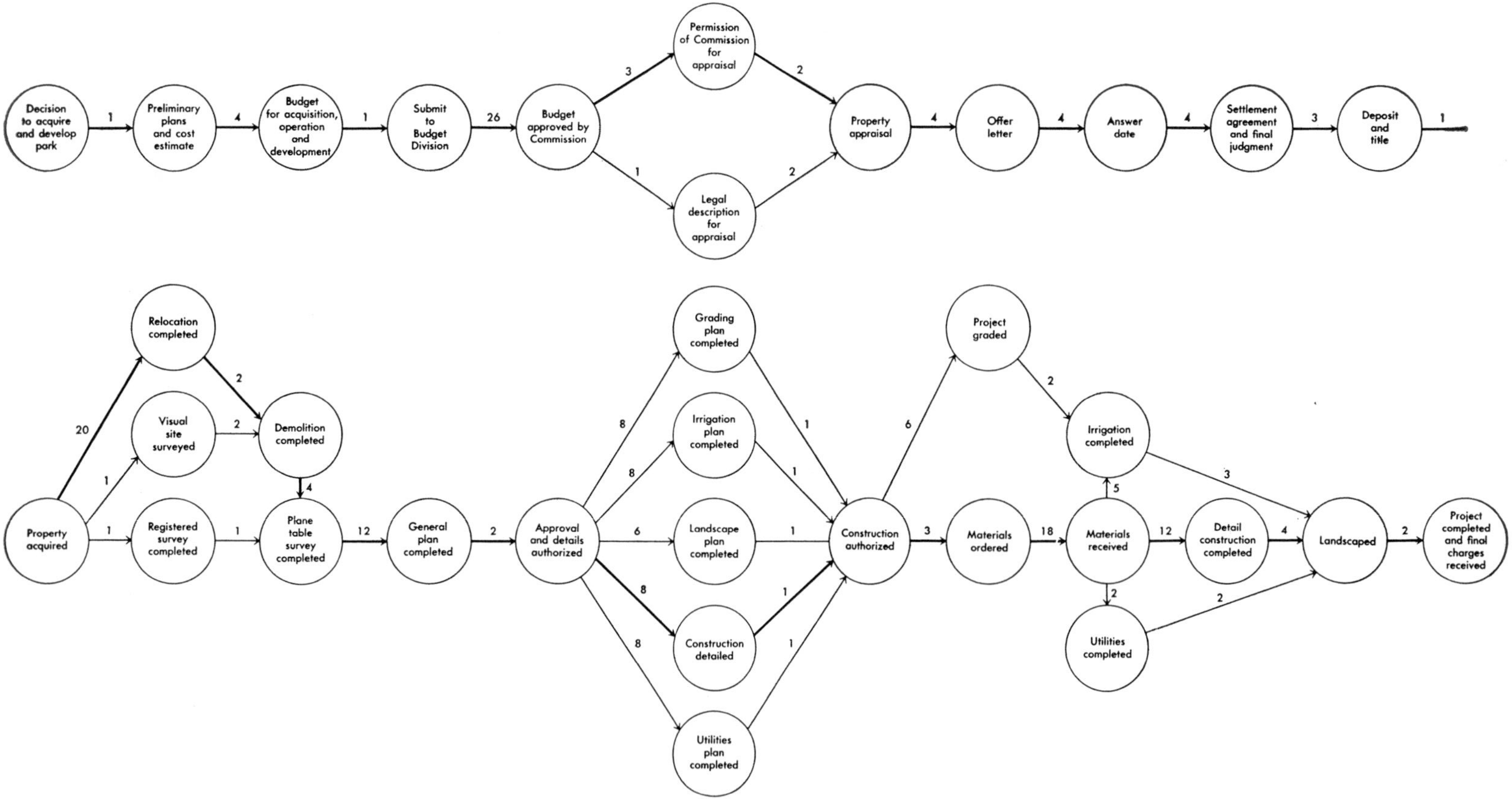

Decision to acquire and develop park
1
Preliminary plans and cost estimate
4
Budget for acquisition, operation and development
1
Submit to Budget Division
26
Budget approved by Commission
3
Permission of Commission for appraisal
2
1
Legal description for appraisal
2
Property appraisal
4
Offer letter
4
Answer date
4
Settlement agreement and final judgment
3
Deposit and title
1

Property acquired
20
Relocation completed
2
1
Visual site surveyed
2
1
Registered survey completed
1
Demolition completed
4
Plane table survey completed
12
General plan completed
2
Approval and details authorized
8
Grading plan completed
1
8
Irrigation plan completed
1
6
Landscape plan completed
1
8
Construction detailed
1
8
Utilities plan completed
1
Construction authorized
6
Project graded
2
3
Materials ordered
18
Materials received
5
Irrigation completed
3
12
Detail construction completed
4
2
Utilities completed
2
Landscaped
2
Project completed and final charges received

This typical park development project consists of thirty-four activities, work functions or processes. All planning and construction are to be accomplished by parks and recreation department forces. The numbers between activities indicate number of weeks to complete an activity. This is determined from an average of maximum and minimum estimates. This is called *realistic time*. The heavy line is called the "critical path" because it indicates the longest sequence of activities. When totaled, it gives time to complete the project, 141 weeks in this case, which are equivalent to 2 years and 8 months. This project is assuming that all timetables are met. Missing commission agendas, delays in ordering equipment and involvement with application for federal funding could prolong project several weeks.

In park and recreation work, the experience method of decision making is most often used. The second method, experimentation, is another way to decide upon alternatives. Sometimes the experimentation method is rather costly, particularly when it does not work and projects or work need to be done over. The experimentation method should be given careful consideration, particularly in the recreation programming phase of the profession.

One of the most promising methods of selecting from alternatives is the research and analysis method. This scientific approach to planning has been extremely successful in other professions and industry. Since many of these other fields are more exact, use of this method is more practical. Leisure service, since it is more of a behavioral science, makes this approach more difficult. In the research and analysis method alternatives are broken into component parts, each one is dealt with individually and then they are fitted back together. Each phase is studied and experimented with more economically and realistically than the whole could be.

Many agencies which are establishing programming and research sections within their department are hiring trained people from the fields of psychology and sociology. This technical training is proving most helpful in instituting research and analysis methods. One example of this approach is the Program Evaluation Reviewing Technique (PERT) to analyze work to be performed.[12] See Table 8-3.

An entire project is divided into component parts and evaluated in terms of what is to be done, who is to do it and how long it will take. Finally all of these parts are combined to give an overall plan of how the project is to be accomplished to obtain a particular goal. This approach has resulted in more effective planning in the area of construction and maintenance. Other experimental research and analysis efforts are being made by many colleges and universities to give us more exact ways of making better decisions. Whatever the method of arriving at the alternatives and selecting from among them, the leisure service manager can make his selection much easier if his goals and objectives are clear. He then can delineate his work and authority, and his employees are sure to do a better job when they know what is expected of them and what their limits are. This will only happen when the planning process has been followed and carried out thoroughly.

Planning for Leisure Services

The planning process, as has been described in this chapter, has dealt generally with planning as a management function. For the most part,

---

[12] Williams, John G. "Try PERT for Meeting Deadlines," *Park Maintenance* September, 1972, p. 10-12.

the principles presented are appropriate for any endeavor or any profession. The first four chapters of the book dealt with the philosophical background of the importance of parks and recreation in today's society. This section has endeavored to present planning more specifically as it applies to leisure services.

The reader should now agree that leisure will have a great effect on society and that recreation is an important opportunity for individuals to satisfy the basic needs of life.

Chapter 7 set forth many standards to justify the need for recreation programs supported and financed by public funds, voluntary contributions and local, state and federal government. We find ourselves arriving at many basic leisure service planning premises with these facts and philosophic concepts in mind. These premises are the outgrowth of broad goals set forth in the establishing authority, whether state enabling laws, city charter, or authority boards of parks and recreation. These premises give us the basis to plan park and recreation programs. As stated before, each community will be different, and will have different needs and requirements. An example of some of these premises might be more free time, less meaningful work, more discretionary money, denser population, less open space, etc., depending upon the particular needs and conditions of a community. With these premises, one can begin to forecast what needs to be done in terms of planning park and recreation services.

The recreation movement in the United States has reflected a program geared toward the middle-class American. This will only be overcome when persons in charge of planning recreation programs really understand these premises and what recreation is, and incorporate basic leisure service principles in planning their programs.

There are certain planning guidelines that are offered in most recreation texts. These are mentioned as guiding principles, not as absolutes. Among the most often mentioned is that in all recreation programs, there should be an opportunity for satisfaction with the common thread of pleasure and enjoyment running throughout. Without this satisfaction, most programs fall by the wayside. Other opportunities should be for joy of creation, fellowship, adventure, self-achievement, physical well being, use of mental powers, emotional experience, enjoyment of beauty, sense of service and relaxation. There are other factors, depending upon the needs of the individual and the community, that could be added to this list, but these points present some of the broad goals that should be kept in mind in good recreation and park planning.

Mentioned earlier in the planning process were the factors of experience, experimentation and research and analysis as methods of choosing from alternatives in decision making, which is a part of the planning process. These factors also are important in the program planning technique. The traditional approach of offering programs that have worked well in the past or in other communities is valid but not always an assurance of good program planning. Often the traditional approach can be combined with a new program that has been found to be successful. Responding to the desires expressed by the individuals who participate in the programs is another method of program planning.[13] Another approach is to initiate recreation activities that meet the greatest and most obvious need first. Another is to offer a program that will meet with success and serve the greatest number of people, starting with programs that people know so as to gain acceptance and success in the undertaking. The program planning can then expand into new areas in an effort to meet special interests of the community as they become recognized by the recreation leaders and participants. New activities and plans never tried can enrich the lives of those participating, creating new avenues of interest and opportunities for them to grow in their total personalities.

Whatever the approach, the planning process must be well conceived, starting with the establishment of goals and objectives to meet the needs of the participants. Next, the course of action is selected, the decisions made and the program put into action.

Summary

This chapter has been devoted to the importance of planning. The other four management functions, organizing, staffing, directing and controlling, are a result of planning and will be no better than the quality of planning itself. *Planning is basically the setting of the organizational, divisional, district, center or park goals and establishing a procedure to accomplish them.* The more the leisure service manager understands the total planning process, the better he is able to analyze it carefully and practice good planning procedures, the more assured he will be of truly accomplishing his goals and objectives as a good manager. It all starts with planning—first things first.

[13] Carlson, R. E., Deppe, T. R., and MacLean, J. R. *Recreation in American Life.* 2nd Ed., Belmont, Calif., Wadsworth Publishing Company, Inc., 1972, p. 396.

CHAPTER 9

Organizing for the Leisure Service Delivery System

The Need for Organizing

Organization is a multifaceted process that involves more than grouping individuals into work units and developing an organization chart. Organizations grow out of the need to develop and improve upon individual competency in an effort to accomplish pre-determined goals and objectives. A leisure service manager attempts to build a team effort and to gain the support and cooperation of the personnel. *Organizing takes into account the formal and informal organization; the span of management authority, responsibility and accountability; line and staff relationships; centralization versus decentralization; and of blending of these factors together to make the organization work.* A shrewd, competent manager will understand these relationships, and attempt to blend them into a cohesive organized unit that is designed to accomplish its goals and objectives.

Many park and recreation departments have attempted to pattern their agency after the organization chart of an already successful department of similar size, only to find that this method is doomed to failure. Not only is each community different, the individuals within a department are unique and therefore have to be understood with respect to their particular characteristics. An understanding of the principles of organizational theory should be developed within the department so that it may be tailored around the individuals and social aggregates to assure success.

Within every agency, whether acknowledged by an organizational chart or not, there is a formal organization, planned and recognized by the members of that organization. There is also an informal organization that is sometimes prevalent, sometimes unorganized, and many times suppressed by those in a leadership position, but inevitably it has an impact on the total operation of the organization.

Formal Organization

"The formal organization is a system of well-defined jobs, each bearing a definite measure of authority, responsibility, and accountability, the whole consciously designed to enable the people of the enterprise to work most effectively together in accomplishing their objectives."[1] The formal organization is structured officially by management and it is generally depicted on paper in the form of an organizational chart. The theory is that the *formal organization defines the jobs of all of an agency's managers and component sections and designates authority and responsibility which delineates the work relationships between these individuals.*

The park and recreation organization usually provides for a director or chief executive who heads the organization and has the total responsibility for its operation. The other individuals in the department, who report to the chief executive, are also indicated in their authority relationships and are shown in their position relative to the carrying out of organizational goals and objectives. These relationships are governed by policies, procedures, rules and regulations.

The formal organization is activated by the goals and objectives of the organization that theoretically make all employees dependent, subordinate and submissive. All of these factors are integrated to make the organization function smoothly. When they do not work, it is most likely the result of poor organizational practice. Some of the greatest mistakes made by the formal organization are outgrowths of restrictions in organizational policies that do not permit from subordinates discretionary power, do not provide subordinates with an opportunity to use their talents or do not recognize their individual preferences and capacities. However, for a manager to assume that a group of individuals can be brought together in a situation with no direction and little guidance indicates that he is unaware of the basic realities of human behavior.

A formal organization is guided by two basic principles, the *first being unity of objectives,*[2] which provides that all of the individuals in the organization need to work towards the same goals and objectives. These goals and objectives should be well formulated and accepted to be most effective by all concerned. While not all individuals will be totally in agreement with these objectives, it is important for the majority of effort to be directed toward their accomplishment, particularly if the organization expects to achieve much success.

The second principle is that of *efficiency.*[3] Efficiency calls for very clear-cut lines of authority. Proper balance of responsibility and authority, adequate involvement in the planning and problem solving processes and security and status are important factors in the motivation of employees. In addition, the organization must be efficient in that it gets

---

[1] Allen, Louis A. *Management and Organization.* New York, McGraw-Hill Book Company, 1958, p. 60-63.

[2] Koontz, H., and O'Donnell, C. *Principles of Management.* 5th Ed., New York, McGraw-Hill Book Company, 1972, p. 242.

[3] Ibid., p. 242-243.

the most for its effort, that its dollars and time are well spent, that waste is eliminated and economy encouraged. In any case, the efficiency will affect the overall organization in the accomplishment of its goals and objectives.

Informal Organization

The informal organization consists of all groups, clerks, clubs and other groupings of employees, sanctioned or unsanctioned by the organization, that affect the organization to its advantage or disadvantage. In many cases, managers in the formal organization refuse to acknowledge the informal organization. By not recognizing existence of the informal organization, managers may endanger the efforts of the agency as well as detract from the basic mission of the formal organization. Informal groups are the result of a basic need of people to belong and feel important, possibly a need not being met in the formal structure. These groups interact in numbers of two or three or more. Many times the informal leader is sympathetic of the problems of personnel within the structure. He may unite individuals in informal groups which may interfere with effective functioning of the formal organization, and possibly create pressure and conflict for the managers.

Generally, informal groups evolve as a result of individuals working in close proximity to each other who have like special interests or other common concerns. Such groups can have a great influence on standards and policies for their benefit. The informal organization can affect the success of an agency and by approaching it from an open, sincere standpoint, a manager, by analyzing their need to organize, can help to integrate their interests and needs in the operation. The informal organization tends to be more prevalent in larger organizations in which a sense of belonging is minimized by the massiveness of the organization. Often organizations run in an overly bureaucratic manner tend to foster informal organizations that are detrimental to the formal organization.

In many park and recreation delivery systems, center directors or park crewmen who have common concerns and problems band together to make their desires known. These individuals initiate informal groups during coffee breaks or in bowling leagues where they come together socially. As a result, an informal leader emerges and begins soliciting support among other groups and eventually they evolve a "formal-informal" organization. In many larger organizations these informal groups are ripe for labor unions or other bargaining agents to pick up their cause, often to the disadvantage of management. As a result, managers of park and recreation agencies are realizing they need to be aware of informal organizations in order to be able to deal with them.

The detrimental effects of the informal organization is offset by following sound organizational practices such as assigning meaningful work which incorporates the task concept as opposed to the more common division of labor approach. The need for informal organization can also be minimized by creating smaller maintenance teams within a given recreation district to accomplish work assignments instead of having a centralized maintenance component which services the entire department. Another approach is to place employees as close as possible to where they can feel the end result to give them a sense of accomplishment and worth. Establishing general guidelines and policies and leaving as much control, decision making and authority as possible to the lower-level supervisors allows employees an opportunity to set their own pace and realize their own accomplishments.

The formal and informal organizations can work together and need not be in conflict with each other. Although the organizational chart may show which individuals are supposedly in positions of authority, the real power may be held by an individual at a much lower level. He may receive recognition from his peers or, by virtue of his prominent position in a labor union, he may control a great deal of the destiny of that organization.

Departmentalization

As any organization grows, ultimately it will need to be divided into more workable units. This happens when the span of management (or span of control) is increased to the point that given managers can no longer efficiently and effectively supervise all of the individuals that report to them. When this happens, it becomes necessary to divide the workload into smaller units and place managers in charge of each unit in accordance with the individual manager's ability to supervise.[4] *Departmentalization in a park and recreation agency is generally accomplished by geographical area.* The city or county is generally divided into districts when it becomes impossible for the recreation or park superintendent to supervise all of the recreation centers and parks in that area. At this point, district supervisors become responsible for a district within the geographical boundaries of the city. The other method of departmentalization is according to activity or function within a recreation and parks department.

As the agency grows, in addition to dividing the city or county into geographical districts, it may also be necessary to divide responsibilities according to activities such as swimming, sports, dramatics, music, etc., and provide a manager for each. Many park and recreation delivery systems are structured into the parks division, the recreation division, the construction division, the special facilities divisions and others.

---

[4] McFarland, Dalton E. *Management Principles and Practices.* 1st Ed., New York, The Macmillan Company, 1958, p. 166.

The manager of a modern park and recreation delivery system should consider many specific items when he is organizing or reorganizing a department to determine how responsibilities should be divided. Some of these considerations are the strength and weakness of the managers, the geographical size to be managed, the number of different types of functions that the department has, the availability of funds. There are advantages and disadvantages in any type of organization. Two types will be presented to provide an idea of the various structures of contemporary leisure service agencies.

Table 9-1 shows a typical large park and recreation delivery system that is organized by *function* at the departmental level with a parks division, a construction division, a recreation division and a special facilities division. The parks and recreation divisions are then organized by *geographical* distribution while the construction and special facilities divisions are organized on a *functional* basis. The advantage of this type of organization is that a higher degree of speciality is possible when all park functions are under the supervision of the park superintendent and all recreation activities under the supervision of the recreation superintendent. This type of organization also assures a great deal of consistency throughout the department in policy and program matters.

There are many disadvantages to the functional type of structuring. For example, Table 9-1 indicates that there is no one individual in charge of Central Park. Each of the park, recreation and special facilities divisions has approximately one third of the overall responsibility for the park and its activities. Unless the three lower-level managers can mutually agree to actions or decisions they are forced upward in the organization to the district supervisors among whom, again, there must be cooperation with respect to decision making. The same is true with the superintendents of the divisions. It is only at the level of director that a single manager has the authority to make a decision affecting all parties concerned. This type of organization is common in park and recreation agencies. It is generally a very cumbersome organization that moves extremely slowly. It also creates a great deal of friction between division and staff which results in many meetings at which decisions are worked out by mutual agreement rather than by the managers alone.

In Table 9-2 a geographically organized department is presented. The advantages of this type of organization are obvious in that there is a much clearer line of authority. All of the operational functions of Central Park are under one manager. Decisions are made at the lowest level, closest to where actual work takes place, and result in much faster action and less need for meetings. This form of structure obviously requires a much more versatile manager at each level of the organization. However, this method of organization adheres to more effective management practices than does the preceding one. Its disadvantages

Table 9-1. *Functional Departmental Organization with Divisional Geographical and Functional Organization**

* No staff functions shown.

Director of Parks and Recreation

Superintendent of Parks Division
- North District
- Central District
- South District

Superintendent of Special Facilities Division
- Pool Section
- Golf Section
- Zoo Section

Superintendent of Recreation Division
- North District
- Central District
- South District

Superintendent of Construction
- Tradesman Section
- Heavy Construction
- Auto Shop

Central Park
85 Acres

Park Manager
3 Park Foremen
2 Truck Drivers
24 Park Attendants

Golf Course
1 Greenskeeper
3 Equipment Operators
8 Park Attendants

Swimming Pool
1 Pool Manager
3 Lifeguards
2 Attendants

Recreation Center and Athletic Facilities
1 Center Director
2 Recreation Leaders
2 Athletic Leaders

Table 9-2. *Geographical Departmental Organization with Divisional Geographical Organization**

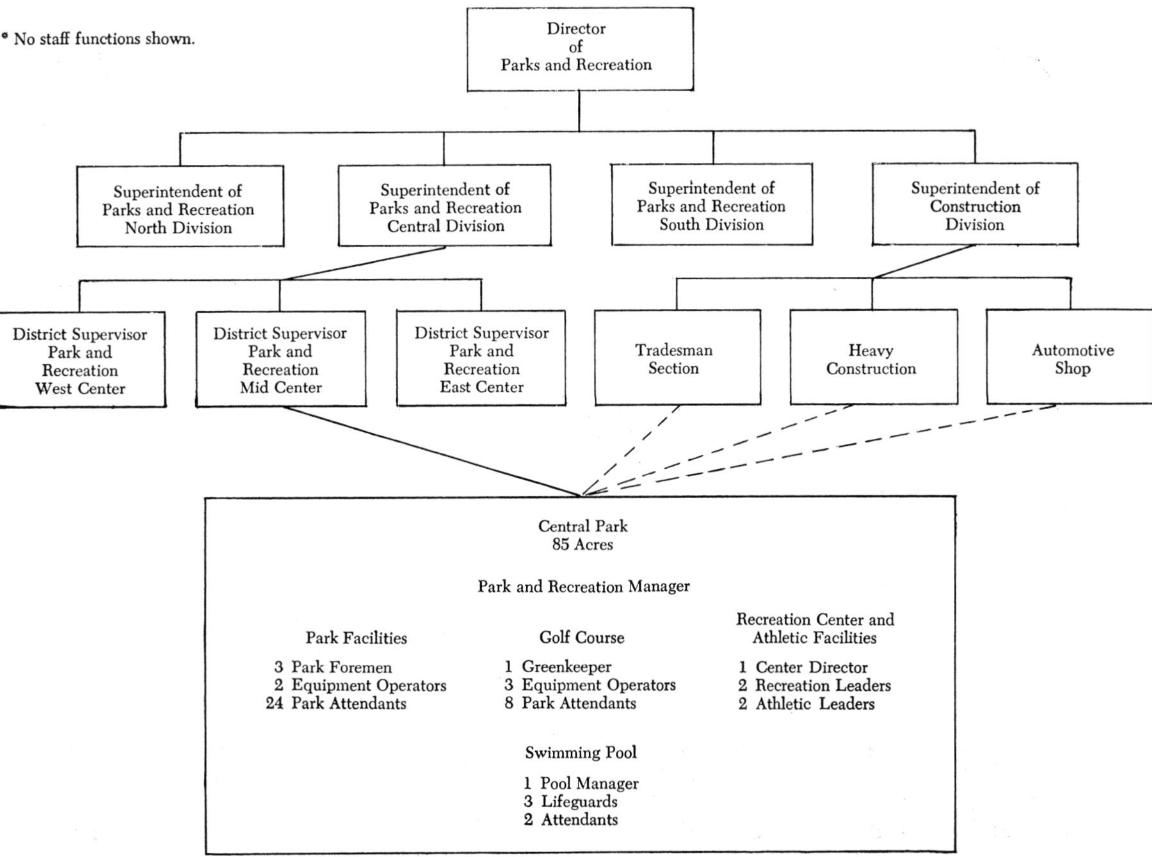

* No staff functions shown.

are that it does not allow for as much specialization. There is also less consistency within the total department. On the other hand, there will probably be more flexibility within the organization. The construction division, which appears in both forms of organizations, is a service department which will be discussed in more detail later in the chapter.

In summary, the departmentalization is designed to divide the organization into smaller units in order to provide more effective managerial supervision. It should be cautioned at this point that departmentalization should not be confused with decentralization or the establishment of service departments. These two areas will be discussed later in this chapter.

Span of Control

As an organization grows, it becomes necessary to group the employees into more manageable units. Managers are assigned to lead and direct these units accordingly. A determination will have to be made of how many individuals one manager can supervise. This is known as *the principle of span of control or span of management.*[5] It is obvious that there is a limit to the number of persons a manager can supervise. The type and complexity of an organization affect span of control. *Generally, it is stated that at upper levels of management in an organization, four to eight individuals are as many as one manager can supervise. At the lower levels of management, a manager can supervise from eight to fifteen.*

These general rules of thumb apply to the total management profession. In park and recreation organizations many other factors influence the span of control. In a large organization the director will generally supervise the superintendents of parks, recreation, administration division and two or three other staff persons. Middle managers such as the superintendents of the various divisions will supervise three or four district supervisors and two or three staff and service sections, such as the parks district supervisors and the supervisors of maintenance and construction, golf course, and landscape sections.

The superintendent of recreation would supervise three or four recreation district supervisors' special program areas such as swimming, arts and crafts and other staff functions. Again the superintendent of recreation would be supervising from four to eight individuals. Lower-level managers such as district supervisors would be supervising eight or more recreation centers or park facilities.

As the leisure service agency grows in size and assumes greater responsibilities, the span of control increases by the addition of more recreation centers, parks, swimming pools, new programs and new facilities.

---

[5] Ibid., p. 173-178.

Ultimately, this requires either the division of supervisory responsibility or the addition of a new district supervisor. The addition of a supervisor may ultimately cause the span of control of the superintendent of parks or recreation to increase to the point that he no longer can effectively supervise that many subordinates. This in turn would probably result in the establishment of another level in the organization. Although the growth of an organization is inevitable, it complicates the effective functioning in many ways. The more levels the organization has, the more expensive it becomes to operate and the more managers it becomes necessary to employ. However, there is little alternative but to add levels and managers in that without proper management, ineffectiveness begins to permeate the organization, resulting in increased costs.

In addition to increasing the costs of operation, additional levels of organization slow down and complicate communications when there are four individuals deliberating about plans instead of three.

For example, a director of parks and recreation is discussing with the superintendent of recreation the desirability of having recreation leaders wear a specific type of uniform. The superintendent of recreation in turn discusses uniforms with his district supervisors and asks them to investigate the possibility with center directors. At this point, one district supervisor misinterprets the intent of the inquiries from the director of parks and recreation and conveys the idea that leaders will wear uniforms whether they like it or not. When the communication is then passed from the center director in that district to the recreation leaders, it is stated that they have to be in uniform by next week. The intent and meaning of the director of parks and recreation were lost in the communication between the four levels.

When there are too many levels in an organization, planning and control are complicated as plans are apportioned between the recreation and parks divisions and passed down through the ranks to the lowest level of employees. For example, the director of parks and recreation might call in his superintendents of parks and recreation and ask them to help him develop plans for a new park. Each superintendent then goes his separate way to plan. The park superintendent, in meeting with his staff, plans for ease of maintenance, esthetics, limited activity and a great deal of water area and no provision for night activity. The superintendent of recreation, meeting with his staff, plans for total use of the park facilities, including night, but with no concern for maintenance.

This difference in approach to planned use of the park is the result of divided function of the department and lack of coordination by the director. An effective and responsive organization is structured as simply as possible, with as few levels in the organization as possible, and as mentioned before, with managers directing only as many subordinates as they can supervise effectively.

There are many factors that determine the number of subordinates that one manager should supervise.[6] One is the similarity of work of the subordinates. In the case of the top-level manager, as was mentioned earlier, the director of parks and recreation supervises the work of the superintendents of recreation, parks, administrative division and possibly two or three other staff sections. This is about as many as he can direct in that each one's work, technical knowledge and daily activities will be considerably different and the director will have to know the terminology, philosophy and technical information of each of the divisions. At the lower level of the organization, however, the district supervisors direct the activities of eight to ten recreation centers, all of which are conducted in a similar manner. The manager will not have to have such a broad knowledge of different technical or program areas to supervise similar work assignments so that his span of control will be more amenable to directing a larger number of subordinates.

Another factor to be considered in managing employees is their geographical distribution. It is much easier for a manager to supervise individuals all housed in offices within the same building. Obviously, this permits him to see his subordinates regularly, either on a formal or informal basis. Generally, the superintendents of the various divisions are housed in one office. On the other hand, district supervisors generally have to travel several miles between various recreation and park facilities, thus limiting the number of facilities or subordinates they can supervise and reducing their span of control.

The complexity of the work assignments of subordinates also affects span of control. Quite obviously, the director of parks and recreation or the superintendents of the divisions of parks, recreation, administration, etc., supervise individuals who have very complex jobs, so their span of control is limited. However, district supervisors of parks or recreation direct the work of subordinates which is less complex. Thus, a park foreman finds it much easier to supervise eight or ten men all doing pick and shovel work because of the simplicity of the work.

Another related factor that affects span of control is the amount of coordination necessary. Obviously, if great amounts of it are required the manager's span of control increases. At the upper level of park and recreation management there is a great need to coordinate the efforts between the parks, the recreation and the administrative divisions. At lower levels, except for special events, coordination is limited at the level of the park manager and center director.

---

[6] Voich, D. Jr., and Wren, D. A. *Principles of Management.* New York, The Ronald Press Company, 1968, p. 211-213.

There are several factors that determine how often and how much time the manager must spend supervising his subordinates.[7] These include the amount of training possessed by the personnel. Generally, individuals with greater education and training require less time and fewer contacts. The amount of authority that can be delegated also affects the amount of supervision subordinates need. The more independently they can work, the less supervision is required. The amount of planning and the number of policy procedures the organization uses may also affect the frequency of supervision, the amount of time necessary to keep up with the latest trends in programming and new facility designs.

The use of objective standards, such as how often the grass needs to be cut and paper picked up helps to cut down on the need for supervision. In the previous chapter, the quantifiable goals were said to make management more effective, particularly from the standpoint of evaluation. Accurate and precise communication techniques and the amount of personal contact supervisors have with their subordinates affect the manager's job, and thus, his span of control. Each of the eight factors mentioned and the variation of each affects how frequently and to what degree the supervisor must spend overseeing his employees.

In any organization, all of these factors must be taken into account in giving each manager a span of control that is reasonable and will assure an adequate job. It is wise to limit the inexperienced or new employee to a narrow span of control and as he proves his capability, to increase it to a point where he can effectively do a good job.

Elements of Delegation

"Delegation is the entrustment of responsibility and authority to another and the creation of accountability for performance."[8] The success of an organization depends, to a great extent, on the manager and his ability to delegate authority. The manager who must deal with the various principles of organization finds that his ability to do so is based on his authority. This authority is paramount and is the key to his job, for he must perform and carry out his work through the people who make up the organization. He can use his authority and force his subordinates to comply or he can persuade them to carry out their tasks in the hope of attaining economic or social gain. In either case, authority is essential and it is extremely important that the leisure service manager understand it—what it is as well as its relationship to responsibility and accountability.

Responsibility is probably one of the most misunderstood terms of

---

[7] Koontz and O'Donnell, Op. cit., p. 254-257.
[8] Allen, Op cit., p. 117.

management. *Responsibility is the obligation of the manager to perform successfully in the carrying out of the task that has been assigned to him.* Authority, on the other hand, is the power or ability to carry out the task.

Authority can be defined as the power to act officially, the sanction to command others, to make commitments, to expend funds, utilize equipment, etc. In any case, the manager has the authority to perform a task. Because of his limited ability, whether it is of a technical, temporal, skill-related or informational nature, particularly at the upper level and middle level of management, it is impossible for him to do all of the tasks necessary personally.

The director of a leisure service agency cannot single-handedly run all of the recreation centers, swimming pools and parks, make the day-to-day decisions to permit them to function properly, answer all of the correspondence or to deal with all of the public. Therefore, he must rely on others to help him in his assignment. He accomplishes this by first employing subordinates, grouping them according to the various organizational principles that were previously discussed and then delegating them the authority to carry out their assigned tasks. His total effectiveness will depend upon how well he can delegate authority.

One can delegate authority, *but one can never delegate responsibility.*[9] Responsibility is something that the manager can share. The director of parks and recreation has the total responsibility for everything that happens and occurs within his department. He can delegate various tasks to his subordinates, but he is always responsible for their actions to the mayor or board of recreation and parks. If one of his subordinates fails or does not perform properly, it is still *his* responsibility and the mayor or board will hold him so. Through the total chain of command, responsibility is shared, but never delegated. Authority, on the other hand, always comes from the top down and can be delegated.

Another term often mentioned along with authority and responsibility is accountability. *Accountability is defined as an obligation to report back to one's superior on the carrying out of a given task.* This will be covered in the chapter concerned with controlling the leisure service delivery system.

Delegation is a basic and fundamental part of organizing. It is necessary for the delegating authority to accomplish the assigned task, activity or assignment. The director of parks and recreation employs a superintendent of parks, and then very carefully defines his job, outlines his goals and objectives and then delegates to the superintendent of parks the task of operating his division. He then grants him or delegates him the authority to carry out the operation of the department. He gives him the ability to hire personnel within the framework of the budget,

---

[9] Koontz and O'Donnell, Op. cit., p. 63.

to requisition the necessary supplies and equipment and all else he needs to run his division. He also holds him responsible for the accomplishments designated by the budget, goals and objectives, etc.

Similarly, the superintendent of parks, because of the magnitude of his job, must divide it into various sections within his division and other staff function, and he in turn assigns tasks, delegates authority and holds other individuals responsible. The process continues all the way down the chain of command to the individual who ultimately cuts the grass, lines the ball field or cleans the restrooms. All of this is made possible because individuals were delegated the authority to carry out their assigned tasks and held accountable for their performance.

The art of delegation is not a simple one. Probably as managers move up the chain of command more prove to be ineffective because of their inability to delegate authority. They try to do too much themselves, causing subordinates to be incapable of making decisions and thus ineffective. It is extremely important that in the delegation of tasks and the corollary authority to perform them there be very clear cut assignments of duties.

The delegation of authority can be either very specific or general. The more specific the delegation the less imaginative and creative the individual can be in carrying out tasks. This usually occurs at the lower levels of management. At the top level of the organization, assignments are relatively general and permit more creativity. They are more feasible at the upper managerial levels where the experience, education and training of the individuals are greater. Quite obviously, the delegation of tasks by the superintendent of recreation will be more general and the authority much broader than that of the center director, whose assignments will be more specific and will involve much less authority. Delegation of authority can be made in written form or handled verbally. There are advantages and disadvantages of each. These will be discussed in much greater detail in Chapter 11, which is concerned with directing.

In the functionally organized parks and recreation department, there is necessarily a split of authority in the carrying out of the overall assignments of the department. In a given case, the recreation division is responsible for programming the softball field which includes the organizing of the teams, providing the equipment and officials, and making sure the teams follow up and play the game. The park division on the other hand is responsible for maintaining the field, making sure the lights work, ascertaining that the field is mowed, lined and watered and seeing that the backstop and other facilities are in good repair. Neither the superintendent of parks nor the superintendent of recreation has the authority or responsibility to tend to all of the factors that will assure a successful softball program. This situation can work if the two superintendents pool their authority and make joint decisions in coordinating their activities to assure a proper and smooth operation or they can rely on a higher authority when mutual agreement cannot be reached. Another solution would be for *re-organization* to permit the recreation division to have the necessary manpower and authority to carry out the total operation of conducting a softball program. This could be accomplished by assigning a maintenance man to the recreation division to perform the necessary work solely within the recreation division. In many cases, this is the best solution.

When it often becomes necessary to pool authority between several managers in an organization some re-organization is obviously necessary. The amount of authority delegated to subordinates should be equal to the task assigned. In other instances, the recovery of delegated authority is necessary.

In organizations in smaller communities, authority is usually centralized to a great extent and retained by the director of a one-man department of parks and recreation. As the organization grows, if it is going to remain effective and efficient, it becomes necessary for the director to decentralize his authority to the various divisions. Decentralization occurs generally as departmentalization takes place. Any organization that continues to centralize its authority is bound to be very slow in arriving at decisions and keeping pace with changing times. As the divisions and sections are formed, it is necessary to delegate the authority for them to function effectively and properly. *Increased citizen requests for more local governmental involvement have made this procedure fundamental to effective program delivery, particularly in the central cities.*

Another factor that affects delegation is the attitude of the manager toward delegation. Obviously, his willingness to delegate is dependent upon several factors. Many managers, as they are promoted, are not willing to let go of their power. An example of this might be the district supervisor who is promoted to superintendent of parks and continues to make the decisions of his replacement regarding the jobs of foremen. He is unwilling to delegate authority to his new replacement. In many instances, the new district supervisor becomes nothing more than a message carrier between the foreman and the superintendent. As a result, too much time is taken to make minor decisions that could and should be delegated to the new district supervisor. On other occasions, managers are unwilling to delegate authority for fear that subordinates will make mistakes. No manager should sit by and allow mistakes that are extremely detrimental to the organization to occur repeatedly. However, the manager who makes too much fuss over mistakes, particularly when they are minor, soon has his subordinates fearful of making decisions.

It is important for managers not to dwell on one or two mistakes, but acknowledge instead the many good decisions. A very closely related point which affects the delegation of authority is the amount of trust the manager has in his subordinates. The more trust he has, the greater, obviously will be his desire to delegate. The astute leisure service manager works at overcoming his weakness in delegation. He does this by defining assignments and delegating authority in accordance with the results he wants and expects. He very carefully selects the right man for the job to be done. He very carefully maintains good communications and establishes quantifiable and proper controls and rewards his subordinates when they carry out their tasks properly in accordance with their delegating authority. It is important to make sure that the *unity of command* (which means that an employee has only one boss) is followed in delegating authority and that subordinates are held responsible for their work. An individual who is responsible to more than one manager will find himself frustrated. He will have conflicting assignments, which will result in his inability to complete either of them. Unity of command is therefore essential in the delegation of authority.

Whatever the task to be performed, the good manager delegates authority in accordance with it, never more than is necessary. He makes sure the subordinate is responsible for performing the task successfully. The manager does this by using the skills of leadership. As mentioned earlier, some managers are more effective by forcing compliance, perhaps even coercing, others by persuading or suggesting; but whatever the means, they should use their authority effectively. In most modern organizations, however, the use of coercion is not recommended or even tolerated. Greater detail will be devoted to the concerns of leadership and leadership techniques in Chapter 11, which deals with directing of the leisure service delivery system.

Line and Staff Relationships

Earlier in the chapter, the organizational concepts of authority, responsibility and accountability were discussed. These concepts tie the organization together, from the director of the department down to the lowest member of the organization. *"These authority relationships, whether vertical or horizontal, are the factors that breathe life into the organization."*[10] In organizations there are two types of authority: the *line authority* and the *staff authority*. The relationships between line and staff are important and have to be reckoned with since probably more confusion results from misunderstandings between the line and staff members than from any other factors in management. It is very important, therefore, that managers understand the difference between the line and staff function.

[10] Ibid., p. 302.

Line functions and line personnel have direct responsibility for the accomplishment of the objectives and goals of the organization, whereas the staff function refers to those parts of the organization that help the line staff to work more efficiently and effectively in carrying out the primary objectives and goals of the organization. Line personnel can be distinguished from staff personnel by the fact that the line personnel have the power to influence people in an authority relationship in a leisure service organization. The director, the superintendent of the various divisions, the recreation and park district supervisors, the center director and park manager are all line personnel. They have the direct responsibility for carrying out the goals and objectives of the organization. Staff personnel would consist of the training officer, department safety officer and various administrative assistants who *aid* the line operation officers in carrying out their function, but who have no direct authority over other personnel in the line operation. They carry out staff assignments that assist the line managers. The authority to manage must rest exclusively with the line officers and their relationship with their subordinates, as indicated earlier. Failure to understand this will cause much friction and disorganization.

As park and recreation agencies grow in size and as the line managers become very involved in day-to-day operations in carrying out their functions, it becomes necessary to give them assistance to take care of detailed work. Therefore, staff personnel are assigned to assist them. Staff personnel are very often highly trained and skilled in given areas. They are hired for their skill and knowledge to help the line personnel function better and more efficiently. As a result of their special skills, they are given exclusive time to devote their efforts and energies in their given area. After they formulate their ideas and prepare their plans for implementation, they present them to the line officers for approval. Staff personnel usually attempt to promote their ideas and convince line officers that they are worthwhile. Their recommendations generally flow upward in the organization to their superiors, who decide whether they are worthwhile to be transformed into action. The staff person who convinces the line officer of the worth of his ideas will more likely have his efforts rewarded than will the person who tries to impose his ideas upon line officers. An example might be that of the safety officer who convinces the line officer of the value of wearing glasses or goggles by a maintenance man to protect him from blinding sparks. If an employee is incapacitated for a while as a result of an accident he will cause a slowdown in the amount of work performed. The line officer will recognize that when his personnel are laid off, the job will not be done. He will readily accept the staff officer's recommendation and will incorporate use of goggles by maintenance men. However, if the staff officer just ordered the employee to wear glasses, the line officer might resent the order and will contradict it. So, it is of value for the staff officer to convince the line officer of his recommendation. He should "sell" the idea rather than imposing the new procedure upon the line officer.

Dangers in Using Staff Functions

Although the need for staff in any large organization has been pointed out, it should also be mentioned that there are certain dangers involved in using staff functions. The first of these is the danger of undermining the line authority. Unity of command is a very important principle and generally, one employee should have one supervisor giving him direction. By introducing the staff functions, the specialist, because of his knowledge in a given area, begins to give additional directions and orders which interject more authority into the organization. If the staff function is not handled carefully, the organization may end up with two individuals giving the same employee direction, thus confusing him and creating problems in terms of work accomplished. *Generally, all direct orders should come from the line supervisor in the organization.* The exception to this would be the case of functional authority, which will be discussed later in this chapter.

If staff personnel cannot convince line personnel of the value of his suggestions or recommendation, the only alternative that he has is to go back to a superior who is a line officer. This line officer can pass the idea down through the chain of command, giving the direct order to the line personnel. An example of this situation would be the staff recommending that a specific dramatics class be implemented in a given recreation center. If the recommendation is not accepted, it might result in the staff personnel's recommending to his superior the need for a dramatics program at this center. If the staff recommendation is accepted by the superior, he in turn would pass the recommendation down through the line side of the organization, insisting that the center implement some form of dramatics program. It should be pointed out at this time, however, that the center director will always resent this type of action. Although he may implement a dramatics program, he may do so only "half-heartedly" and only tacitly support it insofar as it came as a direct order. Had the staff personnel "sold" the center director of the value of the idea he would have implemented it wholeheartedly.

Another limitation of the staff function is that although staff personnel are highly trained in their given area, they very often think in a vacuum. They have a tendency not to realize all of the problems involved in the implementation of a program. It is very important, therefore, that they be made to understand the total problem—all of the factors affecting the operation of a program so as to know how, when and where to implement programs, where they will work and where they will not work. A good procedure would be for the staff personnel to work closely with the line personnel, involve them in the planning of programs, and inquire extensively about the operation so that they make recommendations only after they are well oriented. Since they would work fairly closely with the line, their suggestions would probably be accepted more readily.

It is important for line personnel to keep staff very well informed about what is going on in the operation. As mentioned earlier, staff are there to assist in line operations. If they are not knowledgeable about what is occurring in the organization, they will not be in a good position to recommend procedures in their specialty. Whenever staff are used, it is their responsibility to develop and maintain a favorable working climate and to foster favorable personnel relationships. This can best be done if the staff person takes the approach that it is his job to enable the line manager to do an effective job. He should never attempt to assume credit for ideas or to discredit line officers, for obviously this will develop an unfavorable relationship between staff and line personnel. Again, it cannot be stressed too strongly that the staff person should convince the line officers of the value of his recommendations rather than try to impose them upon the officers.

Functional Authority

Functional authority is an important factor in organizations. This is the authority given to an individual, generally a staff officer, to take specific action within the organization pertaining to matters in which he is the expert. Generally, this functional authority assumes authority over the line organization with respect to procedures in the field of program specialties, accounting, personnel procedures, purchasing or public relations. Because of the knowledge possessed by the staff person in these areas and the need for a certain amount of conformity or consistency within the organization, he is given this functional authority to exercise influence over the line operation.

An example of functional authority might be again the department safety officer. His responsibility is to assure safety practices and procedures by the employees of the organization at all times. He might observe an employee without hard-toe steel shoes in the maintenance division and would instruct him to wear safety shoes the next day or not report to work. He is given this functional authority by the head of the department and has the right to insist that these procedures be followed. In this case the employee must abide by these instructions even though the line officer may have noticed the employee without safety shoes and had taken no action.

Likewise, the finance officer is in a position to request a particular financial report from a given recreation center. When money is being handled directly by the center director, the finance officer is given this functional authority, again, by the department head. In the interest of good budget practices and to assure accountability for all funds, the center director must comply with this order even if the line officer immediately responsible to him is not in favor of it. His only alternative would be to pass his recommendations back up the chain of command to a higher authority where the matter could be resolved one way or the other. Unless this is done, the center director is obligated to comply with the staff person's request to obtain a particular financial report from the line officer. Again, this authority is delegated to assure the maintenance of sound procedures and consistency within the organization.

Service Department

The purpose of the service department within the park and recreation agency is that of grouping activities into one department for economical and performance reasons. The formation of the service department would hopefully be economical and would ensure uniform operation policy throughout the agency. Examples of service departments or sections within the park and recreation department would be the personnel section, the financial section, the planning and research section, the purchasing section or any other section created to facilitate or offer a service to the operating divisions.

Within the park and recreation department, there is a constant need for qualified personnel. In order to recruit, examine, select and train these individuals, a personnel section is maintained. It exists outside the operating division as a separate section because none of the divisions is large enough to justify a personnel section by itself.

The same logic would apply to the establishment of other service sections such as the financial, planning and purchasing units. These service sections are organized by the grouping of activities of specialty, technology or efficiency. As a result, these sections provide a savings in the cost of completing a job. In addition, *the creation of a service section assures standardization of policies and procedures and provides for certain controls.* Within the leisure service delivery system, very often the recreation division and the park division operate independently of each other. However, the central purchasing division within the whole city, county or governmental agency requires that purchasing be done in a standardized manner. There are standardized requisition forms and detailed bidding procedures that are used throughout all the departments of the governmental agency. This is to assure consistency throughout the city. The department of parks and recreation, as a part of the overall city government, is expected to conform to the overall policies and procedures of purchasing. As a result, the city can save several hundred dollars by using bulk purchasing and by the formation of the service department.

The establishment of a service department can also assure control and standardization within the organization. Likewise, within most large city or county governments, there is a civil service commission or merit system that requires personnel to be selected, examined and employed according to set procedures. This results in the establishment of a service department of personnel at the city or county level. Insofar as the city- or county-wide personnel department cannot meet all of the needs of the individual departments, the department of parks and recreation may establish its own personnel division or section to work along with the city- or county-wide department.

Very often there is confusion between the service department function and departmentalization. As mentioned earlier in the chapter, departmentalization has to do with division of an organization into smaller units when it becomes too large for one manager to supervise effectively and efficiently. Within the recreation division, as the organization grows and more recreation centers are added to the system, it becomes necessary to divide them up on a *geographical* basis. This is the purpose of departmentalization. When this is done, additional managers are required to be in charge of each of the districts created. The service department differs from departmentalization in that its functions are divided according to area of specialty or by similarity of activities. The service section would then serve the park and recreation divisions or districts.

Decentralization

"Decentralization refers to the systematic effort to delegate to the lowest level all authority except that which can only be exercised at central points."[11] As the organization grows in size, it becomes obvious that one manager cannot make all of the decisions. As mentioned earlier in this chapter, when this happens, the manager must delegate authority to lower-level managers in order to carry out the goals and objectives of the organization. As the leisure service agency grows in size to the point that the director can no longer manage the entire department, it becomes necessary for him to hire a separate superintendent of parks and a superintendent of recreation. In so doing, he is implementing the departmentalization principle. As a result of this action, it also becomes necessary to form certain service departments.

In the formation of these service sections, delegation of a certain authority to these sections is needed for them to carry out their work. In the creation of such service sections, the parks division and the recreation division each relinquishes authority. The personnel department or any other service department continues to expand as the total department grows. Soon, additional personnel officers, clerks, typists and other

[11] Allen, Op. cit., p. 163-171.

individuals are hired to carry out the burgeoning workload of the entire organization.

As the service department continues to grow, at some point the manager must decide to divide it up and reappropriate it back to each of the operating divisions. By appropriating sections of the service department back to each of the operating divisions, a danger exists that the overhead of operation will increase because of the two separate personnel sections within each of the operating divisions. In addition, there is a danger that a lack of uniformity and policy may occur in the hiring, selection and examination of personnel. Whatever the case, the effective manager is constantly aware of the potential problems in emphasizing decentralization or centralization.

There are several factors to keep in mind when considering the possibilities of decentralization of authority.[12] The first of these is the costliness of the decision. Generally, the decisions involving cost are the most important and they are made by the manager of the organization, whereas lesser decisions can be passed down or delegated to lower-level and middle-level managers. Another factor that must be considered when decisions are to be delegated is how much they cut across or affect the various divisions under that particular manager. In other words, if the director of the leisure service agency has a decision to be made that will affect both the parks and the recreation division, it would be natural and logical that he himself should make such a decision. However, decisions that affect only one or the other of the operating divisions should be delegated down to the appropriate level.

Another factor to be considered in decentralizing authority is the need for uniformity of policy and procedures. If consistency is desirable among the various operating divisions then the management at the highest level should retain such decisions or authority. If a division or section requires a great deal of independence in the area of decision-making to operate, it becomes necessary to decentralize and to delegate authority to it. Failure to delegate or decentralize in this case will stymie that particular operation to the point that it cannot operate effectively. It will require the manager at a lower level to refer constantly to a higher-level manager for decisions. Such efforts would tend to slow down the effectiveness and efficiency of that particular operating section. The greater the decentralization of authority, the more likely will be the degree of independence of a particular section .

Very closely associated with the ability of the top-level manager to decentralize and delegate authority is the availability of competent managers. Quite obviously if lower-level sections or divisions do not have competent managers, the top-level manager will need to make certain

---

[12] Voich and Wren, Op. cit., p. 205-206.

decisions and to centralize his authority. The more competent the manager is at any level of the organization, the greater the likelihood that he will decentralize authority.

Associated with the ability to decentralize authority are the control techniques that the manager has at his disposal to evaluate the competency of decisions being made by the lower-level managers. If effective control techniques and evaluation procedures are available to the manager, he can judge whether his lower-level managers are making appropriate decisions; he can determine to what extent he can decentralize his authority. Decentralization has worked well in instances where there have been highly qualified managers. It goes almost without saying that the *principle of decentralization is the same as the principle of delegation of authority.* When a manager decentralizes he inevitably loses certain controls. The key to effectiveness and efficiency of decentralization is the maintenance of a proper balance between the forces of centralization and decentralization. However, it is becoming increasingly important to bring decision making closer to the participants in order to make leisure service more visible to the people and a vital part of community life.

Boards and Committees

All organizations use boards and committees in one form or another. *A committee is nothing more than two or more individuals gathered together for the purpose of effecting group action.* There is no question that the committee is a definite part of an organization. Committees are formed for many different reasons and for various uses. In the leisure service field, the committee sometimes is formed as the park and recreation board. This board or board of directors is essentially a committee which has been formed by state or local authority or legislation to manage the park and recreation department. This board has certain authority, usually established by enabling legislation. This authority usually calls for policy determination, planning and control and/or evaluation. This committee or board hires a top-level manager who is known usually as the director of parks and recreation. He is the chief executive of the organization. His responsibilities include running the operation on a day-to-day basis. He, in turn, organizes the department, hires the necessary personnel and gives it the leadership necessary for him to implement the policies that have been established by the board. Within the staff organization, the chief executive very often operates by the use of committees.

Whether the committee is at the level of the board of directors or at the staff level, its primary reason for existence falls into several categories.[13] Group deliberation and judgment are functions of a committee in keeping with the old adage that two heads are better than one. The com-

[13] Koontz and O'Donnell, Op. cit., p. 373-376.

mittee can jointly ponder a problem or a situation, provide for alternative approaches and then make a recommendation for the implementation of the proper solution to the problem. In some instances, a committee is delegated authority necessary to make decisions and in other instances the committee is only asked to come up with certain recommendations. These recommendations are then passed up to the executive who appointed the committee. He makes a decision on the basis of the list of recommended alternatives. Often managers rely on a committee to make a decision when they are afraid to take responsiblity for it because it may prove to be unpopular. Although this is an inappropriate reason for the use of a committee, it is often done by poor managers. The fear of authority, in terms of placing decision-making power in the hands of a committee, is also a way for a manager to divide up authority among several individuals rather than delegating too much authority to one individual. It provides the manager the final say in many decisions, but it gives subordinates the feeling that they have a certain amount of power in their role on the committee.

The committee also gives various interest groups an opportunity to become involved in the process of making important decisions. Very often in a large organization where several managers at a lower level have differences of opinion in terms of a solution to a particular problem, the higher-level manager may delegate authority to a representative committee for the purpose of compromising and working out a solution. Although this method can sometimes be effective, it is generally the sign of a weak manager. However, the committee can become a tool for dissemination of information and communication.

The committee also becomes a tool for the consolidation of authority. When a decision cannot be resolved by a single manager who does not have enough authority in his work area, it will be referred to a committee for action. As a result, two managers who have to make a decision together can pool their authority and arrive at a solution. Very often this is done when the magnitude of the decision is not large enough or great enough to push it up the chain of command to the director of the organization. Managers may also use a committee to avoid certain actions. This can be done by referring a decision to a committee. Although this is not an effective managerial technique, it is very often used by weak managers to avoid the making of decisions themselves.

There are many disadvantages in using a committee.[14] Quite obviously, a committee requires that several people come together for group action. This results in high cost in terms of the number of people that need to be together. All of them receive pay while they are serving on the committee, so the manager should be sure that the purpose for which the

[14] Ibid., p. 376-378.

committee is formulated is worth the cost in terms of the money and manpower invested in the committee. Another disadvantage of the committee is that very often it makes compromises to the point that the original intent of the decision is lost or severely "watered down."

The Successful Committee

There are several things that should be taken into consideration when organizing a committee.[15] The first and most obvious is to articulate what the scope and purpose of the committee is as well as to define its authority in decision making. When this is not done, the committee often spends a great deal of its time searching and drifting aimlessly to try to determine what its scope and goals should be. This can all be avoided if the person formulating the committee defines its scope and authority in advance. Another point to consider is the *size of the committee*. Generally an adequate number is between six and 15 people. Fewer than six people often results in poor representation. More than fifteen involves too many people in that too much time is wasted attempting to resolve differences. The selection of the committee members is an important factor to consider. All of the various views of the organization should be considered. Although no attempt should be made to get a pre-determined decision before the committee does its work, it is important that the committee be able to work well together in arriving at its solution.

Another important factor is to select a good chairman for the committee. It is the chairman's responsibility to guide and control the committee. However, the committee should never replace the manager in terms of making decisions that are solely his responsibility. Also, the committee should not be used for unimportant matters or decisions which do not justify or warrant the cost of its existence. Although the committee is a very valuable management tool, it can be misused.

Procedure for Completing Work Assignments

Up to this point, this chapter has covered delegation and decentralization, the relationship between line and staff personnel, responsibility and accountability. In order to integrate these into a workable management configuration, they will be summarized to explain the process of completing work assignments. The first step that needs to be accomplished is definition of work. This is done in accordance with the plans and goals that the manager has determined in the first step of the management process. If the job is too big for him to do by himself, he delegates certain portions of the work to subordinate managers. This

[15] Ibid., p. 391-395.

results in his delegating authority to lower-level managers. The manager only delegates enough authority for the lower-level manager to carry out that specific section of work delegated to him.

In addition to his delegating authority and work to be performed, the manager must create a responsibility in the employee to get the job done. The manager acts according to the pre-determined goals and objectives established in the planning process. At this point, he sets certain timetables, criteria and other standards by which he wants the work accomplished. In addition, he requires accountability so that the manager at the lower level will periodically report back to him as to how the work is proceeding, whether he is having any problems and whether he will be able to meet his deadline for the completion of the work. Once the work is done and has been accounted for, the last and final step is for the manager to measure the results against the pre-determined goals and objectives that set the work in motion. At this point, the work process has been completed.

Summary

In looking at organizational structures in terms of departmentalization, line and staff relationships, the service department and centralization versus decentralization, many factors have to be considered in determining when each of these techniques should be employed. There is a great deal of confusion, misunderstanding and incorrect interchange of each of these four terms. *Departmentalization is the process of dividing an organization up into smaller units* when the span of management gets too large for one manager to supervise effectively. In leisure service agencies this is generally handled according to the operating divisions of parks and recreation. Within the operating divisions there is further division or departmentalization, generally according to geographical areas on the basis of districts. *The service department is created when there is a need for grouping of activities for efficiency, effectiveness or more uniformity of operations throughout the agency.* The service department then services the rest of the operating divisions. Decentralization can take place in either the service department or an operating division of the organization by departmentalization. *The purpose of decentralization of sections or decentralization of authority is to delegate work to lower-level managers within the organization.* It becomes evident and logical that no one manager can perform all the work necessary in an organization. The only way he can accomplish work is to delegate it or decentralize it into smaller, lower-level divisions of the organization. Staff and line relationships take place throughout the organization and are not peculiar to any specific section. *Line function or personnel are those personnel who have direct responsibility for the accomplishing of the objectives of the enterprise whereas the staff function includes those personnel who are there to help the line to work more effectively in accomplishing the primary objectives of the enterprise.* In order for an agency to function effectively, the manager should understand each of these organizational concepts.

CHAPTER 10

Staffing for the Leisure Service Delivery System

Need for Managers

In the field of leisure service as in any other professional field, the quality of managers and other personnel affects the quality of service or product more than any other single factor. This is not an unusual situation since a great deal of the managing process involves personnel. It is the manager who plans, sets goals and objectives, organizes staff, communicates, motivates and leads. Also, he and his personnel deliver the service, promote the program and the budget and are held responsible for all the functions of making the organization work.

The future of any organization depends upon the managers' ability to develop and train personnel from within their organizations to become managers or to secure prospective managers from outside sources. Although the staffing function in many organizations is handled by a personnel department, managers must still do all they can to assist in assuring the selection of the highest quality of personnel in *all* positions, whether at the top level or at the lowest level in the organization.

The individuals within an organization are very much aware of the quality of personnel that are being hired. If they see people of inferior ability being hired, their morale will be affected and the quality of work of the new employees will be influenced negatively. The selection of unqualified personnel as a result of political influence in an organization can seriously hinder its effectiveness. However, if personnel of high quality are hired and fair and equal employment opportunities are prevalent within the organization, the staffing function will most likely be successful.

Types and Levels of Positions

Within the leisure service field there are usually three levels of managers. Each level is important and cannot be overlooked or minimized. There are many common factors and relationships between each level and the difference between them is only in the scope and responsibility of the respective level. In defining a manager earlier, we stated that he is a person who has at his disposal equipment, manpower, money, material, time and space which he handles on a day-to-day basis.

In the leisure service field the *lower-level managers* are considered to be the center directors, park managers and others usually responsible for a single facility and two to ten staff members. These consist of either recreation leaders, instructors, park maintenance men or others who implement work at the face-to-face level in program areas or at the job site in the park setting. The manager at this lower level must carry out his assignment by planning, organizing, directing and controlling. As previously stated the scope of each of these functions is more narrow than at the top level of management and is governed more by policies, procedures and other guidelines. Nevertheless, his role or function is important to the organization. Ultimately, if these lower-level managers learn to manage effectively at the lower level they will advance to higher levels in the organization. Generally, lower-level managers do not supervise or manage other managers. They are responsible only for *non-managerial* personnel and have daily contact with all their personnel and areas of supervision.

Middle-level managers in the leisure service field are park or recreation supervisors. Many of them will come from within the ranks of lower-level managers by promotion. From an organizational standpoint they are responsible for geographic areas or special emphasis areas such as swimming pools, construction or other activities. They *do* supervise other managers and other personnel. They are generally responsible for *broader* areas of work as well as larger budgets, more equipment and facilities than lower-level managers. They generally have greater decision-making responsibility delegated to them and are governed less by policies, procedures and other controls.

The middle-level manager must represent lower-level managers to those at higher level in the organization as well as communicate instructions down the chain of command. Like lower-level managers, they have a responsibility for on-the-job training. Middle-level managers should visit their areas regularly and give assistance where it is needed. Periodically they should make suggestions for change or improvement. Their visits should vary according to the individual needs of facilities and personnel. Some visits, in cases when little help or direction is needed, will be purely for interest and support. Other visits, in instances where help is required, will be for extended periods of time. Middle-level managers will seldom see all their subordinates and facilities daily, but in some instances they will have to "roll up their sleeves" and demonstrate to lower-level managers how to perform adequately. Of course, caution must be taken by managers not to embarrass staff in front of others. Whatever the situation, the middle-level manager should do everything necessary to assure his staff of proper support, assistance and training. His role is vital in the organization; he serves to *link* the agency's goals and objectives with community needs and service requests.

The *top-level managers* in the leisure service field are the directors of parks and recreation and the assistants or superintendents of each of the operating divisions, such as parks, recreation, administration and other major sections. These managers have the broadest responsibilities and authority. They are responsible for long-range planning, establishing of policies, organization structuring and re-structuring, coordination, implementation and many other broad-based managerial functions. They represent the organization to legislative or city managerial authorities. They are responsible for the *overall direction* of the department.

One other level of management that should be mentioned is that of the staff manager. He most likely will be assigned to the top level of the organization. His function, as described in Chapter 9, is to assist the line manager on the basis of his technical knowledge or speciality. Many staff managers come from within the ranks of the organization and will perform well provided they are given appropriate guidelines and direction. Staff managers who are promoted to a high-level position in a line function often have difficulty. One theory suggests that they rely on their particular technical knowledge or specialty to such a point that they lose sight of their appropriate managerial role to the detriment of the overall mission of the organization.

Qualifications and Job Descriptions

Qualifications and job descriptions are extremely important in securing the right person for a particular managerial job. Job qualifications are established by the agency to indicate the desired educational and personal requirements of the employee for a particular assignment and the job description provides a more detailed explanation of the specific performance expectations.[1]

The qualifications for each job should be considered very carefully in advance. There is the danger of not requiring enough qualifications. Occasionally, job qualifications may be too high. In either case, the manager may hire a person who will not perform adequately. The "under-qualified" person may not be able to do what is asked of him because of lack of knowledge or skill. The "over-qualified" person may become bored or dissatisfied with his job or the salary and not perform adequately so that attainment of the overall goals or work of an organization is affected. Therefore, it is extremely important that each job be analyzed very carefully so as to require accurate qualifications for the work to be performed.

There are generally three factors that are used to determine job qualifications. They are knowledge, skill and experience. *Knowledge* is

---

[1] Voich, D., Jr., and Wren, D. A. *Principles of Management.* New York, The Ronald Press Company, p. 381-383.

generally associated with education, including self-education and formal training at institutions of higher learning. Educational requirements may be determined by establishing a basic level of learning to fulfill the job requirements or by giving an examination. The educational requirement may be very specific and expect that the applicant possess a bachelor's degree or a master's degree in park and recreation administration. An examination serves to test a candidate over the relevant subject matter pertaining to a particular position.

Skill also can be tested by examination. In the area of sports a candidate may be asked to perform a given skill and can be evaluated on how well he performs that task. A leisure service manager may be given a problem-solving exam to determine his skill in a given area. The test might include either an objective or subjective evaluation.

Experience involves determining from a job applicant's previous employers whether he has been employed for the period of time indicated on the application. Additionally, a check is made of the applicant's previous work performance. Sometimes, past performance ratings, if they are available, are helpful in appraising the previous work of a job applicant. Letters of reference are also used in many cases. The employer's job is to analyze each new position in detail to determine what skills are needed. If this process is carefully and systematically approached, more realistic job qualifications will be established.

The manager should initiate the process by listing all the duties and activities that are going to be required of a person in a specific position. If there is a similar position somewhere else in the organization or in some other city the manager should examine the qualifications listed for it. The second step involves the determination of whether the applicant has the particular knowledge, skills and experience that will be necessary to perform these duties. Normally, the establishment of performance qualifications will be handled by personnel departments within a city or county governmental unit. Once they are established, a job description will be prepared to fit the necessary job expectations.

As previously indicated *job descriptions* provide a detailed listing of the work requirements for a given position. The job description usually has four parts. The first is the job title or classification. It gives the classification heading of the job and may also provide a working title. For example, the classification for a position may be supervisor and under this classification several working titles may be listed, such as district supervisor, supervisor of arts and crafts, park district supervisor, etc.

In most organizations it is best to have as few classifications as possible since most personnel departments do not like to establish new ones although they are willing to establish new working titles. Usually new classifications have to be presented to legislative bodies while working titles do not.

The next part of a job description is the qualifications. As stated previously, this consists of listing education or knowledge, skills and experience required. Age, sex and health information are also sometimes required.

The job description will then ordinarily list examples of duties to be performed and will provide as much detail about the job as possible so as to help determine whether persons applying for a position are qualified. A job description that is well thought out and carefully researched will serve as a tremendous aid in helping the organization to create new jobs and to attract, screen and hire the best possible candidate. It is extremely important for leisure service agencies not to overlook minority group members. In some regions of the country this may necessitate having bilingual job announcements.

Source of Personnel

The quality of personnel at all levels in an organization will determine its effectiveness, competence and the quality of leisure service offerings that it will make available to the public. The leisure service manager should therefore attempt to be aware of and use every resource available to him. Personnel may be obtained from within the organization through promotion. It is important to boost morale and create "hygienic" incentives for those at lower levels in the agency.[2] On the other hand, an organization occasionally needs new "blood," new ideas and new leadership. A good manager tries to maintain a balance in his organization by hiring the best-qualified persons from within it through promotion and from outside it through open, competitive exams. In any case, personnel within the organization should be given an equal opportunity to compete for new or promotional jobs. Employees will be motivated if they are encouraged by managers to apply for such jobs and thus are able to realize growth opportunities within the organization.

Recruiting

Personnel recruitment is often taken too much for granted. When positions are filled from within the organization, the need for extensive recruitment is not necessary. However, when the manager goes outside the organization to obtain new personnel, a greater degree of recruiting is necessary. Many factors are involved in how the leisure service agency manager decides how extensive the recruiting effort will be

The number of vacancies is an obvious factor in determining the amount of recruiting that will be done. If there are several vacancies a much larger recruitment program is necessary than if there is only one.

---

[2]Kelly, J. *Organizational Behavior.* Homewood, Ill., Richard D. Irwin, Inc., 1969. p. 176.

Particularly if the vacancy is at the lowest level of management, a great amount of recruiting cannot be justified. Obviously, a more vigorous recruitment program should be made for the position of director of parks and recreation than for the position of a recreation leader.

If a personnel manager knows that several persons will retire in the next few years, his recruitment efforts may be affected, particularly if promotion from within the agency will be limited.

If the manager will have to recruit from outside the organization, he will need to promote the organization to interested candidates by a representative who attempts to create a good image of the organization. In meetings with college graduates or prospective employees, this representative conveys the advantages of working for the organization, its benefits, its promotional opportunities and the contribution that the organization makes to the community in terms of the provision of leisure services.

The leisure agency ordinarily has a person who can make such a presentation about the agency. He will have recruitment material on hand to interest prospective candidates. Candidates with outstanding potential may be found at colleges and universities who have leisure studies curricula. With the constant improvement of curricula and other innovations in education, more individuals are being readied to assume lower-level managerial positions immediately after graduation. It is often advantageous for personnel managers to visit colleges and universities even though students might not be selected to fill a particular vacancy. They might apply for a position at a later date because of the image conveyed by the manager. Sending job announcements and other promotional material to colleges to be posted on bulletin boards or for display purposes at conferences is another way for an organization to interest prospective candidates. Advertising in professional journals will also interest a candidate, although this procedure is impersonal. The more specific the information that is provided concerning salaries, job location, etc., the more worthwhile this type of advertising will be. Creating a favorable public image serves as an effective recruitment device. *Representatives of an agency can do much to shape its image at conferences and other professional meetings by their overall conduct.*

One of the best sources of prospective candidates is the National Recreation and Park Association.[3] The NRPA has a personnel services department whose main function is assisting agencies looking for personnel. The NRPA will send the leisure service agency names of candidates who meet the minimum qualifications. The NRPA can also advertise position vacancies in its publications.

---

[3] National Recreation and Park Association, 1601 North Kent St., Arlington, Virgina 22209.

Personnel may also be recruited at national, regional and state conferences. "Job marts" which provide opportunities for interviews for job aspirants are available as part of the overall conference program.

The next step is the screening of prospective candidates to see if they meet the minimum qualifications. This initial screening often saves both the out-of-town or out-of-state candidates and manager excess expense and time if the candidates do not meet the qualifications that the agency has set. There is no reason for a leisure service manager to spend a great deal of time interviewing only to find that the prospective candidate is not interested in the position or does not meet the qualifications. The last phase of recruiting these candidates involves on-the-spot interviewing.

Selecting the Right Person

Selecting the right person for every job is critical because the success or failure of the organization will be determined more than anything else by the quality of leisure service managers and supervisors. The best efforts of promoting the organization and of recruitment and screening prospective employees will be in vain if the final step, selection, is done hastily and improperly. Many methods are used in selecting candidates. These include testing, interviewing and researching the individual's background. Selection is made in some organizations by the personnel officer, in others by a committee or by the manager under whom the person will work. Each procedure has advantages and disadvantages, but whatever method is used, the selection of the best candidate for each position is the central objective of the recruitment program. The final selection should be made by the person under whom the candidate will work. He is the person that will have to work most closely with the new employee and he will be responsible for the employee's work. This should be kept foremost in mind when it comes time for actual selection of the candidate.[4] Good results will be obtained in recruiting if prospective candidates are taken on a tour of the organization's facilities, but recruitment effort will be wasted if the manager for whom the prospective candidate will work does not take sufficient time to interview and select the person properly. This situation will most likely result in the manager's making a poor choice or in the candidate's losing interest because of the manager's abruptness and lack of courtesy.

Written Examinations

Written examinations used in selecting managers have not proven to be very reliable. An examination that might evaluate how familiar a candidate is with management principles, functions and techniques can

---

[4] Koontz and O'Donnell, Op. cit., p. 451.

only measure his knowledge of them, not whether he can apply them properly. Often professional competency examinations are combined with intelligence tests in an effort to measure the critical thinking ability of the prospective manager. This may only measure an individual's ability to take a test, not serve as a valid indicator of his work capability.

A possible alternative is using a combination of a written exam and an oral one, with less emphasis on the written part and more on the oral exam. If written exams are going to be used, they should be reviewed to determine whether they are current and appropriate for the particular position being tested.

Oral Examinations

Oral examinations are often used to evaluate candidates for positions. Generally, the examination is administered by two or three top managers who are considered expert in the specific area in which the position is available. They comprise an *evaluating board* that can meet in conjunction with the local civil service commission, a chief executive of a park and recreation department or with the park and recreation board.

The oral examination measures, to a degree, the candidate's ability to interpret, react to and express himself in a given situation. It may not be able to measure accurately, however, the overall capability of a candidate. It does allow the evaluating board an opportunity to see the top three to five job candidates who have survived the various preliminary application and testing screening procedures.

Performance Ratings

Performance ratings, if systematic, objective and properly administered, are probably the most valuable measurement of a candidate's competence and potential for promotion. Most well-organized departments utilize some form of evaluation that is administered on an annual or semi-annual basis. One difficulty in using performance ratings as part of the selection process is that unless the same person evaluates all of the candidates, the rating will have little validity. An effort should be made to avoid this by making certain that the person who will do the evaluating has an overall understanding of performance rating systems. The most useful types of performance systems are ones with a numerical score rather than a verbal description of the person being rated. Comparison of candidates by use of categories such as "satisfactory," "unsatisfactory," "excellent" or "average" is difficult. If performance ratings are objective, well executed and used periodically, they are the *best* measurement of a person's abilities.

Many times individuals have done outstanding work at a lower-level position in an organization, but when they were promoted or transferred to a position of more responsibility, with additional job pressures, they did not perform as well. Employers should be careful not to promote employees beyond their capabilities. This may seem far fetched but it happens and is referred to as the "Peter principle." It means that managers tend to be promoted to a level of their incompetence.[5] Effort should be made to try to evaluate a candidate's ability with every measurement tool available. An accurate, up-to-date personnel file on all employees can be helpful when it is time to select candidates. Any disciplinary action reported or any letters of commendation can sometimes make the difference as to which candidate will be selected. Generally the best measure of a potential candidate is his past performance record.

Orientation Program and Assignment

The orientation of new employees is very important in park and recreation work. If a position has been vacant for a period of time, the tendency is for an agency to want to have the employee on the job as quickly as possible and to get him too involved before he has really familiarized himself with his job and the agency.

One of the best ways to prevent a poor start is by conducting an organized and effective orientation program. There is a tendency for an organization to try to "cram" too much into too short a period of time. The following are some of the areas that might be presented in the orientation briefing: the department's philosophy, its overall goals and objectives, employee work expectations and a discussion of employee benefits and professional advancement potential within the organization. Two or three days of field trips should be conducted for the employee. The tour should include visits to the various facilities and programs in operation. The personnel officer should sit down with the new employee and explain the "personal benefits" of the organization. A departmental pamphlet which gives additional details on personal benefits that the employee can keep for reference is often helpful. The final phase of the orientation program should be spent in an installation similar to one in which the new employee's permanent assignment will be. See the example of the three-week orientation program (Tables 10-1, 10-2 and 10-3).

The period of orientation provides the new employee with an opportunity to establish rapport with his immediate supervisor. It can also provide the new employee with an idea of how the job can be accomplished and what expectations the agency has of his work. It is designed to get the employee off to a good start and give him confidence. It is also important for the new employee to be placed in the right job. A new, inexperienced park and recreation employee who is assigned to

---

[5]Peter L. J., and Hull, R. *The Peter Principle.* New York: Bantam Books, Inc., 1969.

Table 10-1. *Three-week Orientation Program (First Week)*

Monday	*Tuesday*	*Wednesday*	*Thursday*	*Friday*
Morning 10:00-12 Noon *Group Meeting* 1. Introduction of staff 2. History of organization 3. Philosophy and concepts of leisure and recreation 4. Goals and objectives of department by director of department	1. Assignments to supervisor for tours 2. Tour and visit with park district supervisor	Tour of maintenance and construction operations	Open	*Group Meeting* 1. Discussion and critique of orientation and visits (conducted by training coordinator) 2. Questions and answers 3. Next week's assignments
Afternoon 2:00-5:00 P.M. 1. Tour of office headquarters and introduction of staff 2. Complete forms for employment 3. Physical exams	Continue park district tour	Tour and visit of special facilities (zoo, museums, stadiums, etc.)	*Group Meeting* Administrative workshop 1. Personnel policies and procedures 2. Supervisory process 3. Evaluation 4. Resources for professional growth Directed observation with district supervisor of recreation programs	Group meetings with heads of operating divisions: 1:00 P.M. Recreation 3:00 P.M. Parks
Evening 7:00-10:00 P.M. Open	Open	Open	Continued: 7.00-10:00 P.M. Observation with same district supervisor	Open

Table 10-2. Three-week Orientation Program (Second Week)

Monday	*Tuesday*	*Wednesday*	*Thursday*	*Friday*
Directed observation of specialized programs Examples: 1. Senior citizens 2. Handicapped programs 3. Special crafts	Open	Directed observation of specialized programs Examples: 1. Pre-school programs 2. Women's activities	Open	Open
Divisional Workshop Recreation: 1. Program planning 2. Techniques of directing recreation activities Parks: 1. Maintenance problems 2. Supervisory techniques 3. Technical presentations	Divisional workshop continued	Divisional workshop continued	Divisional workshop continued	*Group Meeting* 1. Discussion and critique of orientation and visits 2. Next week's assignment 3. Questions and answers with the director of department
Open	Visit evening recreation programs	Open	Visit evening recreation programs	Visit and observe selected teen social programs

Table 10-3. Three-week Orientation Program (Third Week)

Forty (40) hours of assignment to select training sites under outstanding supervisors most closely resembling permanent job assignment:

1. Recreation center director assigned to recreation center 2:00 P.M. to 10:00 P.M. four week days and Saturday, 10:00 A.M. to 6:00 P.M.
2. Park manager assigned to park division 8:00 A.M. to 5:00 P.M. four week days and one week-end day.
3. Supervisors assigned to supervisor.
4. Fourth week—permanent assignment.

a brand new facility which has never previously been operated may easily be overwhelmed by the number of problems and pressures in his attempts to get the program "off the ground." If the employee is new to the community, he will not have contacts with its leaders and will be unknown to residents. Therefore, he will also be unfamiliar with the needs and interests of the community and its residents. This fact alone could hinder his initial service efforts. Generally, the most appropriate placement for this new, inexperienced leader would be in a stable, well-organized and well-run facility which has an efficient staff that would permit him to start his work under fairly normal conditions. The new leader should not be made to feel inhibited about offering new ideas. It is important that his first assignment be a pleasant, satisfying experience. If the new leader gets too heavily involved and tries to make too many changes at once he might have a difficult time getting adjusted to the community. It is important for him to work with the community in analyzing and fostering social change. He motivates the community to make its own assessments and attempts to have them acquire the necessary skills to develop a vital, stable pattern of living.

The personality of the new employee should be considered in deciding where he will be placed. Therefore, in addition to determining the assignment of the new manager, heed should also be given to the staff that will be working for him. The other factor to consider in assigning a new manager, whether experienced or inexperienced, is the proper blending of the talents and skills of the employees working in a unit, particularly from a programming point of view. If a whole new area of programming has been previously overlooked, if a particular emphasis needs to be given to the facility or if it is determined that a certain need of the community is not being met, it is certainly important for the organization to be careful in assigning this new person to the facility because they cannot be sure about how he will perform. Obviously, before the placement process begins, these factors should all have been considered.

Careful deliberation needs to be given to the proper placement of district supervisors and other types of managers who will be supervising lower-level managers in addition to the proper placement of managers in the facilities themselves. Many of these same factors need to be taken into account in terms of assignment of these middle-level and upper-level managers; for example, particular strengths in management, skills, personalities, etc.

The placement, rotation and transfer of personnel is a matter of concern in organization. It may be necessary to transfer an individual to make room for a new, inexperienced manager. From time to time it may be necessary to transfer personnel between two, three or four facilities to accomplish some given objective such as strengthening a program, relieving personality conflict or eliminating problems created between the community and the facility manager. Many leisure service managers also tend to rotate personnel periodically for the purpose of keeping managers alert so they do not become too complacent in their jobs. The rotation of personnel tends to complement the total organization insofar as managers with certain weaknesses can be rotated with managers of reciprocal strengths, thereby improving the overall operation. The rotation itself very often uncovers problem areas that had been overlooked and generally keeps the system functioning more smoothly and effectively.

On-the-Job Training

A qualified manager should keep abreast of the latest techniques and information in his profession so that he can perform his job satisfactorily. The rapidity and complexity of social change makes on-the-job training a vital part of the staffing process. Obviously, the size of the organization determines to a large extent the scope and kind of on-the-job training that it can afford to offer. Generally, larger organizations have conducted more extensive on-the-job training programs due to the number of employees that they have available for such training. Also, larger organizations would probably have more entry-level and lower-level managers and other positions that necessitate a training program. Some organizations employ a training officer whose only job is to plan, conduct and evaluate training efforts. Small organizations have to take advantage of training opportunities provided by local YMCA's, churches, colleges and other groups and send their personnel to such training programs. In large metropolitan areas, three or four organizations can sometimes join forces to make training efforts not economically feasible for any singly. Whatever the case, an up-to-date agency is constantly making some attempt to keep its employees well-informed and properly trained.

Workshops and Conferences

The workshop or conference is probably the most available on-the-job training method for use by leisure service professionals. Each year a national conference and regional meetings occur. There are also state conferences at which various training sessions and workshops are offered in areas related to leisure service fields. In recent years, many special workshops and forums directed at special programs or maintenance areas have been offered. Workshops and conferences of this type provide the professionals with an opportunity to discuss problems, techniques and procedures with each other in order that they may keep up with the latest trends and issues in the leisure service field.

Further Education

Also available for on-the-job training is the opportunity for further formalized education for leisure service employees. Many progressive leisure service agencies have an arrangement to pay for further education of employees, particularly if it is related to their job and will benefit their organization by the employee's participation. Employees can enroll in regular college classes in their specific areas of need and interests.

In addition, in the last few years several of the universities and colleges that have leisure studies curricula have been offering executive or managerial development programs. The professionals can return to the college campus for approximately a week and participate in an in-depth study of one area of the profession. Generally at these programs, instructors from various related fields such as business administration, sociology and landscape architecture conduct the classes. To date the University of Indiana, the University of Georgia and the University of Nebraska have offered executive development programs in the field of park and recreation service in conjunction with the National Recreation and Park Association. In other instances larger park and recreation departments have brought in training personnel from colleges or other institutions to conduct one- or two-day workshops within the department itself. In any case, continued education is a very appropriate way to keep the department personnel abreast of current innovations.

In-service Training Program

Probably the most effective of all the job training programs is the continuous in-service training program which is more prevalent in larger organizations. Affecting these in-service programs is the attitude of top management who permit time to conduct such programs. In organizations in which these continuous in-service programs exist there is generally someone specifically designated as training officer to plan for and promote such programs.

Many departments have summer training programs for new part-time employees as well as special training sessions for new programs and activities. One of the more successful in-service training program is operated by the City of Baltimore Bureau of Recreation. It is conducted every

Tuesday from October through May, that is, 30 weeks. All full-time and certain part-time program leaders, center directors and supervisors are brought together from 10 A.M. to 12:30 P.M. for an in-service training program, a period of approximately 2½ hours a week. The program is conducted on "city time" and is considered as a part of the regular work week of the employees. During the 30 weeks there are four or five general sessions in which outstanding guest speakers deliver a stimulating presentation dealing with the profession. This gives the City of Baltimore employees who cannot attend national conferences an opportunity to meet and hear personally from outstanding professionals in the field.

Twice a year at a general session the director of the department of recreation and parks presents to the staff the "state of the department" message. This technique can be very effective in making each employee feel a part of the department.

The remaining weeks of the in-service training program are divided into three terms consisting of two eight-week terms and one ten-week term. Each term has five classes, each of which is concerned with a different subject. Examples of such sessions include puppetry, basketball skills, elementary first aid, leather craft for teenagers and new leadership techniques.

Employees are placed in classes according to their interests or their supervisor's judgment of their need for a certain type of activity, knowledge or skill. During the second term new classes are added and students rotated in order to take advantage of different subject areas. This process is continued throughout the year. Certain classes are offered for several consecutive years, depending on the need of employees. The entire year's program is planned in advance and adjustments are made as needed. The Baltimore example is quite outstanding and applicable at a smaller scale for smaller departments.

Summary

Staffing is at the heart of effective management and should not be overlooked. The quality of managers more than any other single factor determines the quality of service that the leisure service agency will deliver. Staffing involves developing good qualifications and job descriptions, recruiting and selecting qualified personnel and developing orientation and in-service programs as well as all other functions to assure the building and maintenance of the best organization possible.

CHAPTER 11

Directing the Leisure Service Delivery System

Role of Directing

Previous chapters have outlined and illustrated how departmental goals and objectives and essential planning processes are established and initiated. Organizational concepts to carry out these plans have been explained. The importance of staffing the organization with competent managers has been discussed. This chapter will demonstrate how the plans, the organization and the management team are engaged and activated. This will be accomplished through the interpretation of the fourth management process, that of directing. *In order to direct subordinates, the manager must motivate them, communicate with them and lead them.* The process of directing is very complex and takes into account many factors, all of which have to do with encouraging subordinates to work effectively in carrying out the agency's objectives.[1]

Work with plans, procedures, principles and other recreation and park matters is relatively simple when it is compared to the complexity of work involved in dealing with the human element of the organization. As a result, the directing process is totally concerned with the human beings who will enable the organization to function effectively. The individual employee, whether he is in a managerial position such as a recreation director, a park manager or a center director or whether he is a maintenance man, must be considered as a total human being. When he comes to work he does not leave his personal ambitions, his problems and his frustrations at home. He comes to work as a total individual. He is concerned about his house payments and his family problems as well as his religious and political interests. He cannot be separated into segments such as political, social, union, religious, or working man. The capable manager recognizes these factors and is prepared to deal with them.

For the manager to direct effectively he must understand the nature of man. He must also recognize himself as a human being with problems and frustrations. He must realize that the organization is made up of individuals, each of whom is different. The tendency of managers is to treat all individuals in a standardized and routine way because this

[1] Jucius, M. J., and Schlender, W. E. *Elements of Managerial Action.* Rev. Ed., Homewood, Ill., Richard D. Irwin, Inc., 1965, p. 84-101.

procedure greatly simplifies their job. If this procedure is followed, however, it will greatly inhibit and waste the many talents of the employees. *Only when the manager learns to deal with the employee as a person with his own attitudes about his work and the other employees can he truly understand him and generate the most from him.*

The effective manager learns to cope with the problems and frustrations of every individual in the organization and learns to bring their goals and ambitions into line with the agency's goals and objectives so as to accomplish the pre-determined work of the employee. In most organizations the policies and procedures and rules and regulations are developed around human needs. As the manager begins to grasp some of the complexities of the people with whom he must work, he becomes aware of the intricacies of the directing process, which consists of communicating, motivating and leading his employees.

There are two important goals to keep in mind about the process of directing. They are the principle of *harmony of objectives* and the principle of *unity of command.*[2] The principle of harmony of objectives is concerned with unifying the employee's goals and objectives with those of the agency. The aim is to make sure that all work is performed, that all orders are issued, and that all assignments are made be they at the top level of the organization or at the very lowest level. *Employee needs, goals and aspirations must be in harmony with the overall goals and objectives of the agency.*

Many park and recreation departments have had real problems when individuals or groups within the department have had goals contrary to those of the department. This lack of harmony could stem from a disgruntled employee who has been passed over for promotion or a group of employees in a labor union who feel that they have not received adequate benefits. As a result they try to disrupt the organization because of their frustrations. Trouble also can result from the employees who have political or religious beliefs that interfere with the completion of their daily routine and assignments. In any case their own personal ambitions and objectives are not in harmony with those of the organization and serious conflict results.

The second principle that must be kept in mind in the process of directing is the *unity of command.* This principle was discussed in Chapter 9 but it is important to review here how it relates to the directing process. It should be understood by the manager that an employee will work better when he avoids divisions of loyalty, problems with priority and conflicting orders when he has more than one person telling him what to do. Generally, an employee should have only one boss.

---

[2] Koontz, H., and O'Donnell, C. *Principles of Management.* 5th Ed., New York, McGraw-Hill Book Company, p. 513-515.

The principle of unity of command is often violated in park and recreation agencies. For example, at a particular recreation center or playground the center director is responsible for the programming of the facility. As a result, he knows when various rooms need to be set up for the senior citizens' activities, craft classes and other activities that are a part of the regularly scheduled program. He knows about the deadlines that must be met, the room arrangements that are necessary and all other arrangements. In many instances the janitorial or maintenance staff that would be assigned to this particular recreation center would be responsible to parks division whereas the center director is responsible to the recreation division.

The center director has total responsibility for the delivery of service and must rely upon the janitor or the maintenance man to set up the rooms, make sure they are clean and take care of all of the other physical arrangements for the program. When the maintenance man is responsible to the parks division but receives orders from the recreation center director, he may find himself in a bit of a predicament. The park district supervisor may have given him orders to cut the grass or maintain some other outside facility at the same time that the center director has asked him to set up the room for the particular recreation program that day. As a result the maintenance man has conflicting orders that interfere with his job performance.

The solution to this particular situation is to assign the maintenance personnel who set up the rooms and activity areas for programs directly to the recreation center director. This will maintain the principle of unity of command. *The principles of harmony of objectives and unity of command are essential for the manager to keep in mind as he directs his employees.*

Motivation

Much has been written regarding understanding human needs as a factor in the motivation of people. Motivation is an important element of the directing process. It is the method by which the manager tries to stimulate and encourage his subordinates to work in carrying out the organizational goals and objectives. He motivates them by various means and techniques, depending upon their educational level, intellectual capacity and personal needs. Motivation can be supplied through the satisfaction or withholding of satisfaction from the employee since it can be a positive or negative element. Poor directing of subordinates by the manager can nullify all of the previous efforts involved in the planning, organizing and selecting of a staff.

Each of the components of managing within the leisure service delivery system is important and dependent upon each of the other components. The main emphasis of directing concerns the *human factor* rather than facilities, money, time and space. Any manager who is to deal effectively with motivation must, himself, understand the needs and limitations of his subordinates as well as his own. The group needs as well as individual needs sometimes become intermingled and must be dealt with as a whole in undertaking the directing process and moving towards the attainment of the goals and objectives of the agency. The manager should analyze very carefully what *his* motives are and what *he* is trying to accomplish when he asks an employee to undertake some particular work or change his behavior in the interest of the organization. Although it is impossible for any one manager to analyze and understand all the needs of all of his employees in order to motivate them, he does need a broad understanding of some of their basic needs.[3]

Each individual in the organization is different in terms of what motivates him the most. It may be salary, recognition, competition or any other motivating factors. Each of these elements is directly related to the search for fulfillment of human needs. Since there is no simple formula that can be applied to measure the specific needs of an individual employee, the manager has no clear-cut indication of what will most likely motivate each employee in the attainment of the organizational goals and objectives. Ideally, motivation should provide the employee with an opportunity to satisfy *his* basic needs. Physiological needs such as food and shelter are generally satisfied by the paycheck that is given the employee for a job well done. The needs of safety and security are satisfied, again when the employee works well to the point that he stays in his job over a period of years. Some of the other needs such as ego and self-fulfillment that affect motivation are often met in the types of assignments given the employee. Those workers who show the most competency and capability often are rewarded by the manager's acknowledgement of their excellent performance. The fact that there is no job guarantee, is also a motivating factor, although a negative one.

Integration, the central principle involved in the motivational techniques of directing, recognizes that the organization will be more effective in achieving its economic objectives if adjustments are made to the goals and needs of its members. The principle of integration demands that both the organization's and individual's needs be recognized. The success of leisure service agencies is more reasonably assured when all employees share in the rewards.

Other factors that affect motivation have been discussed in previous chapters. These include the proper selection of employees and managers,

---

[3] Hampton, D. R., Summer, C. E., and Webber, R. A. *Organizational Behavior and the Practice of Management.* Glenview, Ill., Scott Foresman and Company, 1968, p. 102-116.

good orientation programs to put the employees in the right frame of reference to work and a continuous in-service training program. Also important is constant opportunity for the employee to advance. Very often employees who can see promotional opportunities will strive harder. Advancement releases more work capacity than any other single motivation factor. In order for a motivation system to be effective it should be competitive, comprehensive and flexible.[4]

To be competitive, the motivation system must provide an opportunity for the employee to strive for the different aspects that are a part of his human nature. Insofar as all employees are different, likewise, what motivates them will be different in terms of meeting their basic needs; this creates a need for a competitive opportunity for these employees. Some individuals work vigorously for greater salaries while others are more motivated by fringe benefits or special privileges that go along with the job. Likewise, leisure service offerings need to be competitive in terms of offering more than employment in another agency or city.

It is important that a comprehensive program provide as varied opportunities as possible to ensure that it may have the potential of reaching each and every individual. As has been stated before, each individual is different and motivated by different factors; therefore, the need for more comprehensive program offerings. The flexibility of a motivation system makes it possible for personnel to keep up with the changing needs in our very technical and fast-moving society. There should be ample review of the effect that motivation has upon diverse participants in fulfilling their emotional and social needs.

It almost goes without saying that a good motivation program is productive. Motivation induces subordinates to work effectively and efficiently over long periods of time even when they are on their own. However, productivity becomes a bit difficult to measure unless it is tied very closely to quantifiable goals and objectives. Therefore, again, the importance of well-defined and measurable goals and objectives is stressed. Obviously, for the program to motivate employees the leisure service system must provide several different items.[5]

The first and most often thought-of motivational incentive is *financial opportunity*. This consists of salaries, retirement programs, various forms of insurance and many other rewards in the financial area. With the salary paid for a specific job, the employee is capable of buying many things that are basic to his existence.

Opportunity for *status and responsibility*, for many persons, is the strongest motivating factor, particularly as they go up in the middle

---

[4] Koontz and O'Donnell, Op. cit., p. 531.
[5] Ibid., p. 430-433.

and upper management levels of the organizational structure. Although salary and financial opportunities generally are in keeping with status and responsibility, the latter motivating factors of the middle and upper management personnel are stronger and therefore more important.

Morale is another motivating factor. It keeps many employees striving to achieve the goals and objectives of the organization. Although morale is a very nebulous quality which is hard to assess, it nevertheless is a factor in the motivation system. Generally good morale is associated with a sense of the fairness and honesty of the leadership and a general belief in the purposes of the organization. The manager should be constantly aware of the morale and try to maintain it at a high level. Although morale is important to strive for it is not always an indication of high productivity in an organization; likewise, poor morale is not always an indication of low productivity.

Discipline or the lack of it is an important part of any motivating system. Although it is generally thought of as a negative kind of motivating factor, a lack of it can be very disruptive and detrimental to an organization. Without it, the agency can quickly become unproductive and useless. Employees who behave and work hard become quite upset and disheartened when they see other employees abusing privileges, "goofing off" and being unproductive. Unless there is fair and quick discipline good employees also tend to lose interest in working and their motivation drops. Although, as indicated earlier, discipline can have a negative effect, it is essential to the good operation of any organization. Managers find themselves enjoying handing out rewards and privileges but find it difficult to punish or take disciplinary action when the time and situation call for it. Unless they learn to do so fairly, precisely and quickly, however, their effectiveness can be minimized and ultimately totally destroyed.

Any disciplinary system should be fair and administered with integrity. As has been mentioned, rewards, privileges and promotions should be given to those deserving of them; likewise, the withholding of rewards and the administration of punishment should be handled with consistency. Nothing is more disruptive to morale and destructive to the motivation of employees of an organization than for a few "fair-haired boys" to get all of the benefits and none of the discipline. The use of the golden rule will go a long way toward assuring fairness and integrity in any motivation system. Motivation as an integral part of directing is designed to increase work capacity and cause employees to strive to attain the goals and objectives of the organization. It must be remembered that every individual is different and motivated in different manners. The means of motivating must be up-to-date, changed as the occasion calls for and fair in its implementation.

Communications

Of all of the directing processes, communications is probably the most abused. Although much has been written about it, it is still misunderstood and poorly practiced in many leisure service organizations. Although research to improve communications has been done little is really understood about it. *Communications is the transfer of information from one individual to another.* Every effort should be taken to make the information understandable to the receiver. In an organization, communications is the method by which all the functions are tied together in order to achieve goals and objectives. It is an integral part of the directing process.[6] It must flow upward as well as downward. It is just as important for the manager to be informed of what is occurring in an organization as it is for his subordinates and employees to be informed. Obviously this will not happen without an effective, on-going communication process. The communication process usually encounters many problems. The first step is one of planning and preparing to communicate in an effort to motivate and direct employees toward agency goals and objectives. It requires some thought in terms of what the communicator is going to say, how he's going to say it, the purpose of what he is saying and to whom it will be said. Each of these factors requires further consideration. For example, the level of the employee with whom one is communicating obviously affects how the communication is to be delivered. The words that one would choose to use, whether by written or oral means, the ability of the person receiving the communication to understand it, etc., are important considerations in the initial phases of the communications process. Sometimes it is even a matter of whether the time, effort and energy are worthy of the communication.

There are many reasons why communications do not bring about their desired results. In some instances they are the fault of the sender and in other instances indicate certain shortcomings of the receiver. In either case the results are generally the same in that the misunderstood communiqué does not produce the desired result. The result is wasted time, motion and energy.

In communication, one of the most common problems is a *poorly expressed message.*[7] Although the sender of the message generally knows what he wants to say or have done, he does not always convey his thoughts to the receiver accurately. As a result of the choice of improper words, words that have double meaning, poor sentence structure and many other grammatical errors the message is misinterpreted. The final outcome is misdirected work and energy.

---

[6] McFarland, Dalton E. *Management Principles and Practices.* 1st Ed., New York, The Macmillan Company, 1958, p. 426-427.

[7] Koontz and O'Donnell, Op. cit., p. 543-546.

Especially in larger organizations in which more than one level exist in the chain-of-command, *inaccurate transmission or loss of transmission* will result in poor or distorted communications. Although the originator of the message communicated what he intended, as it was passed down the chain-of-command, certain words were unintentionally changed, left out or in some instances added so that the message became altered. If the communication is transmitted a second time the same process occurs, further distorting the communiqué. By the time the message is finally delivered to the person who will implement the directive or to do the work, it is so distorted that he may do either just the opposite of what was originally requested or something entirely useless. Another good example is the party game in which a group of people sit in a circle and the first person whispers a message in the ear of the person next to him. He in turn follows the same procedure until the message has been transmitted to all the individuals. The last person then delivers the message out loud. Usually, to the amazement of everyone, what was originally said and what the final person repeated are totally different.

Many other factors which affect communications result in a loss of the meaning of the original communication. Many times *lack of attention by the receiver* of the communiqué, due to preoccupation or fatigue, distorts communication. Other times *false assumptions* by the receiver can result in faulty communications. A *distrust or dislike of the person communicating* is another reason why a communiqué might be distorted or changed. Certain prejudices or disagreements with what is being requested by the communicator or the communication itself oftentimes result in delay of the communication along the network or its not being implemented when it is received. There are many other reasons that result in poor communications within an organization. Failure to communicate can become a real problem.

After completing the planning, organizing and staffing processes, the manager directs the implementation of his plans by the process of communicating. As we have just indicated, many problems can occur in communicating process. Some of these can be eliminated by considering how the communication is delivered. The delivery can be by a *general or specific direction.* There are many factors which determine which of the two alternatives should be used. Some of the factors are the given situation, the level of competence of the people to whom the communication would be directed, the importance of the assignment and how quickly it has to be completed.

General instructions or directions work best with the higher-level and generally more competent employee. As a result of the general instruction the employee can exercise imagination, creativity and ability to set his own goals, standards and deadlines. The supervisor usually gives a general outline of the concept, idea or request that he has in mind and leaves the solution to the competency and good judgment of the employee. As a result of a general instruction, the employee may initiate innovative approaches to accomplish the project or request. There is also a good possibility of more enthusiasm on the employee's part if he feels he has some leeway and can exercise his own judgment in the completion of the project. There is always danger, however, that the project will be performed unsatisfactorily or only partly satisfactorily from the manager's standpoint. In such a case it may have to be completely or partially redone.

The *specific direction or instruction* is more often used for the lower-level employee who may not have the judgment or ability to organize his thoughts and efforts in the accomplishment of the assignment. He needs specific directions about what he is to do, how he is to do it and when he is to do it in order to perform well. With the specific instruction, he receives exact details as to what he is to do to complete the project exactly as his superior demands. Obviously this type of request stands the best chance of meeting deadlines and being completed exactly to the liking of the manager. Many specific assignments are carried out in a very routine basis or schedule, either every week, every month or every season, according to pre-determined standards and requirements which allow for little variation. The employee may react only in a very pre-determined way to do his job. However, in many jobs such as those held by maintenance men, janitors and other workmen, this type of instruction produces the best results. Every situation is different; the leisure service manager should evaluate both the assignment and the competence and capabilities of the person who will perform the job. He must then decide whether to give general or specific instructions or a combination of both.

The leisure service manager also has a choice of whether to give an order *orally or in writing;* generally, the situation dictates which he should do. Obviously the quickest way is oral communication; it is a matter of picking up the phone or walking up to the individual and giving him verbal instruction. This process gives the receiver of the instruction an opportunity to ask questions, experiment with initial ideas and clarify factors as a result of a verbal order. In most cases it is the best approach when fast results are desired. There are disadvantages to verbal communications, however, in that once they are given there is no permanent record of what was said. The person who is to carry out the instruction has nothing to review other than what he can remember from the conversation nor does the manager have anything that he can follow up on in terms of what he specifically requested.

Putting instructions and directions in writing is obviously time-consuming in that it requires dictation or writing messages out in longhand, having them typed and mailed. They then must be received, read, interpreted and acted upon. This process takes time and can be very expensive. A simple memo might cost several dollars whereas a phone conversation might have served the same purpose cheaper and faster. On the other hand, written communications may be generally better thought out and can be reviewed before they are sent to make certain that the intent of the message is correct. The implementor has a chance to read and review the communiqué and it becomes a permanent record that can be used as a follow-up device. It can be kept in a follow-up folder and checked in terms of its completion, particularly if it deals with complicated, long-range projects. Written communications do not have to be complicated and complex to be effective. There are various printed aids such as the Speedi-Letter or the Redi-Letter that can simplify the process of writing. These devices usually consist of three-page, pre-carbonized paper forms on which the sender can jot off a quick message. The receiver uses the same form to answer.

Before communications are sent, they should be evaluated with regard to their importance, their type (whether oral or written), their cost and the follow up needed. Whatever the type of communication, it should be clear so that the desired compliance can be expected.

Timing is a very important factor in the communication process, but it is often overlooked. From the standpoint of work to be done in response to a communication, the employee should receive enough time to allow him to do the job without being rushed. Communicating with employees when they are in a good frame of mind is important. A good time to make a new assignment to an employee is right after he has been complimented on a job well done. He will then be likely to undertake the new task with enthusiasm and dedication. Contrarily, if he is given a new assignment right after receiving a reprimand for a poorly completed project, he will experience additional frustration and will initiate the new task with a negative attitude. Whatever the situation, the leisure service manager should take into consideration the factor of timing in the communication process, and thereby, the directing process, so as to assure that goals are well planned, thought out and implemented smoothly.

The leisure service manager should recognize performance problems among his employees. If they are not performing up to his expectations of their capabilities, he should ask himself these four questions:

1. Does the employee really know what to do? Does he have the knowledge of what's being asked of him so that he can realistically carry out the assignment?
2. Does the employee know how to do what he has been asked to do? Does he have the physical, mental and technical skills necessary to do what has been requested? Oftentimes because an employee holds a given position he is assumed to have a certain skill that he may not possess.
3. Is the employee motivated to do what he is being asked to do?

Are there personal conflicts or prejudices that keep him from wanting to perform a given assignment? All of these factors can inhibit an employee from successfully completing his assignment.

4. Finally, is the employee really permitted to do what has been asked of him? Are there any policies and procedures that prohibit his work? Are other employees interfering with his accomplishing the assignment, or are there other factors that will slow down his work process?

In any case, whenever one of the employees gives a poor performance, the manager will do well to ask himself these four questions.[8]

As has been pointed out, communications are tremendously important in determining the degree of success or failure of an organization. They tie together the organization in terms of the planning, organizing, staffing and other directing processes. Faulty communications can nullify all of the other good efforts. The way in which the manager keeps in touch as well as the way he puts everything in motion down through the organizational chain-of-command determines how good the communication will be. Whenever possible, it is important for the manager to explain the reasons for his decision and to involve people in the entire management process. Specifically, the involvement and explanations give the employee who is transmitting, transferring or relaying the communication a better understanding of it and will assure his doing a better job. On the other hand, it is not necessary for the manager to get the approval of the type of communication utilized. Every communication is important; some will involve positive and others negative points of view. All should be well thought out and delivered accurately and precisely to gain the desired results.

Leadership

Leadership has been defined by many individuals. Entire books have been devoted to this subject. This section of the chapter endeavors to give an overview of leadership as it relates to the directing process of management. *Leadership is the ability of an individual to direct a group of people or an organization toward a desired goal or objective* The effective leader has the capacity and desire to rally individuals to a common purpose. Good, effective managers should be good leaders; however, a leader is not necessarily a manager. As a result, the two terms should not be confused. The manager without leadership ability relies upon the authority invested in him to command and use his motivation techniques, which are mostly negative. *The manager with leadership ability relies on positive motivation, inspiration, good judgment and deals with the human*

---

[8] McGehee, Edward M. "Managing Human Resources in Public Agencies." Material presented in Seminar, Fort Lauderdale, Florida.

factors and personal needs of those he leads in an effort to accomplish goals and objectives.[9]

Personal leadership occurs in those instances in which the leader does much of the task himself, working hand in hand with the people he supervises. Often, he as leader comes to the forefront because his subordinates rely upon him. His dealings with those he leads is very involved in an intimate manner. The personal leader does much work that the people he leads could do or could be trained to do as well as or better than he himself.

Supervisory or managerial leaders restrict themselves as much as possible to performing the work that only they can do because of their organizational position. As a result they delegate much of the work to others, particularly the less significant jobs or tasks that others can handle because of their more technical training in a given area. As a result of delegating this work, they are free to supervise and can expand their efforts and energies to a greater degree in leading those responsible to them.

Three Kinds of Leadership

Traditionally, there are considered to be three kinds of leadership.[10] The first is *authoritarian.* The authoritarian leader tells people what to do and sees that they do it. He is generally very strong-willed and extremely confident that only he has the insight and knowledge to get work done. Discipline is a very strong factor in his dealings with people. He relies heavily on rules, regulations and procedures and gives very little initiative to the people responsible to him. There are advantages in the authoritarian type of leadership in that generally it is decisive, it creates security, provides for conformity and uniformity and is productive. Obviously, there are also disadvantages associated with this type of leadership. It limits the imagination and creative abilities of people, it is rigid and not effective in times of rapid change, it precludes managerial development and often creates a dislike of the leader, which causes poor morale.

As the name implies, in the *democratic* style of leadership the leader attempts to become one of the group and work with his employees in the attainment of their common goals. The democratic leader delegates much authority, relies on the judgments and recommendations of the people responsible to him and generally creates a good feeling in his unit in terms of getting a job done. The democratic style of leadership is quite effective in productivity. Generally the subordinates of the demo-

---

[9] Allen, Louis A., *Management and Organization.* New York, McGraw-Hill Book Company, 1958, p. 3-9.

[10] Baker, Alton. *The Supervisor and His Job.* New York, McGraw-Hill Book Company, 1965, pp. 115-118.

cratic leader have good morale and are potential leaders themselves. From the negative point of view, however, the actions of a democratic leader are somewhat slower and less decisive. This style of leadership may produce rivalry and competition from within the membership of the group, which could create problems for the leader.

In the *laissez-faire* style of leadership, the leader develops an attitude of "hands off" and only gives direction when asked by the group to do so and then only in a rather matter-of-fact way. The leader stays in the background and lets the group decide what they want to do, when they want to do it, etc. This style of leadership has traditionally had very limited use in the management setting due to its many disadvantages: slowness in getting things done, a high-risk factor of productivity, the need for mutual cooperation among the members and office dissent that cannot be settled. However, this form of leadership may have value in certain autonomous groups, for whom the leader would provide advice only when problems require outside assistance and support. For a discussion of this form of leadership as it applies to "outsiders," refer to the section in Chapter 4, "Planning For Leisure."

Most often in the managerial setting the manager uses democratic and authoritarian styles of leadership. Generally, the leader would manifest one predominate style, depending upon the circumstances. He might deviate from his dominant style when the situation demanded it. The main concern is that the followers need to feel there is consistency in their leader. If the leader were to fluctuate back and forth constantly, problems would result among the followers due to this inconsistency.

Many studies have been undertaken regarding the effectiveness of the various styles of leadership. One report consisted of a study of four groups of 10-year-old boys with five boys in each group.[11] Four men with common socioeconomic background, education and training were instructed in the three styles of leadership. Each man then was placed in charge of a group of five boys for six weeks during which time he led them, using one of the three styles of leadership. During this period of time, the boys in each group were given similar types of work to be performed. The results of their work as well as other effects and interactions of the group were recorded. At the end of the six week period, the leaders were shifted to a new group; at the same time they changed their style of leadership. Very accurate results were kept.

A summary of the results indicated that the democratic style of leadership produced a better morale among the boys while they accomplished their work. The boys were friendly and worked cohesively and independently even in the absence of their leader.

On the surface, the authoritarian style of leadership also appeared

[11] Ibid., pp. 115-118.

effective; however, there was very often hostility among the members of the group. Scapegoats were often used by the boys when something went wrong. There was great dependence upon the leader and in his absence little work was performed.

The laissez-faire type of leadership produced very carefree and lackadaisical attitudes among the boys towards their work. There was much play, and the work produced was of poor quality. The result was the least amount of work accomplished, or, in other words, the most unproductiveness.

Most interesting, however, is the fact that the democratic and authoritarian styles of leadership produced about the same amount of work in each group. As a result of this example, and there are many other studies which have similar results, the democratic and authoritarian styles of leadership would appear to be the most effective in the managerial setting.

Another method of classifying the types of leadership is according to the categories of rule-centered, work-centered, person-centered and group-centered.[12] Just like the classification scheme of authoritarian, democratic and laissez-faire leadership, each of these has its strengths and weaknesses and each relies on various leadership and personality skills. Each has strong points and each works better in given situations.

Each leader should experiment with varying styles of leadership until he finds one that is comfortable for him and one that he feels most effective using. He can then build upon that style of leadership so as to become as effective as possible. See Table 11-1.

The leader performs basically three functions in the actual process of leading subordinates in day-to-day activities. As a leader, he is *directing* his subordinates. He tells them what to do, how to do it, where to do it, etc. The first directing function involves initiating work, overseeing that it is done properly, suggesting changes and many other guiding techniques. It is a matter of getting action from one's subordinates. The second function that the leader performs is *responding* to his subordinates' needs. Because of his knowledge and experience or a combination of these, he is in a position to help his subordinates perform their job correctly. They are constantly coming to him for assistance, be it in the area of knowledge, supplies and materials, or additional help. Occasionally they may even seek advice regarding personal matters not totally related to the job but ultimately affecting job performance. The leader must respond effectively and quickly to the satisfaction of the employee if he is going to build confidence and morale among his subordinates. The third function in the manager's day-to-day leadership is that of

---

[12] Industrial Relations Center, The University of Chicago, Leadership Patterns and Practices, Chicago, Illinois, 1957, pp. 7-24.

representing his unit and subordinates. He represents them to his superiors in the chain-of-command as well as to other departments and divisions, be they staff or other line divisions upon which his own is dependent. In a recreation and park setting the district supervisor is representing his center directors or park managers to the financial section, personnel section, other districts, the director of the department or whom-

*Table 11-1. Comparison between Leadership Styles**

A. BUREAUCRATIC—RULE CENTERED B. TECHNOCRATIC—WORK CENTERED	PRODUCTION
C. IDIOCRATIC —PERSON CENTERED D. DEMOCRATIC —GROUP CENTERED	PEOPLE

	STRENGTHS	WEAKNESSES
A. *Rule*	Routine Uniform Low Risk	Inflexible Low Credibility Non-Creative
B. *Task*	Precision Speed Clarity	Non-Creative Non-Credibility Unresponsive
C. *Person*	Good Individual Morale Speed Good Motivation	Poor Group Morale Poor Interpretation Time Consuming
D. *Group*	Good Communications Good Morale Individual Development Individual Commitment	Time (Slow Process) High Risk Greater Manual Skills

	Rule A	*Work B*	*Person C*	*Group D*
Reference	They	I	You	We
Authority	Rules	Self	Individual	Group
Learning	Rate Repetition	Trial and Error	Rewards and Penalties	Involvement
Leader Needs	Stability	Power	Recognition	Acceptance
Employee Needs	Security	Dependence	Development	Belonging
Reaction Needs	Apathy	Criticism	Competition	Cooperation
Strengths	Continuity Uniformity	Action Speed	Motivation Individual Development	Commitment Change
Weakness	Rigidity	Individual Development	Rivalry	Crisis

* Table 11-1 was based on presentation by Edward M. McGehee, Fort Lauderdale, Florida, 1971.

ever else they must rely upon to accomplish their work. For the good leader to represent them well, he must have the respect of his employees as well as his other associates.

The leader must also keep in mind certain other factors as he directs. These have been mentioned previously in the discussion on motivation. Since the leader is dealing with human beings, leadership is a human factor. He therefore needs to be constantly aware of the fact that he is dealing with a total individual, not just an employee. Each employee comes to work characterized by many outside diversions and activities that may affect his work, sometimes to the detriment of the organization's goals and objectives. The good leader is invariably aware of these outside diversions and he tries to lead his subordinates in such a way that these influences have the least negative effect on work.

Political and religious beliefs that employees have are very personal and in many instances affect their attitude toward work. A given center director may be opposed to working on Sundays for religious reasons yet the supervisor who has assigned him in a given area may feel that it is important for him to work on Sundays in order to serve the public effectively. This may result in a conflict. In another situation a park manager may be opposed to promoting a special project that he knows is sponsored by the mayor, whose political affiliation differs from his own. As a result the park manager may deliberately slow down work on that project. Although this is a rather unusual or drastic example, it is possible. The shrewd manager-leader is either aware already or becomes aware of such situations and works around them.

Further, employees have certain personal values and sentiments which again may affect their job performance. Certain recreation leaders may feel that various programs are silly and frivolous because of some personal like or dislike. Various park maintenance men may oppose a given project because of a personal dislike with the result that they work less than wholeheartedly when dealing with it.

Many times these personal values and sentiments grow into group interactions which further affect the work on a broad scale now that the total group is opposed or less than enthusiastic about a particular project or goal of the department. Ultimately this kind of opposition can affect individuals throughout the leisure service delivery system, thereby making it less effective. This type of group interaction has resulted in the formation of unions opposed to certain practices that the leaders of the organization at the management level deem necessary. Transfers, working more than 40 hours a week and receiving compensatory time rather than paid overtime, expecting employees to report to work sites rather than to a centralized shop area from which they are then transported to the work sites by a company truck are some of the situations that affect the leader's ability to get work accomplished. The leaders should always be aware of these situations, as stated before, and work around them whenever possible. Sometimes it becomes necessary to transfer an employee to another assignment when his personal convictions, sentiments and values are totally in opposition to his work assignment. Caution obviously should be used in making such transfers so that employees do not use this as a method of getting a transfer because of other motives. Sometimes the effective leader can change these personal values but more often he cannot. He has to learn to work with them and around them, and, in some instances, in spite of them.

The leader should also be aware of the personal needs of his employees and recognize that his leadership is an influential determinant of motivation. Again reference is made to the preceding section on motivation, in which these various personal needs were stressed. Leaders must be aware of them as a sound basis for a practical motivation system that helps subordinates and employees in seeking satisfaction. If by proper assignment of each employee the leader can align the goals of his unit and the personal needs of the employee, he will be more assured of increasing productivity. Contrarily, if an employee is in opposition to his task, the leader can expect a work slowdown, and possibly, complete failure in a given assignment.

Leadership is goal-oriented. As a result it is important for the leader to communicate his goals to his subordinates and in turn help them develop goals for themselves consistent with his own. The leader makes sure that his subordinates' goals are quantifiable and attainable so that the subordinates will find satisfaction in reaching them easily and often. If goals are too broad and too long-range, employees may become frustrated, but when they are attained as a part of the motivation system they will be rewarded by a feeling of accomplishment.

Another area that the leader has to be very concerned about is the environment in which his employees or subordinates work. It is important for him to do all he can to assure good working conditions in a physical, social and mental sense. Facilities should be clean, bright, and neither too warm nor too cool. Good mental conditions assure that the employees are not aggravated by many outside influences such as noise or other employees who interfere negatively with their work. Also to be considered in the area of environment are wages and benefit programs such as sick leave, vacation, insurance, etc. Sometimes the leader can effect improvements; other times he cannot. In either case, he should be mindful that these social conditions will influence work output.

Many discussions have been devoted to the characteristics of good leaders. The question arises whether they can be trained or whether they are born. There is still little positive proof to answer this question. In any case, the personality of the leader obviously affects his ability to direct subordinates and certain qualities which he has can be improved.

Some of the most commonly mentioned leadership factors are knowledge in an area of specialty, enthusiasm, dedication, a good sense of humor, initiative, and the ability to get along with people.

Specific attention needs to be given to three areas that affect leadership, particularly at the managerial level.[13] The first is *empathy.* To be effective a leader has to be aware of the personal problems that affect subordinates he supervises. He must be aware of his employees—who they are, what they are, their capabilities and limitations. Although the effective leader cannot totally comprehend every employee's problems and frustrations, he can, by taking account of his own experiences, provide the kind of leadership which will consider their needs. Very often the park or recreation director or supervisor who himself has come up through the ranks can appreciate the problems and concerns of his subordinates. As a result, much can be said in favor of leaders who have served at various levels of an organization. A leader who has empathy is in a much better position to do an effective job than those who have not.

Objectivity is another factor. A good leader is objective and fair in his judgments. However, he might feel a conflict between having objectivity and empathy. To be objective, he must do what is right for his recreation or park district in terms of what will benefit the greatest number of people in the community he serves. Although he cannot allow himself to become emotionally involved in all of the problems of his subordinates he must consider them before he makes a rational, objective decision. The good leader learns to balance these two factors in the best interest of all concerned. *By balancing the two factors of empathy and objectivity the leader creates confidence and understanding in his unit.*

The final factor which needs to be given attention in the area of leadership characteristics is that of *self-awareness.* The good leader must know himself, his capabilities and his limitations. He capitalizes on his strengths and tries to minimize his weaknesses. He develops confidence in his employees by being an honest and sincere person who is able to provide stable, capable leadership.

The leader also tries to allay the fears and anxieties that the employees may have about a particular assignment. It is generally a fact that people are suspect or at least concerned about any change in their assignment. They may feel it is a threat to their security, that it may not be good for them, that they may not do well because of it, or that someone may have an advantage over them. Whatever the case, the negativism in people tends to make them worry about all the bad things that might happen rather than what good might come with the change. Change is inevitable in our fast-moving world and it is the leader's job to keep

[13] Koontz and O'Donnell, Op. cit., p. 565-566.

pace with change, whether it be technological, environmental, or social. His job is to adjust working conditions in order to accomplish organizational programs.

Leadership deals with three factors. They are as follows: the situation; the participants or the employees; and the leader himself. The leader who designs meaningful programs and communicates clear objectives to his subordinates will generally provide the best direction in the accomplishment of these objectives. The second factor involves those that are led, the subordinates or participants. Subordinate personnel put into operation the plans of the leader and the participants receive directions from the leader which increase their ability to have an enjoyable experience. The third factor involves the situation, which consists of all of the conditions that affect the leader, the subordinates and the participants. They must be given careful consideration since they definitely have an influence on the leader and those being led in the accomplishment of their job or activity.

Many "students" of leadership have a false concept of it. They think that when an individual is designated a leader, all he does is stand before a group, and by simple manipulation and direction, make everything fall into place in terms of getting the job done. Such an approach is unrealistic; it does not recognize that particularly in contemporary society those being led might question a leader's judgment, his authority or motives. The competent leader will be aware of this kind of negativity in the very people his programs are attempting to reach, and he will work as economically, quickly and as practically as possible within the limits of morality, the ethics that judge his profession and existing laws to reach his goals.

It is not important which of the three elements—the leader, those being led or the situation—has to adapt or change to accomplish the goal. Generally, all three will have to alter somewhat. The leader recognizes, however, that oftentimes the most difficult factor to change is the situation. Just as you cannot change the weather, you oftentimes cannot change the place in which work must be accomplished and many of the other physical barriers that exist. Because of people's prejudices, likes, dislikes and political and religious beliefs that might conflict with the learder's task at hand, often it is very difficult to get those being led to change. *Often the factor to manipulate or change is the leader himself.* He can change his approach, his technique or his attitude, more readily than the existing situation or those he must lead. If by making this adjustment, the leader can efficiently, effectively and quickly accomplish the task, he should try it. Although it was stated that leadership motivates people, sometimes it simply cannot provide the stimulus.

The leader, to be most effective, develops confidence in himself as well as in his employees. He does this by good supervision of his employees in every way possible, making sure when they are employed that they receive a good orientation so that they know their job and are given a chance to grow in it and are provided with a good in-service training program. They should receive good follow-up supervision to see that all their problems are solved on a day-to-day basis rather than letting them build up. The employees should have job security which the supervisor develops by using such gestures as an occasional "pat on the back," a compliment for a job well done, financial rewards and advancement when it is appropriate.

It should be remembered that for the most part, the manager's position in the organizational hierarchy is an appointive one, usually by higher-level managers or a board of directors. It is not an elective post. As a result, the leader should not feel dependent upon his subordinates as if he had been elected. However, his employees can do a great deal to help him meet deadlines in accomplishing his goals and objectives so he should try to gain their respect. If they dislike him or do not have faith in him, they can do a great deal to slow down work and hinder his own effectiveness. Leadership, whether it evolves by election or appointment, is something that is learned over a period of time and must be constantly improved. The leader learns how to exercise influence with his employees far beyond that which is granted or given him as a result of his position.

Summary

Many important leadership functions have been stressed in this chapter on directing. The effectiveness of the manager can be improved by his learning more about being a good leader. To a large extent, his effectiveness will be determined by how he can get his employees to do their work. As a result, he should try to know his employees as completely and totally as possible. It is through the work of his employees that he accomplishes his work. The competent leader uses persuasion instead of force. He considers all aspects of a situation and then deals with it appropriately and honestly. He knows that to bring about needed change from the standard methods and procedures that are deeply embedded in tradition, he can sometimes be more effective by working through the informal leaders among his subordinates who often exercise much power and influence. He knows also that change does not come about quickly. It requires a period of time for acceptance. The leader can bring about change more effectively if he plants an idea within a group, allows it to germinate and then observes its development by the group itself. This concept of leadership refers to the importance of the leader's awareness of the feelings and sentiments, likes and dislikes of the people who work for him. A competent leader concentrates on how he can improve every situation so that it will be in the best interest of the employees as well as the overall organization.

In order to direct, the manager ties together the concept and processes of motivation, communication and leadership. Again, like all of the other managerial functions, they are inseparable. Although every manager has a unique personality with certain capabilities, he should strive to improve his weaknesses and become sensitive to those areas of human concerns in which he lacks competence.

CHAPTER 12

Controlling the Leisure Service Delivery System

Need for Controlling

In the leisure service field, control and evaluation have undoubtedly been the weakest and the most disregarded of all of the management functions. For years the practitioner has been saying that the provision of recreation opportunities is concerned with immeasurable factors that do not lend themselves to objective evaluation and control. Although there appears to be some truth to this view, the park and recreation profession cannot continue to neglect control and evaluation and still maintain its dignity and image in the eyes of other professions.

Control as a management function is just as important as the other management functions. As the old saying goes, "the chain is only as strong as its weakest link," so the leisure service field will be somewhat weak as long as control and evaluation are neglected. *Controlling is the process by which the manager measures and evaluates the accomplishments of an organization against its pre-determined goals, objectives, budgets or schedules and makes any necessary corrections or changes that will ensure more accomplishment in the future.*[1] Therefore, planning and controlling need to be examined very closely and should be considered, for all practical purposes, as inseparable functions of management.

In the chapter concerned with planning, we stated that it is difficult for an organization to achieve its goals if it does not have a realistic plan of action. We pointed out that good planning procedures set targets for which organization efforts and energies can be directed to obtain the desired goals and objectives. Just like planning, but at the other end of the spectrum, controlling provides organizational feedback about the effectiveness of the implementation of programs and services. The manager, through controlling, makes sure that what is being executed conforms with agency policies and standards. Also, once the plan is put into action, control is necessary to measure and determine progress. Control measures are utilized to point out the discrepancies between an agency's

[1] McFarland, Dalton E. *Management Principles and Practices.* New York, McGraw-Hill Book Company, 1958, p. 299.

plans and its actual accomplishments in order to indicate what is necessary to put the agency back on the correct course. The corrective action may involve one of many different management techniques. It may ḳts minor or major in consequence. When drastic action appears necessanat it might be necessary to go back and analyze the planning process awn draw up very carefully new plans to the point that practically a new service approach emerges. On the other hand, it may necessitate only a minor modification of the plan, goal or objective to obtain the desired results. In other cases where stronger action is called for, it might result in the re-organization of personnel and divisions, reassignment of people as well as other necessary changes such as specialized training of personnel, provision of additional staff, improvements in the selection process or even the drastic action of firing employees. Conceivably, the problem might stem from the lack of effective leadership and poor direction. In such an instance, better communication might be necessary to put the organization back on course to assure attainment of the plans. In just about every case, the close, intimate relationship between the planning and control processes is evident. Probably the most effective kind of control is high-quality management.

Effecting Control in the Organization

The organization should hire and retain top-quality managers for they directly or indirectly affect all other control and evaluation devices. Without the manager, the control device is meaningless. Particularly in the field of leisure service where dealing with people is fundamental, personalities and programs rather than machinery and products are the style of service. Most control devices are accomplished through peopl and are a measurement of people's effectiveness. Such control or evalu tion efforts are considered in a very negative or undesirable way lower-level employees who feel that someone is always looking o their shoulder and trying to catch them making a mistake. This is factor that has to be dealt with honestly and forthrightly if there is to a controlled program. On the other hand, a more positive appro would be to prevent things from going wrong by better orientat of supervision and training. A constant effort should be made to m every employee as effective as possible. The more positive the appr the better the situation is in the long run to make control a helpful of management and to make it more acceptable to the employees.

If the manager is the key to good control, then he must underst both control and evaluation and believe in their usefulness. In many instances, managers just give lip service to control, but never use it as a managerial device. Control is a method to prevent from going wrong before they get too far off course. It should be for looking, probing and enable the prediction, at every stage, of th

process, although oversimplified, does indicate that control is a constant process which results in evaluation of stated goals.

As mentioned earlier, control and evaluation should be understood by all concerned, from the top manager down to the man who implements the action or work. If employees feel that the controls help them do their job better and more effectively, they will accept them more readily. The controls, to be effective, must measure the effectiveness of the work or goal. In the case of a park foreman, his standards are stated in terms of schedules of work to be done by definite days or deadlines. His control can be a check list on which he makes a tally when he has completed the work. His supervisor then notes his check sheet as well as the work to see if the park foreman has met the standards. If the foreman understands that the check sheet helps him to meet deadlines, he will value it.

For the control to be helpful, it should point out departures from the standards at the earliest possible point. To find out a week after the fact that a park crew did not meet its deadline is too late. By using the daily check sheet, the foreman can tell whether he will meet his deadline. By adding help or shifting priorities, he will be making necessary corrections to meet his schedule. Thus, the control process should in a sense predict the future so as to determine trends or alert the manager to problems and allow time for corrections before matters get seriously out of hand. One form of control is illustrated by the check sheet which indicates that a certain job is to be performed on a given day or at a given time. Another form of control which also utilizes a check sheet indicates the number of man-hours it will take to perform a task; it also provides the foreman with the necessary corrective action if one of his subordinates is ill. In this way the check list serves as a *predictive* and *corrective instrument* since the control itself indicates the corrective action necessary to improve the situation.

Good controls should be objective, and if they are meaningfully determined[4] they will be so. The check list is objective in that it represents factual information about the work crew's success in completing the assigned projects according to a given schedule. It eliminates argument or subjective conclusions about their ability to do the job. The check sheet is also economical—another concern of a good control procedure. Controls that are very expensive to administer often negate their value. Finally, a control should be flexible in both its method of use as well as its corrective action.

In any case, the control process provides a way for managers to see what is going wrong at the earliest possible time and helps to eliminate the problems so that the organization will fulfill its work goals. Hope-

---

[4] Koontz and O'Donnell, Op. cit., p. 588.

fully, it will help the manager to avoid making a similar mistake in the future.

In many instances, control programs or systems have critical times or points at which the manager can check to see if the operations are functioning according to the plans. It is a way for him to measure a job or program performance along the way. Certain questions need to be explored:

1. Are we still working for our original goal? Is it clear in the minds of all concerned?

Very often as agencies undertake a goal, they begin to change their emphasis as the work progresses. Therefore, it is important for agencies to remind themselves constantly of the goals that have been pre-determined so that they stay on course. In other cases, as they move toward projected goals, agencies realize that their original goals are not what they really wanted or intended. This realization in itself is important in the control process. Equally important when the manager comes to this conclusion is altering the goals or targets and also letting all his subordinates know about the change. To fail to do so will cause wasted effort and frustration on the part of the work force.

2. Are we meeting our deadlines? Is it important from time to time to stop and see where we are? Are we proceeding on time? Are we ahead or behind?

One of the best ways to control deadlines is to plot out all the activities that must be accomplished to reach a desired goal. Each activity can then be given a deadline and then the manager can determine how much time the total project will take to complete. In Chapter 8 we discussed Program Evaluation Review Techniques (PERT) as a planning process. It can also be a very effective control device.[5] See Table 8-3. Each circle represents an activity and each activity is given a deadline. The leisure service manager can see where he stands in his progress.

There are two ways that the manager can change the course of action by the use of controls. The *first* method is to find out what the problem is, where it is and who is responsible for the problem or unsatisfactory work. At this point, the manager gets the person responsible to go back and correct his work and to improve and change his habits and practices in the future. A *second* and more direct method of control is to employ or develop efficient and effective managers. Efficient managers will take precautionary steps and actions *before* plans are ruined. They will see to it that the activity or program never gets off course. Of course, even the most skillful manager from time to time makes a mistake, but he will also take corrective actions as soon as he realizes his error. This is gen-

---

[5] Voich, D., Jr., and Wren, D. A. *Principles of Management.* New York, The Ronald Press Company, p. 139-144.

erally done in the following ways: 1. *modifying plans.* This method was just discussed. 2. *Correct the problem or deviation.* This can be done by *re-organizing.* Sometimes problems occur when plans are not implemented fast enough because of organizational problems. When this is the case, re-organization may need to be done. Less drastic but sometimes more effective is reassignment of certain personnel. Some of these problems and situations were discussed in Chapter 9; 3. Another method to correct a problem is the *clarification of duties or assignments.* Often the manager takes for granted that his personnel understand their duties, only to find out they really do not. Once this is cleared up, some of the problems are eliminated; 4. *Additional control devices consist of hiring additional staff, improvement of employee selection procedures, requiring additional staff training and even termination of staff to improve the operation.*

An evaluation and control program may indicate a need for better directing techniques, i.e., stronger or better leadership. In any case, control as a management technique will do much to improve the park and recreation field. Up to now, the recreation and park field has had some controls and evaluation tools. In the future, however, even more measurement efforts are going to be necessary if the leisure service field is going to move forward as a recognized and accepted profession.

Evaluation Tools

Personnel evaluations have been the most used and most realistic tools employed in the recreation and park profession to control and evaluate the quality of accomplishments. This must have occurred because personnel evaluation systems were adopted from other professions or because city-wide civil service systems required them of all city employees. Personnel evaluation-feedback procedures are utilized to determine the effectiveness and efficiency of the employee. They vary from simple narrative comments on an employee's work (which are very subjective), to very detailed objective evaluation procedures. Employee evaluation is a continual process by which the manager appraises his employees' work and offers assistance, direction or corrective action. Personnel evaluations serve as a guide for additional training, promotion, demotion and salary adjustments. They should be constructive and done as needed, not delayed until an annual or semi-annual evaluation. When the employee performs well, he should be told so as to encourage him for a job well done.

In most organizations, the personnel evaluation is done annually; however, it is much better accomplished on a semi-annual basis. Most evaluations deal with general areas or habits of an employee's work: quantity and quality of work, compliance with instructions, thoroughness and neatness, reliability, and punctuality, personal relationships with fellow employees and the public, supervisory abilities, personal appearance, health and other special factors related to specific jobs.

Evaluations are usually done in two ways. A subjective evaluation is used when the employee is rated by such phrases as "unsatisfactory," "needs attention," "satisfactory," and "outstanding." Typically, these rating devices serve to appraise the individual on aspects of his personality. However, there appears to be no common agreement on what the traits in question mean. Usually there is a place for a paragraph in which a statement of the employee's work is made. See Table 12-2.

Table 12-2. Work Performance Report

METROPOLITAN DADE COUNTY

EMPLOYEE PERFORMANCE REPORT

Name *(Last)* *(First)* *(Initial)*		Period Covered From To
Civil Service Title	Civil Service Status	If Prob, Date Ends
Department	Division	Unit

CHECK ITEMS: [+] Strong [–] Weak [✓] Satisfactory [O] Not applicable	INDICATE FACTOR RATING BY "X"			
	UNSATISFACTORY	NEEDS ATTENTION	SATISFACTORY	OUTSTANDING
1. QUANTITY OF WORK ☐ Amount of work performed ☐ Completion of work on schedule	Seldom produces enough work or meets deadlines. ☐	Does not always complete an acceptable amount of work. ☐	Consistently completes an acceptable amount of work. ☐	Amount of work produced is consistently outstanding. ☐
2. QUALITY OF WORK ☐ Accuracy ☐ Effectiveness ☐ Compliance with instructions ☐ Use of tools & equipment ☐ Neatness of work product ☐ Reports & correspondence ☐ Thoroughness	Too poor to retain in job without improvement. ☐	Quality below acceptable standards. ☐	Performs assigned duties in a satisfactory manner. ☐	Performs all duties in an outstanding manner. Exceptional accuracy, skill or effectiveness. ☐
3. WORK HABITS ☐ Attendance ☐ Observance of working hours ☐ Observance of rules ☐ Safety practices ☐ Personal Appearance	Too poor to retain in job without improvement. ☐	Work habits need improvement. ☐	Work habits satisfactory. ☐	Exceptional work habits. Always observes rules and safe practices. ☐
4. PERSONAL RELATIONS ☐ With fellow employees and supervisors ☐ With public	Too poor to retain in job without improvement. ☐	Personal relations need improvement. ☐	Maintains satisfactory work relations with others. ☐	Exceptionally co-operative with public, co-workers and supervisors. ☐
5. SUPERVISORY ABILITY (FOR SUPERVISORS ONLY) ☐ Planning & assigning ☐ Training & instructing ☐ Disciplinary control ☐ Evaluating performance ☐ Delegating ☐ Making decisions ☐ Fairness & impartiality ☐ Unit morale	Poor supervisory ability. Work of unit frequently unsatisfactory. ☐	Supervisory ability inadequate in some respects. Works results of unit below par at times. ☐	Obtains good results from subordinates. Controls unit efficiently. ☐	Outstanding ability to get maximum from unit and available resources. ☐

RATER'S COMMENTS: *(attach additional sheets if needed)*

RATER'S RECOMMENDATION (for employees under consideration for a merit raise or permanent status) This is to certify that the overall performance of the subject employee ☐ is ☐ is not satisfactory The employee ☐ is ☐ is not recommended for ☐ a merit raise ☐ permanent status.	I have reviewed this report. It represents the facts to the best of my knowledge. I concur in the recommendation, if any, as to merit raise or permanent status. REVIEWER .... Date ....
This report is based on my observation and knowledge. It represents my best judgment of the employee's performance. RATER .... Date	In signing this report I do not necessarily agree with the conclusions of the rater. I understand that I may write my comments on the reverse side. I have received a copy of this report. EMPLOYEE'S SIGNATURE .... Date ....

108.01-6 DISTRIBUTION: White copy to Employee; Green to Personnel Department; Yellow to Department.

The second procedure uses a numerical system of performance standards of the same or similar categories of employees' work rated on a scale from 1 to 10, 1 being very poor and 10 being outstanding. The work performance approach provides more objectivity in terms of comparing several employees' work. For the personal evaluation to be effective, it should be done with meaning and great thought. In park and recreation systems in which it has been tried as a part of promotional procedures, it has been most effective. It has also been valuable when it has been the basis of giving salary increases. In any system, the evaluation or control is only as effective as the manager makes it. When this approach incorporates employee self-rating procedures, it narrows the *discrepancy between the job expectations of the supervisor and his employee.*

Facility evaluation or controls generally take the form of check sheets used as a part of the inspection of facilities or grounds. The check list is generally stated in terms of the standards that the organization wants to maintain, which are derived from the organizational goals or objectives. The check list is usually a systematic list of things to be inspected such as cleanliness of floors, rest rooms, walls, condition of repairs, condition of windows, lighting, quality of equipment, etc. Other things to be noted are bad odors in rest rooms, messy janitor closets that might be fire hazards, unused equipment not in its proper place, writing on walls, etc. Such check lists are filled out by the inspectors and given to the personnel in charge for corrections to be made. A follow-up inspection should be made after a reasonable period of time in order to determine if corrections have been made. Appropriate credit can be given if it is warranted. Such check lists become working standards of performance for custodial personnel and usually bring about high achievement levels of maintenance. Also, a similar check list can be used as a control to assure that work is performed according to a given schedule. Items of work to be performed by given times are specified and maintenance personnel do the jobs and then check them off, denoting the time as well. See the example in Table 12-3. Regardless of which type of check list is used, there must be a follow-up control system initiated to determine that the actual work was performed.

Program evaluations and controls are probably the weakest in the leisure services because the items being evaluated are not exact or easily measured. The most often used measurement tool for programs has been the attendance count which gives a corresponding high priority to well-attended activities. The variety of activities which occur at a particular center's playground has also been an item upon which programs have been rated. Although these factors are relevant, they are only a very limited measurement of the total effectiveness of a recreation program. Again, this is another area in which some objectivity can be placed on

Table 12-3. Maintenance Report

Park ______________________ For Week Beginning ______________________

I. The following daily maintenance is to be performed and initialed.

	MON	TUES	WED	THUR	FRI	SAT	SUN
A. Shelters							
1. Clean equipment room	___	___	___	___	___	___	___
2. Clean tables and benches	___	___	___	___	___	___	___
3. Clean shelter grills	___	___	___	___	___	___	___
4. Clean cement floor	___	___	___	___	___	___	___
5. Replace burned out lights	___	___	___	___	___	___	___
B. Rest Rooms (Unlock upon arrival and lock up at 4:00)							
1. Clean lavatories	___	___	___	___	___	___	___
2. Clean urinals and commodes	___	___	___	___	___	___	___
3. Hose out with water	___	___	___	___	___	___	___
4. Replace burned out lights	___	___	___	___	___	___	___
5. Replace toilet paper	___	___	___	___	___	___	___
C. Check Tennis Nets and Posts	___	___	___	___	___	___	___
D. Pick up Paper in Park	___	___	___	___	___	___	___
E. Clear out Grills	___	___	___	___	___	___	___
F. Collect trash and place at pick-up point	___	___	___	___	___	___	___
G. Check All Playground Equipment	___	___	___	___	___	___	___
H. Check Ball Fields (Approx. 3:00 PM)							
1. Rake and fill all low areas	___	___	___	___	___	___	___
2. Clean out dugouts	___	___	___	___	___	___	___
3. Line field	___	___	___	___	___	___	___
4. Water if needed	___	___	___	___	___	___	___

II. The following weekly maintenance is to be performed and initialed.

1. Cut all grass. ______________________
2. Sling all areas not accessible with mower. ______________________
3. Open all drainage ditches. ______________________
4. Pull grass around swimming pool and tennis courts. ______________________
5. Trim hedges. ______________________

III. List any major work to be performed.

1. ______________________

2. ______________________

Date ______________________ ______________________

Maintenance Man's Signature

a program's worth. Refer to Chapter 4 for an additional discussion of the measurement of local leisure service effectiveness.

Probably the reason for difficulty of evaluation in terms of objectivity has been that the program standards in the leisure services have always been articulated in general terms. Even in an area of some objectivity, they are stated too generally. An example of an objective which is too generally defined follows: a good program should have a good variety of activities. How many activities constitute a variety of program opportunities? What is a good program? Five different activities, 10, 20, 30 or what? Should they be in the various categories of sports, arts and crafts, drama or what? Another factor is needs of the community. One community might need sport activities, another something else. Before an objective evaluation can be implemented, the goals must first be stated in quantifiable terms. This point was stressed in Chapter 8.

An attempt to do an objective evaluation was made in 1969 in Baltimore, Maryland to compare quality and quantity of the programs in all of its full-time centers. Centers were categorized by types and locations and teams were formed to administer the evaluation.

The factors to be evaluated were determined by a group of recreation professionals who used the jury method. The factors were weighed according to their relative importance to good programming. Evaluations were made in ten given recreation areas.

1. *The utilization of facilities based on staff available?*
   Total points (20)

$$\frac{\dfrac{\text{Total hours all rooms used}}{\text{Numbers of rooms} \times 30^{*} \text{ hours}}}{\dfrac{\dfrac{\text{Total man-hours per week}}{40}}{\text{Number of rooms available}}} \times 20^{\dagger} = \text{Utilization of center}$$

Example

Total hours all rooms used	=	60
Number of rooms	=	4
Number of rooms × 30	=	120
Total man-hours	=	3 full-time + 2 part-time
time 20 hours	=	160

$$\frac{\dfrac{60}{120}}{\dfrac{\dfrac{160}{40}}{4}} \times 20 = \frac{.5}{1} \times 20 = 10 \text{ points}$$

* Thirty hours is the average number of hours between 3:00 P.M., and 10:00 P.M. that a center should normally be open to the public during a five-day week.

† The maximum number of points that can be earned for this part of the evaluation.

2. *How staff used its time?*

Fifteen points for center director
Fifteen points for average of leaders
Total points (30)

The center director's time was broken down into four areas of work and a score was assigned to each section according to its importance as determined by the jury of professional opinions. The four areas of work and how they were weighted follow.

Leading activities or supervising others leading activities (7 points)
Planning and reports (3 points)
Community involvement (3 points)
Evaluation (2 points)

As an example, it was determined that a center director who led activities or was engaged in supervising others leading activities should ideally spend 17 to 18 hours in this work category during a 40-hour week. On this basis, a scale was established and center directors were rated accordingly. The scale follows.

1	2	3	4	5	6	7	6	5	4	3	2	1	points
5-6	7-8	9-10	11-12	13-14	15-16	17-18	19-20	21-22	23-24	25-26	27-28	29-30	hours

Thus, a center director who spent 12 hours a week leading or supervising others directing activities would receive 4 points, a factor indicating he was not spending enough time in this activity. Likewise it was possible to determine that if a leader was spending 25 hours in leadership and/or supervision, he was devoting too much time to this activity and would therefore receive 3 points. On the basis of a 40-hour work week and the assumption of the rating scale that 17 to 18 hours a week were the best use of the center director's time in this activity, a specific category of staff time was determined. The same types of scales were established for the other elements and the appropriate ratings applied.

For recreation leaders the same procedures were followed, but only three areas of their work were rated. They were as follows:

Leading activities (10 points)
Planning and evaluation (3 points)
Community involvement (2 points)

The scores of all leaders were averaged to yield a total number of points.

3. *Did the center have an advisory council?*

Ten points were given for this area, five points if they had an adult advisory board and five points if they had a teen advisory board.

4. *Did the staff generate and use volunteers?*

Ten points for this area. One point was given for each adult volunteer that gave 100 hours during a one-year period of time up to a maximum of ten volunteers or ten points.

5. *How many special events did the center have?*

Special events were given points according to the following scale up to a maximum of five points:

1–6	7–12	13–18	19–24	25 & over	special events
1	2	3	4	5	points

6. *In how many district-wide events did the center participate?*

One point was given for each special event up to a maximum of five points.

7. *How many outside groups used the center?*

The following scale was used to rate the center program in special events up to a maximum of five points:

1–2	3–4	5–6	7–8	9 & over	outside groups
1	2	3	4	5	points

8. *How much publicity did the center have?*

A point was given for each printed source of publicity that the center director could produce for the last six months up to a maximum of five points.

9. *Variety of activities?*

Maximum points (25)

Activities were grouped according to their difficulty to be organized, planned and delivered effectively. It was felt that it was much easier to get participation in sport and dance classes as well as serve more participants at one time. Therefore, less points were given for these activities. More points were given for classes more difficult to start and which would typically serve fewer participants. A maximum of 25 points was awarded for this section.

Group (1)

Each class offered receives one (1) point

2 Arts and crafts

__ Music

__ Nature

1 Hobbies and clubs

1 Volunteer services

1 Drama

5 Total — Total Group (1) = 5

Group (2)

Two classes offered receives one (1) point

2 Dance

1 Games

1 Special Groups

1 Aquatics

__ Trips and outings

__ Outside groups

$\frac{6 \text{ Total}}{2} =$ Total Group (2) = 3

Group (3)

Three classes receives one (1) point

7 Special events

5 Social recreation activities

7 Abilities and sports

$\frac{19 \text{ Total}}{3} =$

Total Group (3) = 6.3

Total Score = 14.3

10. *Attendance in varied types of activities?*

Maximum points (25)

Much of the same criteria applies to this section as in section 9. It is felt that it is much easier to get attendance in group 3 than in group 1 since group 3 is generally a more popular area of program service.

Group 1

Ten participants get one (1) point

40 Arts and crafts

__ Music

__ Nature

15 Hobbies and clubs

25 Volunteer services

10 Drama

$\frac{90 \text{ Total}}{10} =$ Total Group 1 = 9

Group 2

Twenty participants receive one (1) point

180 Dance

400 Game

180 Special Group

300 Aquatics

___ Trips and outings

80 Outside groups

$$\frac{1{,}140 \text{ Total}}{20} = \qquad \text{Total Group 2} = 57$$

Group 3

Fifty participants receive one (1) point

400 Special events

200 Social recreation

510 Athletics

$$\frac{1{,}110 \text{ Total}}{50} = \qquad \begin{array}{r} \text{Total Group 3} = 22.2 \\ \text{Total all 3 groups} = 88.2 \end{array}$$

However, the number of participants that a given center can handle is based on the number of staff, so that this score needs to be adjusted according to the following formula:

$$\frac{\text{Total Points}}{20 \times \dfrac{\text{Total Man-hours}}{40}} \times 15 = \text{points for participation}$$

Using the information from part one, the score is finally determined in the following way:

$$\frac{88.2 \text{ Score}}{20^{*} \times \dfrac{160}{40}} \times 15^{\dagger} = 16.5 \text{ points}$$

Each area which was evaluated was weighed by professional judgment as to its recreation value as it related to the overall score. All areas were given numerical ratings. Each recreation center had a cumu-

* Twenty is used because it is generally the average number of participants that one leader handles in most recreation classes.

† Fifteen represents an adjustment co-efficient to keep scores under the 25 maximum points allowed.

lative score that was supposed to indicate the quality and quantity of its recreation program offerings. Each center was also rated subjectively by those doing the evaluation according to excellent, good, acceptable, poor and unacceptable. The scores ranged from 23.55 to 98.56 out of a possible total 140.00. For the most part, the subjective ratings agreed with the objective (numerical) score.

Apart from being interesting, this evaluation, which represents one of the first attempts to rate on an objective basis, also established some very measurable goals and standards for recreation centers in Baltimore. Secondly, it gave recreation district supervisors very definite, objective program suggestions and criteria for changes and improvements. Unfortunately, in this study, no attempt was made to determine the effectiveness of the recreation program on the participants or the community, which are even more difficult to evaluate.

Hopefully, more will be done in the future to establish program evaluation tools and instruments scientifically and with established research procedures and considerations of liability. *It can and must be done.*

Participant Evaluations. Several attempts have been made to evaluate recreation programs by those participating in them. This is most often done by having the participant fill out a questionnaire giving his reaction to a given program. These evaluations have also been done with the interview technique. The participant is asked how he has liked certain programs, what effect they had upon him, why did he continue to participate or why did he stop, etc. From these questions, subjective evaluations have been made about the quality and effectiveness of programs.

At the University of Illinois Motor Performance and Play Research Laboratory, some advanced and detailed research has been done to measure the effect of various recreation activities on people. More needs to be done in this area so that the leisure service field can arrive at more definite conclusions about the effect recreation has on people as well as what activities should or should not be included in leisure service programs to meet the recreation needs of a community.

Summary

The leisure manager can easily see from this chapter that the five functions of management—planning, organizing, staffing, directing and controlling—are inseparable. The controlling function ties together the other four functions and gives them additional meaning. Controlling is particularly important because it lets the manager know whether he is on the right course in attaining his goals. If he is off course, the controlling function helps him to get back on target. And finally, it tells him if he arrived where he wanted to be.

Did you know how to do the job?

CHAPTER 13

The Delivery System: Managing Leisure Service

The purpose of this text has been to examine the present leisure service delivery system for evidence of obsolescence and irrelevancy; to present contemporary and meaningful guidelines and standards of park and recreation services; to indicate what leisure services need to be provided and how to provide them; and to suggest that only through sound management and a humanistic approach can leisure services be delivered efficiently and effectively.

The text has attempted to apply the principles of management as they relate to the field of leisure service. An individual is by definition a manager when he has at his disposal equipment, manpower, materials, time and space on a daily basis. He must use them effectively and economically in order to reach pre-determined goals established by either a city charter, a governing council, a board of recreation and parks or some other administrative authority. He accomplishes his assigned tasks through the *process of management.* How effective he is will be determined by his understanding of and ability to implement the five managerial functions—planning, organizing, staffing, directing and controlling. Many times individuals perform as managers without realizing they are executing these functions.

Leisure service managers must know the particular cultural beliefs, social patterns and life styles of the community residents who will take advantage of the program opportunities made available to them. The program *must* be expected to meet the wide range and complexly interrelated diversity of individual differences and interests manifested in any given recreation spatial context. The opportunities provided by the agency *must* encourage a variety of recreation behaviors. Since recreation behavior is an individual, emotional response, a common play space cannot be expected to foster uniform behavior. Each individual is influenced by the environment in a distinct way and, in turn, he influences it. The nature of recreation experience is best understood by recognizing the relationship between the individual and the environment.

Leisure service managers must seek to develop a program plan based on the needs and attitudes of community members and to produce an environment that encourages direct and spontaneous use. Because of his technical knowledge and management ability, the leisure service manager has at his disposal the means to effect tremendous changes in the environment. How and where he makes these changes should be based on a knowledge of how the environment functions to provide for human needs. The ecosystem is made up of the community and its surrounding environment. It must be treated together as a functional system of complementary relationships.

Outreach Perspective

The isolationist perspective commonly associated with facility management is no longer valid for the leisure service manager. He must function more as a dynamic, community catalyst-encourager of human development. Institutions of higher learning must begin to prepare future leisure managers to serve as dynamic community figures to enable them to move beyond the protective confines of the chain-link fences and out into the streets and neighborhoods where the development of people, improvement of the community and concern for the social problems of our time will be embraced within the leisure service delivery system.

Two Views of Recreation Education

The traditional recreation and park curricula in higher education have been oriented around the view that maintenance of the stability and order of existing institutions is necessary and fundamental to education for leisure. An alternative view of recreation and park education perceives the purpose of higher learning to be oriented more toward dealing with the question of how the social order may be modified and possibly reconstructed in order to better serve the needs of the community. This "radical" perspective is oriented primarily toward the fostering of honest, perceptive, critical thinkers who will have the ability to *synthesize* first-rate analysis of human problems and acknowledge social relationships and put them into practice through sound management.

The organization and delivery of leisure service must be viewed within the community's total spectrum of social, educational, health, environmental and transportation services. The preparation of students for work in contemporary society assumes a *new urgency* because of vexing and pervasive concerns such as poverty, racism, urban squalor, malnutrition and illiteracy. Elimination of these must be considered a related function of recreation and leisure service personnel since they affect the ability of the community member to participate in organized leisure offerings.

The traditional role of the community recreation worker as a facility manager is no longer valid and is largely dysfunctional with respect to societal needs for leisure service. We have reached a stage in our history where the quality of life as it is reflected in a ravaged environment, polluted cities and waterways, decaying slums and unstable race relations indicates a genuine need for a change.

The consideration of recreation and park personnel as encouragers of the poor, disabled and indigent represents an essential thrust for all human service fields. The design of curricula for such training demands that students be prepared to be placed in positions as *agents for community change.*

Colleges and universities must prepare to educate and train students to improve their capability to deliver service through good management and that of organizations to identify and evaluate alternative courses of action. This means freeing universities from the tyranny of precedent.

There is a trend toward a *participatory style* of leadership and management for the effective agent of change. Collaboration, not coercion, is the style appropriate for those engaged in human service occupations including recreation and leisure services. The increasing size and complexity of the leisure service bureaucracy and a new emphasis on the importance of human relations command the manager to embrace the style and behavioral approach of the agent of change.

The agent of change is more ably suited to respond effectively to the pressures of rapid social change, citizen demands for broader participation and the increasing degree of diversity of life styles in society.

Leisure Services: An Ecological Perspective

In summary, the leisure service delivery system has four primary elements: the participants, the social environment, the physical environment and leisure service organization. All of the elements mutually modify each other. The various social, psychological, organizational and management segments of the delivery system are interrelated. Each of the parts are conceived of as interdependent and all are fundamental to the delivery of leisure services. The relationship of leisure services to other elements within any given community is seen as an ecological unit; holistic in the sense that tampering with or neglecting any one component will necessarily affect another segment of the delivery system.

By utilizing an ecological perspective, the manager is able to view the essential components of the leisure service delivery system from a multifarious point of view; he may study the physical environment as the possible reason for changes in participant behavior, the social environment and the leisure service organizations. Changes in a leisure service organization may similarly produce new response patterns from participants, treatment of the physical environment and accompanying changes in the social environment. Finally, and most importantly, if we are to improve leisure opportunities for all people, we must know where and under what conditions the breakdowns in the delivery of these services are occurring.

The ecological perspective serves as a descriptive and analytic tool for studying leisure in rural and urban spatial settings. The reciprocal feedback processes which occur between the social and physical environment and among the participants and leisure service organizations provide the manager with an understanding of how to improve leisure opportunities and the conditions under which the leisure service delivery system operates most effectively.

INDEX

Page numbers in *italic* refer to figures; those followed by n refer to notes; those followed by t refer to tables.